Palgrave Advances in Criminology and Criminal Justice in Asia

Series Editors
Bill Hebenton
Criminology & Criminal Justice
University of Manchester
Manchester, UK

Susyan Jou
School of Criminology
National Taipei University
Taipei, Taiwan

Lennon Y. C. Chang
School of Social Sciences
Monash University
Melbourne, Australia

This bold and innovative series provides a much needed intellectual space for global scholars to showcase criminological scholarship in and on Asia. Reflecting upon the broad variety of methodological traditions in Asia, the series aims to create a greater multi-directional, cross-national understanding between Eastern and Western scholars and enhance the field of comparative criminology. The series welcomes contributions across all aspects of criminology and criminal justice as well as interdisciplinary studies in sociology, law, crime science and psychology, which cover the wider Asia region including China, Hong Kong, India, Japan, Korea, Macao, Malaysia, Pakistan, Singapore, Taiwan, Thailand and Vietnam.

More information about this series at
http://www.palgrave.com/gp/series/14719

Laura Bui · David P. Farrington

Crime in Japan

A Psychological Perspective

Laura Bui
Centre for Criminology and Criminal
Justice
University of Manchester
Manchester, UK

David P. Farrington
Institute of Criminology
University of Cambridge
Cambridge, UK

Palgrave Advances in Criminology and Criminal Justice in Asia
ISBN 978-3-030-14096-0   ISBN 978-3-030-14097-7   (eBook)
https://doi.org/10.1007/978-3-030-14097-7

Cover credit: Alamy ACTG0F

This Palgrave Macmillan imprint is published by the registered company Springer Nature Switzerland AG
The registered company address is: Gewerbestrasse 11, 6330 Cham, Switzerland

Preface

Almost ten years ago, we took knowledge on crime from a psychological perspective and compared it to our findings from Japan. There were many similarities in psychosocial factors for youth offending and violence. The major difference, however, was a higher level of violence among young Japanese males compared to that among young American males. Albeit with limitations (what research doesn't have its limitations), this finding contrasted with the dominant research literature and stereotypes on Japan: namely that the country had low crime compared to Western industrialised countries, because its citizens were group-oriented and harmonious due to its collectivistculture, its social institutions were benevolent and organised, and its public spaces were spotless and efficient. Counter-narratives that questioned this particular account existed, and so we continued our investigation.

Our research interest in Japan stemmed from narratives in the US on Asian-Americans. This population has lower offending rates than other American racial groups (Yoo et al. 2010). In addition, educational attainment and socio-economic status are comparatively high in this population. Because of these assets, Asian-Americans have been dubbed as 'model minorities'. A cultural explanation was assigned to this phenomenon: collectivist values such as group harmony, dependence, and high self-control were responsible for the success of this group. Confucian values of strong familial ties were also suggested when referring specifically to Americans of East-Asian ancestry (Ng et al. 2007). In fact, whenever an issue is raised by Asian-American communities, it is questioned because, unfortunately, it is believed that they should have nothing to complain about. The feeling is that they should be glad for their success as a minority group.

If cultural values explained the comparatively low crime rate of Asian-Americans, this should apply to Asian countries as well—lower crime rates should be found among countries of the 'East' than in the 'West', and these values should play a prominent role. Within the criminological literature, it appeared that the most targeted Asian country on the 'low crime because of culture' discourse had been Japan.

Our line of investigation revealed how powerful the narratives of the dominant group were. The model minority myth has been spread to demonstrate that the US is, indeed, a meritocracy and that success is accessible to anyone if only they worked harder (Wu 2014). Likewise, Japan was perceived as a 'criminal justice utopia' (Goold 2004) by Western scholars and its institutions were used as global models to aspire towards and replicate. A significant amount of this literature promoted Japan through an uncritical Western gaze. Much of what is understood about crime in Japan in the English language further demonstrates the challenges of creating a universal knowledge base for criminology. Cross-national crime studies are essential.

Cross-national studies of crime are valuable because they are able to establish universals and culture-specific phenomena (Farrington 2015). They are not carried out enough because differences between countries make proper comparisons difficult. Other issues with cross-national studies include methodological challenges, lack of transparency in the publication of crime statistics in less developed countries, and the costliness of conducting such studies.

Liu (2007) observed that these issues are a hindrance to the development of criminology. To overcome them, he argued that case studies should be used; they had unparalleled strengths because they offered in-depth knowledge of one country without the methodological headaches in comparing two or more countries. They were able to provide a wealth of information about a country's crime and criminal justice, as well as an understanding of its historical and cultural context. In fact, he considered the case study to be the most productive approach in developing comparative criminology, for it had limitless possibilities of investigating criminological topics. A case study should be able to, first, examine and expand on criminological concepts and theories; second, examine crimes particular to that country; and third, investigate how social control and the criminal justice system function.

Our book is a case study on Japan. The main aim is to review research on psychology and crime in Japan, published in the English language, and to compare the results with comparable research from Western industrialised countries. We focus on English language research in order to make Japanese studies accessible to an English language audience. The book takes a different angle in that it offers an understanding of crime from a psychological perspective. Criminology often follows a sociological perspective. Indeed, the majority of criminologists have a background in sociology or were trained as sociologists. Some of these sociologists believe that psychology has no place in criminology and that only societal phenomena explain crime. A more cynical view is that psychology blames the individual for social ills—people are poor, uneducated, offenders, and failures because they choose to be; something is wrong with them, rather than with the social system, that should be fixed. This, however, is a simplistic view of what psychology can contribute to criminological knowledge.

Human behaviour and the individual seem pertinent to emerging criminological phenomena in Japan, and this warrants a psychological approach. Psychological explanations of crime are more useful in understanding individual-level crime phenomena because they emphasise influences from cognition and biology, as well as from social relationships and the immediate environment. This is not to say that crime is the product of only psychological factors. At the same time, sociological factors may manifest as psychological factors to affect people personally; psychology could be seen as an articulation of the effects of sociological phenomena. For example, deprived neighbourhoods, because of social inequality, affect accessibility to nutrients, which in turn may manifest in individuals as aggressive behaviour, poor executive functioning, and low self-control. Perhaps this contributes to the significant relationship between poverty and violence. We can observe the individual, who may reflect larger social forces that are not readily apparent.

In this book we present what is known about crime and antisocial behaviour in Japan from a psychological perspective, and aim to explain how this fits into the broader understanding of crime. Chapters 2–8 cover known explanations for crime. Including them was based on how pertinent they were to understanding crime in Japan and to psychological criminology. Some chapters, like the one on mental disorders, were more concerned with highlighting the relevance of psychological phenomena rather than being a known explanation for crime in Japan.

Chapter 1 introduces explanations for crime by setting the context. We discuss Japan's influence on the West, and vice versa, and how these influences have affected the study of crime in Japan and comparative criminology. Chapter 2 revisits the cultural explanation for crime. Although cultural traits have not been dismissed entirely by Japanese scholars, the consensus seems to be that culture is an incomplete explanation. Part of the issue has been the implications of using a cultural explanation for certain countries and not for others. A lot of knowledge on cultural differences and similarities has been gathered in the area of cross-cultural psychology, and only recently have criminologists begun to implement this in promising theories.

The chapter after discusses the life course and how it explains offending. Examining crime through developmental phases requires studies that are long-term, known as longitudinal studies. In Japan, however, these studies are difficult to conduct due to government policy. In addition, elderly crime is a recent emerging issue, possibly because of modern societal changes. Chapter 4 delves into family explanations, starting with types of family violence and then family risk factors for later offending. A primary challenge in effectively addressing family violence is societal perceptions of the family and women.

Chapter 5 focuses on young people, as social discourse has blamed them for the perceived societal breakdown and rise in crime. Attention to youth crime is important because of findings from developmental and life course criminology, which suggest that early prevention is important in stopping the development of persistent, serious offenders. The debate on the use of crime prevention is also explored. School factors are discussed in Chapter 6, and we look into the development of self-control as a personality trait. The rigidity of the educational system has been criticised for contributing to the rise in violence at school, particularly bullying, and at home with school refusal.

Mental disorders are examined in Chapter 7. Special attention is given to the 2005 Medical Treatment and Supervision (MTS) Act, which addressed previous limitations in dealing with offenders who were diagnosed with a mental disorder. Poor mental health, as reflected in significant cases of suicide and social withdrawal, is, too, reviewed. In the penultimate chapter, biosocial interactions are the focus. Very little research has been done directly on the biosocial approach, but studies from the fields of psychology and psychiatry indicate promising future avenues in examining these interactions. Psychopathy and sexual offending are examined within the context of biosocial explanations. Chapter 9 is the concluding chapter, which discusses future needed research to advance knowledge, and to contribute to a universal knowledge base, if it is even possible.

We are aware of our position as Westerners in the UK writing a book about Japan. This is the challenge of international, comparative criminology. Investigations of an unfamiliar terrain are open to all scholars, but care must be taken to depict as accurately as possible the subject of study. Under-representation, however, is a problem in criminology. Scholars who are not versed in the English language, or do not have collaborators who are, find themselves limited in their ability to contribute to collective knowledge on crime and criminal justice, because criminology primarily represents a certain group of scholars—those from the English-speaking Western world. Fortunately, this is changing. Although the growth of criminological knowledge in Asia has been slower than in North America and Europe, there is now more research conducted and made available in and from Asia, enabling a better understanding of crime phenomena than before (Liu 2009).

In addition to contributing to the area of comparative criminology, we would like our book to inspire further discussions on integrating psychological insights into crime and justice research.

Lastly we would like to thank Liqun Cao, Emiko Kobayashi, Daniel Marshall, Adrian Raine, Natalia Vibla, and the Palgrave team for their advice and comments on earlier versions of this work.

Manchester, UK   Laura Bui
Cambridge, UK   David P. Farrington
December 2018

References

Farrington, David P. 2015. "Cross-National Comparative Research on Criminal Careers, Risk Factors, Crime and Punishment." *European Journal of Criminology* 12 (4): 386–99.

Goold, Benjamin. 2004. "Idealizing the Other? Western Images of the Japanese Criminal Justice System." *Criminal Justice Ethics* 23 (2): 14–25.

Liu, Jianhong. 2007. "Developing Comparative Criminology and the Case of China: An Introduction." *International Journal of Offender Therapy and Comparative Criminology* 51 (1): 3–8.

———. 2009. "Asian Criminology—Challenges, Opportunities, and Directions." *Asian Journal of Criminology* 4 (1): 1–9.

Ng, Jennifer C., Sharon S. Lee, and Yoon K. Pak. 2007. "Contesting the Model Minority and Perpetual Foreigner Stereotypes: A Critical Review of Literature on Asian Americans in Education." *Review of Research in Education* 31 (1): 95–130.

Wu, Ellen D. 2014. *The Color of Success: Asian Americans and the Origins of the Model Minority*. Princeton: Princeton University Press.

Yoo, Hyung Chol, Kimberly S. Burrola, and Michael F. Steger. 2010. "A Preliminary Report on a New Measure: Internalization of the Model Minority Myth Measure (IM-4) and Its Psychological Correlates Among Asian American College Students." *Journal of Counseling Psychology* 57 (1): 114–27.

Contents

1

Introduction

The British and the Japanese may not be particularly alike, but the two races are exceedingly comparable. The British must actually believe this, for why else would they be displaying such a curious desperation to deny it? No doubt, they sense that to look at Japanese culture too closely would threaten a long-cherished complacency about their own. Hence the energy expended on sustaining an image of Japan as a place of fanatical businessmen, of hara-kiri and sci-fi gadgetry. Books, articles, and television programmes focus on whatever is most extreme and bizarre in Japanese life; the Japanese people may be viewed as amusing or alarming, expert or devious, but they must above all be seen to be non-human. While they remain non-human, their values and ways will remain safely irrelevant.

—Kazuo Ishiguro, *London Review of Books*, 1985

© The Author(s) 2019
L. Bui and D. P. Farrington, *Crime in Japan*, Palgrave Advances in Criminology and Criminal Justice in Asia, https://doi.org/10.1007/978-3-030-14097-7_1

Influence of Japan on Criminology

In recent times, criminology in Asia has substantially grown, and it is a hybrid of Western[1] influence and native interest from scholars and policy makers (Liu 2009). The post-war era witnessed Japan's rise as an economic superpower followed by the four 'Asian Tigers': Taiwan, Hong Kong, South Korea, and Singapore (Lee and Laider 2013; Liu 2009; Sheptycki 2008). These countries evidenced comparatively low crime rates, which supported the idea of 'Asian exceptionalism'. Despite differences between these countries, 'Asian values' and 'Confucian traditions' were thought to contribute to low crime as well as to a different social order (Fukayama 1998; Karstedt 2001).

Criminologists from the Western World were particularly interested in Japan because of its low crime rate (Sheptycki 2008). It had been theorised that modernisation would increase crime, and this was confirmed by observations of increasing crime rates since the Second World War in every Western country that transformed from agricultural to industrial (Shahidullah 2014). Japan was the first non-Western country to modernise, but defied established knowledge by having comparatively low crime (Finch 2000; Westermann and Burfeind 1991), which has remained true even today. According to recent statistics released from the United Nations Office on Drugs and Crime (UNODC 2016), Japan had lower rates of major offences[2] than the US, England and Wales, Germany, and France. Comparing low crime countries to high crime ones, Freda Adler (1983) attributed Japan's low crime to *synnomie*, comprising norm conformity, cohesion, intact social controls, and norm integration. These traits did not seem to be prominent among countries with high crime.

---

[1]In this book, the use of the terms 'Western' and 'the West' refer to Europe and North America, as the volume of criminological knowledge derives from them.

[2]Major offences were assault, robbery, and theft, whose rates were obtained in 2014, as well as homicide, whose rate was obtained in 2013.

Low Crime and Orientalism: A Brief History

Modernised and low crime Japan underscored a major issue in criminology: its ethnocentrism. Much knowledge about crime is derived from Western countries. Criminology, as a contemporary social science discipline, primarily developed in North America and Europe (Liu 2009). Many theoretical and methodological advances have been attributed to American criminologists, almost to the point that criminology is thought of as 'American criminology', despite the fact that the discipline originated from Europe (Stamatel 2009; Marshall 2001). Consequently, there is an assumption that what applies in the American context is universally applicable (Liu 2007). The 'Westernisation' of knowledge is observed in cross-national studies of crime, whereby the underrepresentation of non-Western countries (Liu 2007) and the imposing of Western theories onto non-Western societies (Agozino 2004) are critical obstacles to creating a comprehensive and inclusive criminological knowledge base.

Japan, as an exception to modernisation theory, needed an explanation. Western scholars pointed to differences between countries as reasons for Japan's low crime rate. They noted that Japanese culture prioritised the group and conformity, unlike Western cultures, such as the US, which prioritised the individual and autonomy (Miller and Kanazawa 2000). It was proposed that crime was low in Japan because committing crimes deviated from group norms and conventions, and therefore was widely disapproved.

Japanese values were also linked to overall 'Asian values', in which Confucian beliefs, particularly ones promoting strong familial ties, were reasons for the country's successes in not only boosting its economy, but also curbing crime (Karstedt 2001; Martinez 2007). Reference was, too, made to Japan's homogeneous population, because it supported an integrated society, which prevented the breakdown of social norms, or anomie[3] (Leonardsen 2002). Another popular explanation was the strong

---

[3]Emile Durkheim (1951) theorised that anomie occurs when there is a breakdown in social organisation and social control is no longer effective in restraining individuals from deviant behaviour.

preservation of cultural traditions derived from Shinto, Buddhist, and Confucian beliefs (Smith and Sueda 2008). Japanese scholars, however, have attributed their recent weakening social ties and poor childhood socialisation to the deterioration of their cultural traditions, even arguing that Western Europe was better at preserving theirs (Smith and Sueda 2008).

There are several problems with these explanations from Western scholars. First, it was assumed that only one trajectory for modernisation existed; the implication was that modernisation, as observed in the West, was the universal model (Karstedt 2001). Second, explanations for Japan's low crime were overly simplistic, because they did not elaborate the precise mechanisms that produced low crime (Komiya 1999). Third, cultural explanations were mere observations and had not been empirically validated, yet they were treated as facts (Takano and Osaka 1999). The homogeneity explanation was also based on mere widespread beliefs because, in actuality, Japan has several minority groups, such as the Ainu, resident Koreans, foreign workers, and *Burakumin*, that make up about 4% of the population (Sugimoto 2014). Although this is a small proportion compared to multi-ethnic societies such as the US and UK, Japan is not as homogeneous as it has been purported to be.

The danger with these types of explanations is that they encourage the treatment of people and cultures judged to be different from the dominant group as 'other'. Such perceptions, in turn, may lead to unfair discrimination and dehumanisation, which may directly and negatively affect life chances. Regrettably, these explanations are common in Western discourse on Japan. Take, for example, an excerpt from the beginning of the renowned anthropological study on Japan, *The Chrysanthemum and the Sword*, by American Ruth Benedict (1946), who conducted this post-war research without ever learning Japanese or setting foot in Japan (Lie 2001):

> The Japanese were the most alien enemy the United States had ever fought in an all-out struggle. No other war with a major foe had it been necessary to take into account such exceedingly different habits of acting and thinking. (Benedict 1946: 1)

Such descriptions emphasise differences. They promote dissimilarities, with the intention of reducing non-Western cultures and people to stereotypes and two-dimensional caricatures. In the case with Japan, Benjamin Goold (2004) referred to it as 'idealising the other'. Goold argued that criminological texts on Japan, particularly David Bayley's *Forces of Order: Policing Modern Japan* (1976) and John Braithwaite's *Crime, Shame, and Reintegration* (1989), romanticised Japan and the Japanese, arguing that low crime was seen as the result of differences from the West. Although Bayley concluded that low crime was the result of an efficient but lenient criminal justice system, whereas Braithwaite concluded that low crime was the result of a reintegrative shaming approach towards offenders (Hamai and Ellis 2008), Goold examined passages from these texts to support his argument that their underlying tone promoted a Western 'us' and Oriental 'them'—the Japanese were less likely to be selfish or individualistic and more likely to sacrifice themselves to group needs, and this produced low crime; these traits were thought to be unlike those found in Western societies.

The underlying 'Orientalism'[4] in these explanations implies that the Japanese are inherently different from Westerners, and that these differences in cultural traits, and in language, are reasons for the low crime rate. Goold (2004) also noted that, oddly, cultural traits tended to be used to explain non-Western contexts like Japan, but they were seldom used to understand Western contexts like England—research trying to comprehend English attitudes towards the police, for example, would not suggest a singular cultural trait, such as the belief in 'fair play', as an explanation.

Japanese scholars, however, did not seem to mind. Instead, they promoted the Japanese as unique. They were so unique that many Japanese themselves believed this, and a large body of literature existed to discuss their uniqueness (Sugimoto 2014). This literature, *Nihonjinron*, meaning 'theories on the Japanese' (Naito and Gielen 2005), had assumed

---

[4]This is in reference to Edward Said's (1979) work entitled, *Orientalism*. In his book, he argues that the West—primarily the US, France, and the UK—views the Middle East and Asia with prejudice and racism, and the purpose of their representations of 'the Orient' is to impose their vision of reality on to these regions as a method of domination and control.

that all Japanese shared the same attributes, which did not vary in degree, and that these attributes had existed in Japan for an unspecified period of time (Sugimoto 2014). In addition, it was believed that a relatively low prevalence of these attributes was found in Western societies, which was why these attributes were 'uniquely Japanese'.

Scholars of Nihonjinron have tried to pinpoint exactly what attributes distinguished the Japanese. The three most influential attributes belonged to a framework that classified Japan as a group-oriented society. First, the Japanese lacked an independent self. According to Doi (1973), they possessed *amae*, which referred to a psychological need to be indulged by superiors, as in the relationship between children and their parents. Amae encouraged interdependence; second, the Japanese were group-oriented, and the maintenance and nurture of harmonious relationships within groups were of foremost importance (Nakane 1970); and third, just as harmonious relationships were important within these groups, they, too, were important between groups, and the high level of societal stability and cohesion was credited to these between-group dynamics (Sugimoto 2014).

Evidence for the uniqueness of Japan was supported, not only by low crime, but also by the economy, which transformed the country into a rising economic superpower (Thang and Gan 2003). Consequently, towards the end of the 1970s, numerous 'Learn from Japan' campaigns emerged, which provided opportunities for other societies to emulate Japanese educational programmes, management practices, and industrial relations (Sugimoto 2014). It was no surprise that another explanation for Japan's low crime rate was the successful economy (Sheptycki 2008). Examining several economic factors, Tsushima (1996) found that unemployment was the single most important explanation for violent crime, whereas economic inequality was related to property crimes. In other words, Japan had lower violent crime rates possibly because it had comparatively more economic opportunities and less inequality.

In addition to the economic structure, Roberts and LaFree (2004) tested three other known macro-level explanations for Japan's low violent crime rate: culture, specifically informal social control; certainty of punishment, which was attributed to high police clearance rates; and an ageing population, because crime was known to be committed disproportionately by young males. Their findings showed that all explanations, except for culture, were significantly related to post-war violent crime rates. Similar to Tsushima's (1996) study, declining levels of economic stress, as measured by unemployment and inequality, was the strongest predictor of low homicide rates. They concluded that increases in economic stress would lead to higher levels of crime. Johnson (2006), however, noted that, in addition to limitations in their other findings, Roberts and LaFree's prediction was wrong because the subsequent bursting of the economic bubble in the 1990s increased unemployment and inequality, but not homicide rates.

Does Japan Have Low Crime?

Subsequent decades after the 'Learn from Japan' campaigns brought a critical assessment of Japan's alleged uniqueness (Sugimoto 2014). About this time, the low crime rate also came under scrutiny. To examine whether Japan really had low crime, Fujimoto and Park (1994) compared 15 industrial countries to Japan on homicide, sex crime, and theft rates between 1950 and 1988. They highlighted that the crime rate had not always been low, as theft between 1950 and 1970 in Japan was higher than seven other countries, including the US. Instead of solely focusing on the rate itself, they also focused on trends and public safety. Their results showed that crime trends in Japan were similar to those in other industrialised countries, characterised by a predominant amount of property crimes and a low prevalence of violent crimes. Although homicide rates were relatively low in Japan, they argued that the country could not be considered safe as claimed by previous researchers: including motor vehicle and industrial related accidents, as well as suicide between 1980 and 1988, increased the overall death rate to the median among all countries. Thus, when criminologists state that Japan has low crime, it is unclear whether this refers to overall crime or specific types of crime. White-collar crime, especially institutional corruption (Fenwick 2013), for example, may be relatively high in Japan (Leonardsen 2002).

Some Western and Japanese scholars have questioned the reliability of Japan's official crime statistics, even though previous Western researchers had relied on them—thought to be uniquely accurate—to support Japan's relatively low crime rate (Finch 2000; Hamai and Ellis 2008). Critical scholars suspected that, because of under-recording, a significant 'dark figure' of crime existed, particularly among crimes where reporting by victims was low, such as white-collar crime, domestic violence, and sexual assault (Aldous and Leishman 2000; Kitamura et al. 1999).

Instead of using official crime statistics, a couple of studies have used self-reports to compare crime. The self-report method is considered the closest data source to actual behaviour, after observation of the crime as it occurs (Thornberry and Krohn 2000). The use of self-reports arose from the need to seek alternative measures of crime, as official data were unreliable (Farrington 1973). Bui et al. (2014) compared self-reports of violence between roughly 400 American and 400 Japanese high school male youths. Contrary to the low crime discourse, they found that Japanese males self-reported a higher prevalence of violence than American males (48% vs. 35%). Previously, Ramirez et al. (2001) compared self-reports of aggression between 200 Japanese and 200 Spanish university students. Surprisingly, they found that Japanese students were more likely to be physically aggressive than Spanish students. Even Japanese females were more physically aggressive than their Spanish counterparts. Verbal aggression, however, had a higher prevalence among the Spanish than Japanese students.

Official crime rates were affected after a string of police scandals between 1999 and 2001. The admissions of corruption in the handling of crime statistics (Johnson 2007) resulted in a substantial loss of public trust in the police (Johnson 2003). Quantitative comparative studies on public confidence in the police in Japan and America have even shown that confidence in the police was lower in Japan than in America, despite previous observations to the contrary (Cao and Stack 2005; Cao et al. 1998). Reacting to this, Japan's National Police Agency (NPA) created new policies whereby reported incidents were recorded without police discretion at 'consultation desks' (Hamai and Ellis 2006). About 90% of these reported incidents were eventually recorded as a crime, and this led to noticeable increases in the crime rate, specifically for violent crime (Hamai and Ellis 2006).

As the crime rate superficially increased, so did the fear of crime. The high level of fear, however, was disproportionate to the actual risk of victimisation, as Japan has one of the lowest victimisation rates among industrialised countries (Sheptycki 2008). Despite these low rates, the 'Iron Quadrangle' (Hamai and Ellis 2006)—the media, victims and their rights movement, police and politicians, and crime experts—aggravated fears by highlighting crime as the foremost societal concern.

Crime and Deviance in Modern Japan

Fear of crime is related to other issues in Japanese society. The country has the highest proportion of people aged 65 and over in the world, as well as a declining fertility rate (Muramatsu and Akiyama 2011). The primary reason for this is the growing trend among young men and women to postpone marriage and delay having children. Although Japan is traditionally a patriarchal society (Tsutomi et al. 2013), in which women were expected to be housewives and discouraged from full-time work (Sugimoto 2014), a higher proportion of women today have chosen to remain single for the long term because of their educational advancement and participation in the workforce (White 2002).

Related to this, young people, in particular, have been the primary focus of the discourse on the 'law and order collapse' (Johnson 2006, 2008). Young people have been regarded as the reason for the rise in violent crimes. The mass media had been the main culprit in spreading this idea (Yoder 2011). Consequently, the public has the impression that societal conditions are deteriorating because of the state of their young people (Toyama-Bialke 2003). As the public is disproportionately older, fear of crime may be intertwined with older people's concerns about social change, economic decline, and their poorer quality of life (Pain 1995), and as a result youth are perceived as the cause of that fear (Pain 2000).

Homicide statistics, though, indicate that the vast majority of murderers are middle-aged men around the ages of 40 and 50 (Johnson

2006). Cross-national studies of homicide rates show that, not only do Japanese youth commit less murders than their older counterparts, but also they commit fewer murders than youth in other countries (Johnson 2006). Overall, the Japan homicide rate has dropped to less than a third of the number of murders recorded in 1955, and this has been attributed to the significant decrease of the male youth population (Hiraiwa-Hasegawa 2005). It is established that a gender discrepancy in crime exists, whereby males commit a disproportionate number of offences compared to females (Farrington and Welsh 2007), and delinquency reaches a peak during adolescence and early adulthood (Farrington 1986; Wolfgang et al. 1985). Fujimoto and Park (1994) concluded from their study, however, that, although Japan had lower homicide rates, this did not indicate a particularly safe country: the suicide rate is among the highest in the world.

Some deviant and violent behaviours are also specific problems in Japan: school-related issues include *ijime*, which is roughly translated as bullying (Morita 1996; Naito and Gielen 2005). Unlike bullying in Western societies, which is perpetrated by one or two individuals, bullying in Japan may be perpetrated by a group or the entire class, and even by teachers (Mino 2006). These issues may lead to forms of psychopathology that may be associated with shame (Crystal et al. 2001). Examples are cases where students refuse to or cannot attend school, which are referred to as *tōkō kyohi* (Yamamiya 2003), meaning 'school refusal'. This phenomenon has been gradually increasing since the 1980s (Yoneyama 2000). A similar occurrence to tōkō kyohi is *hikikomori*, meaning social withdrawal. Hikikomori is primarily observed among males during puberty and adolescence, in which the sufferer completely withdraws from society for six or more months (Koyama et al. 2010).

Western Influence on Japanese Criminology

Asian criminology may be seen as an extension of Western criminology, because one source of developing criminology in Asia was Western influence (Liu 2009). Since the post-war era, Japanese criminology has concentrated on reading, translating, and attempting to apply American theories and frameworks such as Edward Sutherland's principles of criminology and Robert Merton's anomie (Lee and Laider 2013). The spread of Western influence is attributed to Asian scholars, including the Japanese, who studied in Western universities and brought back what they learned to teach and organise programmes on criminology in Asia (Liu 2009). These scholars, who had studied abroad, tended to conduct empirical work testing US criminological theories, and the most popular of these was Travis Hirschi's social bonding and control theory (Lee and Laider 2013). Japanese criminology, though, has a specific Western influence: it is highly Americanised (Konishi 2013).

Although the field of criminology is supposedly a collection of different disciplines, whose similarity lies in their interest in crime, criminology is often considered synonymous with sociological criminology (Wortley 2011). Prior to the Second World War, Japanese psychiatrists initially developed criminology and forensic medicine in their country (Yokoyama 2013). During that time, Japanese criminology took on a psychological perspective, in which criminal careers and biological influences were studied, but under the context of eugenics; in agreement with Nazi Germany in 1940, Japan enacted the National Eugenics Law, which required the sterilisation of those who seemed likely to produce criminal offspring.

The post-war era experienced a surge of sociological explanations that have formed the current state of criminology today. When the Second World War ended, Japan became a democracy and there was more freedom to study and research; during this time, however, poverty was a significant issue, and this attracted the interest of sociologists to the study of crime (Yokoyama 2013). This trend paralleled that of the US: the rise of sociological explanations for crime occurred shortly after the end of the Second World War when, in the US, earlier developments from the Chicago School linking crime to social conditions flourished (Hollin 2002). Sociological criminology in the US was considered a reaction of opposition to Nazi ideology that included eugenics and execution of those with mental and physical disabilities (Jones 2008). Nazi ideology was influenced by psychobiological theories from Cesare Lombroso, an Italian physician in the nineteenth century, who believed that certain genetic characteristics distinguished offenders from non-offenders, and that offenders were 'born criminals' (Hollin 2013; Jones 2008). Consequently, psychological perspectives on crime became less influential in the US after the Second World War.

Although some prominent psychological theories emerged during the 1960s and 1970s, they were not integrated into mainstream criminology; rather they remained within the discipline of psychology (Hollin 2002). Psychology was still used to understand crime, though separately from criminology, and it was primarily applied to offender rehabilitation (Andrews and Bonta 2010). In the 1970s, however, the US experienced the rise of punitive approaches to criminal justice. Loïc Wacquant (2009) attributed the growth of punitiveness and neoliberalism to a group of 'Reagan-era conservative think tanks', particularly the Manhattan Institute. These think tanks influenced American government policies by encouraging economic deregulation and severe cuts to social programmes. Penal policies also reflected this influence, in that the application of 'broken windows' and 'zero tolerance policies' were aimed to further punish those most at risk of becoming victims or offenders of crime: the poor. As American global influence grew, it was able to spread its punitive penal policies through Western Europe via the UK, as well as to the rest of the world. Further support for 'get tough' justice policies were also fuelled by findings from studies of rehabilitation that were interpreted as showing little evidence that treatment programmes could reduce reoffending (Mair 1995). As a result, in the 1970s rehabilitation was rejected in favour of harsh and punitive treatment of offenders (Andrews and Bonta 2010).

Psychological and Sociological Understandings of Crime

Sociologists have been critical of the psychological perspective because they believe that it neglects group-level factors (e.g., social disadvantage) in explaining crime, and psychology's focus on the individual assumes that it is the individual's fault, which may further alienate the vulnerable and powerless. Psychologists, however, argue that the sociological perspective ignores significant individual differences in criminal conduct and is more susceptible to ideology rather than scientific evidence (Wortley 2011).

Roughly, sociological explanations for crime are concerned with society and how it may produce or influence the occurrence of crime and distribution of criminality. Its focus of study is on social structure, and it seeks to change the environment to reduce crime (Hollin 2002). For example, racial and urban inequality are considered sociological explanations for the disproportionate number of black Americans as victims and offenders in violent crime (Sampson and Wilson 1995). From this perspective, crime is seen as a result of social conditions such as social class or the economy.

Psychological Criminology

Recent decades, however, have witnessed an increased interest in psychological explanations for crime. In the US, the punitive policies of the get-tough movement have largely failed and were expensive. The supposed war on drugs and crime seemed to actually be a war on race, in which black Americans were disproportionately represented in prisons, death row, and arrests compared to white Americans (Andrews and Bonta 2010).

Clive Hollin (2002) describes the return of psychology to criminology, beginning in the 1990s, whereby psychologists challenged what they thought was a criminological bias against their discipline: during this time, criminologists also began to revisit studies of the individual offender in light of the increased popularity of biological theories, textbooks dedicated to biosocial factors, and psychological factors that focused on cognition. In response to Robert Martinson's (1974) original findings that were interpreted to mean 'nothing works' in reducing recidivism, the 'What Works' movement was created, which gathered support about components of interventions that were effective in reducing offending (Andrews and Bonta 2010). Findings from meta-analyses on offender rehabilitation, which statistically summarised the overall effectiveness of treatment, showed that treatment did significantly reduce offending (Raynor 2002). In addition to developments from the 'What Works' initiative, some British psychologists and criminologists began to collaborate because of growing research on Developmental and Life-Course Criminologies, which subsequently combined to form one criminological area (see Farrington 2005).

Psychological explanations for crime focus on the individual and behaviour. They use psychology—the science of the mind and behaviour—to understand crime and criminals. The discipline of psychology is concerned with understanding behaviour and applying what is learned about it to intervene in and improve people's lives (Matsumoto and Juang 2013).

This minority approach to the study of crime is defined as 'the scientific study of behaviour and mental processes that contribute to an understanding of crime and criminals' (Wortley 2011). One of the goals of psychological criminology is to intervene directly with offenders and those at risk of offending; this is achieved by predicting and preventing criminal behaviour. Thus, understanding crime and criminals by studying behaviour and mental processes is a hallmark of psychological criminology (Hollin 2013). For example, a psychological explanation for the discrepancy in self-reported violence between black and white Americans is that black Americans are more likely to experience adverse familial, school, and individual factors. For officially recorded violence, however, no factors fully explained the between-group difference in violence, which suggests that racism may play a role during the arrest and court referral stages (Farrington et al. 2003).

Psychological explanations for crime include not only the family, peer, and school environments as influences on criminality, but also individual and biological factors, such as brain functioning in violent offenders (Raine 2013), forensic mental health (Towl and Crighton 2015), impulsiveness (Jolliffe and Farrington 2009), and the transmission of criminality from parents to their children (Besemer et al. 2011). They are also useful in the study of individual differences in offending; the development of offending from childhood to adulthood; and interactions between the individual and environment in causing offending (Farrington 2005).

Contributions to psychological criminology do exist in Japan as well. In the Japanese Association of Criminal Psychology (JACP), founded in 1963,[5] as well as government organisations such as the Ministry of Justice and National Research Institute of Police Science, psychologists have contributed to knowledge about screening, classifying adult and juvenile offenders, and offender treatment (Misumi 1989; Yokoyama 2013). Recent times have witnessed emerging criminological phenomena in Japan that may be better understood by integrating a psychological perspective: violent youth-on-youth murders (Ohbuchi and Kondo 2015), serious youth offending (Bui et al. 2016), bullying (Naito and Gielen 2005), and family violence (Kumagai 2016). These are a few examples whose current knowledge would benefit from the field of psychology.

Conclusion

Explanations for the low crime rate in Japan derive from a variety of reasons. These, in fact, show that the current situation in the country is complex, whereby many social issues may act as drivers and by-products of crime. Another reason for the different explanations is Western impact and participation: much of Japanese criminology has been influenced by advances in theory from the West, particularly from America. In addition, the popular explanation for Japan's low crime rate by Westerners tends to be culture, which, to some extent, has been promoted by the Japanese and *nihonjinron*. A significant proportion of criminological phenomena, however, cannot be adequately explained by sociological understandings of crime that dominate the field. Rather, psychology also has much to offer in the understanding of crime.

---

[5]The majority of sources have stated that the JACP was established in 1963 (see Konishi 2013; Imada and Tanaka-Matsumi 2016; Misumi 1989).

References

Adler, Freda. 1983. *Nations Not Obsessed with Crime*. Littleton: Fred B. Rothman and Co.

Agozino, Biko. 2004. "Imperialism, Crime and Criminology: Towards the Decolonisation of Criminology." *Crime, Law and Social Change* 41 (4): 343–58.

Aldous, Christopher, and Frank Leishman. 2000. "Enigma Variations: Reassessing the Kôban." Oxford: Nissan Institute of Japanese Studies.

Andrews, Donald A., and James Bonta. 2010. "Rehabilitating Criminal Justice Policy and Practice." *Psychology, Public Policy, and Law* 16 (1): 39–55.

Bayley, David H. 1976. *Forces of Order: Policing Modern Japan*. Berkeley: University of California Press.

Benedict, Ruth. 1946. *The Chrysanthemum and the Sword*. Boston: Houghton Mifflin.

Besemer, Sytske, Victor van der Geest, Joseph Murray, Catrien Bijleveld, and David P. Farrington. 2011. "The Relationship Between Parental Imprisonment and Offspring in England and the Netherlands." *British Journal of Criminology* 51: 413–37.

Braithwaite, John. 1989. *Crime, Shame and Reintegration*. Cambridge: Cambridge University Press.

Bui, Laura, David P. Farrington, Mitsuaki Ueda, and Karl G. Hill. 2014. "Prevalence and Risk Factors for Self-Reported Violence of Osaka and Seattle Male Youths." *International Journal of Offender Therapy and Comparative Criminology* 58 (12): 1540–57.

Bui, Laura, David P. Farrington, and Mitsuaki Ueda. 2016. "Potential Risk and Promotive Factors for Serious Delinquency in Japanese Female Youth." *International Journal of Comparative and Applied Criminal Justice* 40 (3): 209–24.

Cao, Liqun, and Steven Stack. 2005. "Confidence in the Police Between America and Japan." *Policing: An International Journal of Police Strategies & Management* 28 (1): 139–51.

Cao, Liqun, Steven Stack, and Yi Sun. 1998. "Public Attitudes Toward the Police: A Comparative Study Between Japan and America." *Journal of Criminal Justice* 26 (4): 279–89.

Crystal, David S., Gerrod W. Parrott, Yukiko Okazaki, and Hirozumi Watanabe. 2001. "Examining Relations Between Shame and Personality Among University Students in the United States and Japan: A

Developmental Perspective." *International Journal of Behavioral Development* 25 (2): 113–23.

Doi, Takeo. 1973. *The Anatomy of Dependence*. Tokyo: Kodansha.

Durkheim, Emile. 1951. *Suicide: A Study in Sociology*. Glencoe: Free Press.

Farrington, David P. 1973. "Self-Reports of Deviant Behavior: Predictive and Stable?" *Journal of Criminal Law and Criminology* 64 (1): 99–110.

———. 1986. "Age and Crime." In *Crime and Justice, Vol. 7*, edited by Michael Tonry and Norval Morris, 189–250. Chicago: University of Chicago Press.

———. 2005. *Integrated Developmental and Life-Course Theories of Offending*. New Brunswick: Transaction.

Farrington, David P., and Brandon C. Welsh. 2007. *Saving Children from a Life of Crime*. New York: Oxford University Press.

Farrington, David P., Rolf Loeber, and Magda Stouthamer-Loeber. 2003. "How Can the Relationship Between Race and Violence Be Explained?" In *Violent Crime: Assessing Race and Ethnic Differences*, edited by Darnell F. Hawkins, 213–37. Cambridge: Cambridge University Press.

Fenwick, Mark. 2013. "'Penal Populism' and Penological Change in Contemporary Japan." *Theoretical Criminology* 17 (2): 215–31.

Finch, Andrew. 2000. "Criminal Statistics in Japan: The White Paper on Crime, Hanzai Hakusho and Hanzai Tokeisho." *Social Science Japan Journal* 3 (2): 237–49.

Fujimoto, Tetsuya, and Won-Kyu Park. 1994. "Is Japan Exceptional? Reconsidering Japanese Crime Rates." *Social Justice* 21 (2 (56)): 110–35.

Fukayama, Francis. 1998. "Asian Values and Civilization." In *ICAS Fall Symposium, Asia's Challenges Ahead*. University of Pennsylvania.

Goold, Benjamin. 2004. "Idealizing the Other? Western Images of the Japanese Criminal Justice System." *Criminal Justice Ethics* 23 (2): 14–25.

Hamai, Koichi, and Thomas Ellis. 2006. "Crime and Criminal Justice in Modern Japan: From Re-integrative Shaming to Popular Punitivism." *International Journal of the Sociology of Law* 34 (3): 157–78.

———. 2008. "Japanese Criminal Justice: Was Reintegrative Shaming a Chimera?" *Punishment & Society* 10 (1): 25–46.

Hiraiwa-Hasegawa, Mariko. 2005. "Homicide by Men in Japan, and Its Relationship to Age, Resources and Risk Taking." *Evolution and Human Behavior* 26 (4): 332–43.

Hollin, Clive R. 2002. "Criminological Psychology." In *The Oxford Handbook in Criminology and Criminal Justice*, edited by Mike Maguire, Rod Morgan, and Robert Reiner, 144–74. Oxford: Oxford University Press.

———. 2013. *Psychology and Crime: An Introduction to Criminological Psychology*. London: Routledge.

Imada, Hiroshi, and Junko Tanaka-Matsumi. 2016. "Psychology in Japan." *International Journal of Psychology* 51 (3): 220–31.

Johnson, David T. 2003. "Above the Law? Police Integrity in Japan." *Social Science Japan Journal* 6 (1): 19–37.

———. 2006. "The Vanishing Killer: Japan's Postwar Homicide Decline." *Social Science Japan Journal* 9 (1): 73–90.

———. 2007. "Book Review: Park, W.-K. (2006). Trends in Crime Rates in Postwar Japan: A Structural Perspective. The Law and Political Science Series of the University of Kitakyushu, 20. Morioka City, Iwate Prefecture, Japan: Shinzansha Co., Pp. Xii, 255." *International Criminal Justice Review* 17 (2): 153–55.

———. 2008. "The Homicide Drop in Postwar Japan." *Homicide Studies* 12 (1): 146–60.

Jolliffe, Darrick, and David P. Farrington. 2009. "A Systematic Review of the Relationship Between Childhood Impulsiveness and Later Violence." In *Personality, Personality Disorder and Violence*, edited by Mary McMurran and Richard C. Howard, 38–61. Chichester: Wiley.

Jones, David W. 2008. *Understanding Criminal Behaviour: Psychosocial Approaches to Criminality*. Cullompton: Willan.

Karstedt, Susanne. 2001. "Comparing Cultures, Comparing Crime: Challenges, Prospects and Problems for a Global Criminology." *Crime, Law and Social Change* 36 (3): 285–308.

Kitamura, Toshinori, Nobuhiko Kijima, Noboru Iwata, Yukiko Senda, Koji Takahashi, and Ikue Hayashi. 1999. "Frequencies of Child Abuse in Japan: Hidden but Prevalent Crime." *International Journal of Offender Therapy and Comparative Criminology* 43 (1): 21–33.

Komiya, Nobuo. 1999. "A Cultural Study of the Low Crime Rate in Japan." *British Journal of Criminology* 39 (3): 369–90.

Konishi, Tokikazu. 2013. "Diversity Within an Asian Country: Japanese Criminal Justice and Criminology." In *Handbook of Asian Criminology*, edited by Jianhong Liu, Bill Hebenton, and Susyan Jou, 213–22. New York: Springer.

Koyama, Asuka, Yuko Miyake, Norito Kawakami, Masao Tsuchiya, Hisateru Tachimori, and Tadashi Takeshima. 2010. "Lifetime Prevalence, Psychiatric Comorbidity and Demographic Correlates of 'Hikikomori' in a Community Population in Japan." *Psychiatry Research* 176 (1): 69–74.

Kumagai, Fumie. 2016. "Introduction: Toward a Better Understanding of Family Violence in Japan." In *Family Violence in Japan: A Life Course Perspective*, edited by Fumie Kumagai and Masako Ishii-Kuntz, 1–48. Singapore: Springer.

Lee, Maggy, and Karen Joe Laider. 2013. "Doing Criminology from the Periphery: Crime and Punishment in Asia." *Theoretical Criminology* 17 (2): 141–57.

Leonardsen, Dag. 2002. "The Impossible Case of Japan." *Australian and New Zealand Journal of Criminology* 35 (2): 203–29.

Lie, John. 2001. "Ruth Benedict's Legacy of Shame: Orientalism and Occidentalism in the Study of Japan." *Asian Journal of Social Science* 29 (2): 249–61.

Liu, Jianhong. 2007. "Developing Comparative Criminology and the Case of China: An Introduction." *International Journal of Offender Therapy and Comparative Criminology* 51 (1): 3–8.

———. 2009. "Asian Criminology—Challenges, Opportunities, and Directions." *Asian Journal of Criminology* 4 (1): 1–9.

Mair, George. 1995. "Evaluating the Impact of Community Penalties." *The University of Chicago Law School Roundtable* 2 (2): Article 6.

Marshall, Ineke Haen. 2001. "The Criminological Enterprise in Europe and the United States: A Contextual Exploration." *European Journal on Criminal Policy and Research* 9 (3): 235–58.

Martinez, Dolores P. 2007. *Modern Japan Culture and Society*. London: Routledge.

Martinson, Robert M. 1974. "What Works?—Questions and Answers About Prison Reform." *The Public Interest*, no. 35: 22–54.

Matsumoto, David, and Linda Juang. 2013. *Culture and Psychology*. Belmont: Wadsworth/Thompson Learning.

Miller, Alan, and Satoshi Kanazawa. 2000. *Order by Accident: The Origins and Consequences of Conformity in Contemporary Japan*. Boulder: Westview.

Mino, Tamaki. 2006. "Ijime (Bullying) in Japanese Schools: A Product of Japanese Education Based on Group Conformity." In *Rhizomes: Re-visioning Boundaries*, 24–25. http://espace.library.uq.edu.au/view/UQ:7721.

Misumi, Jyuji. 1989. "Introduction: Applied Psychology in Japan." *Applied Psychology* 38 (4): 309–20.

Morita, Yohji. 1996. "Bullying as a Contemporary Behaviour Problem in the Context of Increasing 'Societal Privatization' in Japan." *Prospects* 26 (2): 311–29.

Muramatsu, Naoko, and Hiroko Akiyama. 2011. "Japan: Super-Aging Society Preparing for the Future." *The Gerontologist* 51 (4): 425–32.

Naito, Takashi, and Uwe P. Gielen. 2005. "Bullying and Ijime in Japanese Schools." In *Violence in Schools: Cross-National and Cross-Cultural Perspectives*, edited by Florence L. Denmark, Herbert H. Krauss, Robert W. Wesner, Elizabeth Midlarsky, and Uwe P. Gielen, 169–90. Boston: Springer.

Nakane, Chie. 1970. *Japanese Society*. Tokyo: Tuttle.

Ohbuchi, Ken-ichi, and Hideo Kondo. 2015. "Psychological Analysis of Serious Juvenile Violence in Japan." *Asian Journal of Criminology* 10: 149–62.

Pain, Rachel. 1995. "Fear of Crime and Local Contexts: Elderly People in North East England." *Northern Economic Review* 24: 96–111.

———. 2000. "Place, Social Relations and the Fear of Crime: A Review." *Progress in Human Geography* 24 (3): 365–87.

Raine, Adrian. 2013. *The Anatomy of Violence: The Biological Roots of Crime*. New York: Vintage Books.

Ramirez, J. Martin, Jose Manuel Andreu, and Takehiro Fujihara. 2001. "Cultural and Sex Differences in Aggression: A Comparison Between Japanese and Spanish Students Using Two Different Inventories." *Aggressive Behavior* 27: 313–22.

Raynor, Peter. 2002. "Community Penalties: Probation, Punishment, and 'What Works'." In *The Oxford Handbook of Criminology*, edited by Mike Maguire, Rod Morgan, and Robert Reiner, 1168–206. Oxford: Oxford University Press.

Roberts, Aki, and Gary LaFree. 2004. "Explaining Japan's Postwar Violent Crime Trends." *Criminology* 42 (1): 179–210.

Said, Edward. 1979. *Orientalism*. New York: Vintage Books.

Sampson, Robert J., and William Julius Wilson. 1995. "Toward a Theory of Race, Crime, and Urban Inequality." In *Crime and Inequality*, edited by John Hagan and Ruth D. Peterson, 37–56. Stanford: Stanford University Press.

Shahidullah, Shahid M. 2014. "Comparative Criminal Justice: Theoretical Perspectives." In *Comparative Criminal Justice Systems: Global and Local Perspectives*, 55–86. Burlington: Jones and Barnett Learning.

Sheptycki, James. 2008. "Transnationalisation, Orientalism and Crime." *Asian Journal of Criminology* 3 (1): 13–35.

Smith, David, and Kiyoko Sueda. 2008. "The Killing of Children by Children as a Symptom of National Crisis: Reactions in Britain and Japan." *Criminology and Criminal Justice* 8 (1): 5–25.

Stamatel, Janet. 2009. "Contributions of Cross-National Research to Criminology at the Beginning of the 21st Century." In *Handbook on Crime and Deviance*, edited by Marvin D. Krohn, Alan J. Lizotte, and Gina Penly Hall, 3–22. Handbooks of Sociology and Social Research. New York: Springer.

Sugimoto, Yoshio. 2014. *An Introduction to Japanese Society*. 4th ed. Cambridge: Cambridge University Press.

Takano, Yotaro, and Eiko Osaka. 1999. "An Unsupported Common View: Comparing Japan and the US on Individualism/Collectivism." *Asian Journal of Social Psychology* 2: 311–41.

Thang, Leng Leng, and S. K. Gan. 2003. "Deconstructing 'Japanisation': Reflections from the 'Learn from Japan' Campaign in Singapore." *New Zealand Journal of Asian Studies* 5 (1): 91–106.

Thornberry, Terence P., and Marvin D. Krohn. 2000. "The Self-Report Method for Measuring Delinquency and Crime." *Criminal Justice* 4 (1): 33–83.

Towl, Graham J., and David A. Crighton. 2015. "Introduction." In *Forensic Psychology*, edited by David A. Crighton and Graham J. Towl, 2nd ed., 1–12. West Sussex: Wiley.

Toyama- Bialke, Chisaki. 2003. "The 'Japanese Triangle' for Preventing Adolescent Delinquency—Strengths and Weaknesses of the Family-School Adolescent Relationship from a Comparative Perspective." In *Juvenile Delinquency in Japan: Reconsidering the "crisis"*, edited by Gesine Foljanty-Jost, 19–50. Leiden: Brill.

Tsushima, Masahiro. 1996. "Economic Structure and Crime: The Case of Japan." *Journal of Socio-Economics* 25 (4): 497–515.

Tsutomi, Hiroshi, Laura Bui, Mitsuaki Ueda, and David P. Farrington. 2013. "The Application of Criminological Theory to a Japanese Context: Power-Control Theory." *International Journal of Criminological and Sociological Theory* 6 (4): 128–44.

United Nations Office on Drugs and Crime. 2016. "United Nations Office on Drugs and Crime Statistics on Crime." Vienna: Author.

Wacquant, Loïc. 2009. *Prisons of Poverty*. Minneapolis: University of Minnesota Press.

Westermann, Ted D., and James W. Burfeind. 1991. *Crime and Justice in Two Societies*. Pacific Grove, CA: Brooks/Cole.

White, Merry 2002. *Perfectly Japanese: Making Families in an Era of Upheaval*. Berkeley, CA: University of California Press.

Wolfgang, Marvin E., Robert M. Figlio, Paul Tracy, and Simon I. Singer. 1985. *The National Survey of Crime Severity*. Washington, DC: U.S. Bureau of Justice Statistics.

Wortley, Richard. 2011. *Psychological Criminology: An Integrative Approach*. Oxon: Routledge.

Yamamiya, Yuko. 2003. "Juvenile Delinquency in Japan." *Journal of Prevention & Intervention in the Community* 25 (2): 27–46.

Yoder, Robert. 2011. *Deviance and Inequality in Japan: Japanese Youth and Foreign Migrants*. Bristol: The Policy Press.

Yokoyama, Minoru. 2013. "Development of Criminology in Japan from a Sociological Perspective." In *Handbook of Asian Criminology*, edited by Jianhong Liu, Bill Hebenton, and Susyan Jou, 223–30. New York: Springer.

Yoneyama, Shoko. 2000. "Student Discourse on Tokokyohi (School Phobia/Refusal) in Japan: Burnout or Empowerment?" *British Journal of Sociology of Education* 21 (1): 77–94.

2

Culture

Probably the most complicated explanation for crime is culture. It is complicated not only from a research standpoint, but from the multiple standpoints that can be taken: Sociologists have their approaches and psychologists have theirs, but scholars from the Western world, who are used to global dominance in social narratives, may take a standpoint characterised by ethnocentrism—that the 'Far East' is full of the 'other'. Although Japan had promoted uniqueness, in the views of the West, it is considered as 'different'.

Of all countries that have been subjected to comparative analysis by Western criminologists, Japan has suffered the most instrumental stereotyping (Goold 2004). It is seen as the 'other', and observed differences have been used to explain its crime and criminal justice phenomena. The reason for attention in criminology was that Japan, seen as different but industrialised, was doing exceptionally better in reducing crime than Western industrialised countries. This narrative rings very familiar to those who study race relations in the US: compared to other American racial groups, Americans whose ethnicity originates from 'the Far East' are academically and socio-economically more successful (Bui 2018), but as they are a minority group, they are unfairly discriminated

© The Author(s) 2019
L. Bui and D. P. Farrington, *Crime in Japan*, Palgrave Advances in Criminology
and Criminal Justice in Asia, https://doi.org/10.1007/978-3-030-14097-7_2

against because they are still considered as perpetual foreigners (Chol et al. 2009). In other words, if the dominant group is unable to explain the success obtained by a group perceived to be weaker, it will attribute this success to some essential freak and alien characteristic.

The Problem with Cultural Explanations

Studying culture has merit because it helps to locate how everyday experiences and practices shape the development of important social and executive skills in different societies (Lewis et al. 2009). The problem of using culture to explain crime in Japan, however, is epitomised in a couple of book reviews of known texts on the topic: in a review of five books on Japanese criminal justice, Steinhoff (1993) divided criminological research on Japan into two categories: the first type of research sought solutions to (primarily) American crime problems in Japanese institutions, whereas the second type prioritised gaining insight into how criminal justice institutions operated in the Japanese context. The aim of the former research was to identify what was working to reduce crime in Japan and export it, in the hope that these Japanese-derived institutions could also reduce crime in the American context. Essentially, this form of research concentrated on learning from Japan to solve social ills abroad. Steinhoff, however, took aim at this form of criminological research, as it depicted Japanese criminal justice romantically; there seemed to be no attempt to scrutinise observations—often idealised—about these institutions. An example is the neighbourhood police box known as *kōban*.

Much has been written about the kōban. Western scholars have praised—and have uncritically accepted—this form of policing, in which Japanese police emphasise community involvement and patrolling to reduce crime; the impression is that Japanese law enforcement is in touch with the people and that is why crime is low. Rake (1987), for example, a television producer, wrote enthusiastically in *The ANNALS* about the crime-reducing effects of implementing community policing like the kōban from Tokyo to Santa Ana, California in the US. He had been inspired by Bayley's (1976) research, and produced a documentary based on it. These observations about the kōban, however, have been criticised for their lack of awareness of the historical context and larger police system in Japan (Aldous and Leishman 2000).

The reviewed books that fell into this category of research were Ted Westermann and James Burfeind's (1991) comparative work, *Crime and Justice in Two Societies: Japan and the United States*, and, notably, David Bayley's (1976) work, *Forces of Order*, based on interviews with Japanese police officers. While Steinhoff had positive comments to make about these two works, this was not true for Robert Thornton and Katsuya Endo's (1992) comparative work on US–Japan sister cities, Salem in Oregon and Kawagoe, which she found lacked scholarly rigour.

Steinhoff noted that this kind of criminological research tended to emphasise culture as the reason for why these institutions operated as they did: 'If you begin with the assumption that culture subsumes everything, you will find a cultural explanation for everything, even if more powerful alternative explanations abound' (p. 848). Most of this research seemed to have been based on assumptions that the Japanese were inherently different because of their cultural values, which each and every one of them internalised. Therefore, criminal justice and crime were products of this internalising of exotic cultural traits. This reasoning appears to be circular, and this is what Steinhoff had underscored.

Kochi Hamai (2011) reviewed the book, *Crime in Japan: Paradise Lost?*, by Norwegian Criminologist, Dag Leonardsen. Published in 2010, this was the most recent book in the English language on the topic until Liu and Miyazawa's (2018) co-edited *Crime and Justice in Contemporary Japan*. Leonardsen's main premise was that increasing punitive measures by the Japanese government may actually have negative consequences, particularly among those who were at high risk for suicidal behaviour.

Hamai commented that the book was ambitious and that he appreciated the attention given to how reactions to crime affected the well-being of vulnerable citizens. He highlighted, however, that for such a complex issue, crime and suicide were heavily explained by culture—perceived Japanese traits of perseverance, discipline, and group-dependence. Hamai further wrote that, as a criminologist, he instead would have examined statistics on socio-demographic changes.

His review reveals an ongoing issue in the use of culture to explain crime in Japan by Western scholars. The use of the cultural explanation has been criticised as a form of 'orientalism' (Goold 2004), or generally as 'intellectual imperialism' (Zedner 1995), in which Japanese and non-Westerners are reduced to cultural simplifications and caricatures. Using culture to explain crime in non-Western societies suggests that these societies are perceived to be relatively less complex than that of Western societies.

This is not to say that Leonardsen intended to simplify and caricature the Japanese; rather, his work could be interpreted as a fascination with such a complex society, whose social ills manifest and are responded to slightly differently. Perhaps when trying to understand crime in new terrain, social phenomena like the economy or urban migration are considered 'mundane' and not sufficient to explain the observed differences. Another way of putting it is that what is used normally to explain crime in the familiar is thought to be unable to explain crime sufficiently in the unfamiliar.

It is believed that a better understanding of phenomena in a different place requires an understanding of the culture. This is a reasonable starting point. The problem is how best to examine cultural influences in spite of the threat of ethnocentric biases, which may contribute to unintentional simplification and caricature. Another obstacle is how to treat culture as a credible explanation so that it can be included into a broader explanatory framework for crime. These are difficult challenges when undertaking comparative research.

Miller and Kanazawa (2000) pointed to two limitations of the cultural explanation. First, it was considered incomplete. The main component of this explanation argues that Confucian values have contributed to Japan's low crime rate. These values, though, are found in other East Asian countries. Although these countries have relatively low crime compared to Western counterparts, their cultures differ significantly from that of Japan's, and they cannot be lumped together into a monolithic East Asian culture. Second, the cultural explanation was vague. How exactly does culture contribute to the crime rate? This has never been made clear.

The issue is not that the cultural explanation is invalid. Rather, the problem is how culture has been used to understand crime in Japan. Steinhoff (1993) suggested that criminological research on Japan should focus less on polarised differences (criminal justice in America vs. criminal justice in Japan) and focus more on the everyday context and its influence on the choices people make, and how those choices, in turn, affect institutional influences. This suggestion is in line with the second type of criminological research that she identified, which aimed to understand criminal justice institutions in their natural settings.

The cultural discourse on crime in Japan is one example of a larger discussion about the merits of studying culture in criminology. The extent to which crime and criminal justice are influenced by culture and vice versa, as well as how best to study culture, are current issues in the field.

Comparing Cultures

Differences in levels of crime between countries, as well as groups, exist. This is uncontested. Howard et al. (2000) believed that most would agree that cultural variation does affect levels and types of violence among countries, but the primary obstacle in studying cultural influences is that countries are not culturally homogeneous. Crime and social control are considered expressions of culture, as their manifestations reflect values and beliefs that are relevant and important in a specific context. What is contested, however, is the extent to which these crime differences are consequences of cultural differences (Karstedt 2001).

Comparing countries is not only susceptible to the usual problems—data collection pitfalls, for example—it is also susceptible to our own understanding of the world. The researcher herself becomes the limitation: what lies outside her cultural knowledge and understanding can become misinterpreted; even translations may hide vital subtleties of meaning. Zedner (1995) noted that establishing universal truths—what is common among all cultures—may be interpreted in two ways. First, it may conceal ethnocentrism, which assumes that one's culture is superior to others, and this superiority is what one uses to make sense of his world; and, second, it may reveal comfort in finding familiarity in foreign settings.

The danger is that, once similarities are identified, they are left unexamined. Proper care and attention to underlying similarities and differences are abandoned especially if study results confirm one's original predictions. Nelken (2009) suggested that, to make more accurate interpretations of criminological observations, understanding what the people relevant to the observation were trying to accomplish was needed. He provided an example from his research that sought to understand why the imprisonment rate of young people in England and Wales was among the highest in Europe. In making sense of this phenomenon, he asked juvenile justice practitioners for their opinions. The practitioners actually did not view the system as punitive or intolerant, but attributed the high rate to persistent young offenders and pressure to process these cases quickly. The mentality that youth offenders needed official intervention also played a role in the high juvenile incarceration rate.

Cultural explanations for crime phenomena have a long history. Culture was used to explain variations in the prevalence of violence between northern and southern regions of the US, Italy, and France in the nineteenth century (Howard et al. 2000). Take for example the culture of 'honour and violence' in the American South (Nisbett and Cohen 1996). It was observed that violence rates in the American South[1] were higher than in the American North, because of a distinctive cultural code referred to as the 'culture of honour'. This code encouraged violent behaviour in order to protect one's reputation, family, and values.

This code, however, ignored the use of violence in interpersonal relationships, as well as excessive use of violence. The culture of honour was theorised to have originated from a time when the South was primarily

---

[1]Specifically, the fourteen US states Alabama, Arkansas, Georgia, Kentucky, Louisiana, Maryland, Mississippi, North Carolina, Oklahoma, South Carolina, Tennessee, Texas, Virginia, and West Virginia.

a herding economy, in which the rule of law was weak. In contrast, the North created a civilisation that primarily comprised farmers and craftsmen. Consequently, to protect livestock against theft in the South, violence became instrumental. Although the culture of honour has been re-examined and disputed (Chu et al. 2000), it is an apt example of how culture is used to explain crime differences.

What Is Meant by Culture?

Culture from a psychological stance is 'a unique meaning and information system, shared by a group and transmitted across generations, that allows the group to meet basic needs of survival, pursue happiness and well-being and derive meaning from life' (Matsumoto and Juang 2013: 12). An analogy to better understand culture is that it 'is to society as memory is to individuals' (Kluckhohn 1954, cited in Triandis 2001). Cultures differ from place to place, as culture is affected by the specific social and environmental factors, such as the physical environment, community size, and climate.

Culture contains ideas, norms, and practices that are needed to survive in a particular context, and because this information has proven useful, it is preserved, often over generations (Kiyama and Park 2007; Triandis 2001). Although the term *society* is sometimes used interchangeably with culture, society comprises people whereas culture is a shared information system that a society uses (Shiraev and Levy 2010). Another way to understand the difference between society and culture is that society is observed as a complex system of multiple relationships among people whereas culture refers to the meanings and interpretations related to these relationships (Matsumoto and Juang 2013).

From a sociological approach, culture is seen as both the consequence as well as the primary cause of human activity. Social institutions are created that reflect a society's cultural values and beliefs, and institutions, in turn, influence the behaviours of society as well as its individual members. As the relationship between humans and culture is reciprocal, society uses these institutions to regulate individual members through cultural norms and behaviours (Shiraev and Levy 2010).

An example of a sociological theory of culture is modernisation. Emile Durkheim (1924) proposed that, before the industrial revolution, societies were able to use culture to regulate behaviour, as societies were primarily homogeneous and the influence of cultural norms were relatively strong. Once societies industrialised, however, rapid socioeconomic change resulted in improved living conditions and more personal freedom, their populations became more heterogeneous, and as a result, shared norms and values were difficult to establish and individual members were less likely to conform.

A further example is research on Japan. Roberts and LaFree (2004) examined whether changes in culture explained changes in the violence rates in Japan. As a measure of culture, they used indicators related to social disorganisation theory: divorce, female labour force participation, and urbanisation. Previous scholars have noted that the Japanese were more likely to conform to group norms and avoid committing deviance, and, as a result, informal social control was high. This concept, found at the individual level, was directly linked to social disorganisation theories at the macro-level. It is thought that social disorganisation, in which a society experienced a breakdown of norms and informal social controls, increased the likelihood of deviance and crime. Roberts and LaFree provided evidence that, in recent times, Japan seemed to be experiencing a weakening of key social institutions such as the family and community; the divorce rate had steadily increased, while the rate of community service and stay-at-home wives had decreased.

They then set out to examine homicide and robbery trends from 1951 to 2000. Findings showed that, while violence rates decreased over the years, rates of divorce, female labour participation, and urbanisation increased, demonstrating that strong informal social control was unrelated to the violence decline, as the trends moved in opposite directions. Poor economic conditions, a young male population, and the certainty of punishment were suggested as better explanations for Japan's violent crime trends. Johnson (2006), however, argued that the social disorganisation measures were unrepresentative of culture, as they failed to capture the 'control' aspects of Japanese culture. Although this may be a limitation, the measures seem to be appropriate indicators of culture, capturing changes from group-orientated to a more individualistic culture; observations in the scholarly literature have used changing norms of marriage, for example, in which love-based marriages have become more commonplace than arranged marriages, as indications of increasing individualism in Japanese culture (Hamamura 2012).

Individualism–Collectivism

The term *individualism–collectivism* became well-known after Geert Hofstede (1983) conducted a global and extensive study on work-related values from the responses of 116,000 IBM employees from 50 countries. His initial study produced four cultural dimensions, in which one of them was individualism–collectivism. This dimension reflects the extent to which cultures encourage members to prioritise only themselves and their immediate family (more individualistic), or prioritise in-groups that look after its members (more collectivist) (Matsumoto and Juang 2013).

Individualism refers to cultures characterised by independence from in-groups. People in individualist cultures prioritise their personal goals over the goals of their in-groups, which form one's inner circle (Komiya 1999), such as work colleagues, family, or one's tribe, and they behave based on their attitudes instead of on in-group norms (Triandis 2001). Individualist cultures tend to be found in the West, and countries that are considered highly individualistic are the US and UK (Triandis 1994). In contrast, collectivism refers to cultures characterised by interdependence and in-groups. Those in collectivist cultures tend to prioritise their in-groups, adhere to in-group norms and behaviours, and are particularly concerned with relationships within these groups (Triandis 1994). These cultures are also considered harmonious, confrontational-avoidant, and conformist (Harzing 2006). They are likely to be found in Asia, Africa, and South America (Triandis 2001).

The cross-cultural psychologist, Harry Triandis (2001), considered the dimension to be the most significant cultural difference among cultures: individualism–collectivism is the most popular dimension compared to other cultural dimensions, as it is probably the most researched dimension used to compare East Asians to North Americans in psychological research (Hamamura 2012). According to this dimension, these distinct traits are taught from an early age. For example, Imada (2012) examined stories in educational textbooks in Japan and in the US. American narratives differed from Japanese ones because they often took a first-person perspective and featured strong and unique protagonists who were capable of fulfilling their goals. Japanese stories often took a third-person perspective and featured lessons focused on being a considerate and altruistic member of the group, and recognising the importance of friendships.

Triandis (2001), however, emphasised that not everyone in a particular culture would embody completely those particular beliefs and values. For example, it is expected that people in a collectivist culture will vary in their degree of collectivism, and the same would be true of those in an individualist culture.[2] If this is the case, culture itself will not be the only factor that produces crime. Thus, the intervening processes between culture and crime require elaboration.

Tightness–Looseness

Most of the time, in psychological research, culture is treated as a phenomenon at the individual level (one's thought or perception about oneself or others). Gelfand et al. (2006) proposed a theory on how external norms and constraints explain differences in behaviour. In essence, they link the two cultural constructs, tightness–looseness to individualism–collectivism to explain how societal institutions influence the socialisation of cultural norms among individuals.

---

[2]Psychologists have used the terms *allocentrism* and *idiocentrism* to describe cultural variation at the individual level. Allocentrism is the individual-level version of collectivism whereas idiocentrism is the individual-level version of individualism. These terms account for personality differences. These terms were developed after discovering that, at the country-level, individualism and collectivism were the polar extremes of one dimension. At the individual-level, however, characteristics from both of these types of cultures—such as self-reliance, competitiveness, family integrity, and interdependence—emerged and were independent from each other. In other words, they were not two sides of the same coin, or two ends of the same continuum.

The construct, tightness–looseness, measures the extent to which cultures enforce clear social norms and reliably use sanctions for deviation from these norms (Chan et al. 1996). Cultures that are tight have strong social norms and a low tolerance for deviant behaviour, while cultures that are loose have weak social norms and a high tolerance of deviant behaviour (Gelfand et al. 2011). The consequences related to tightness are order, conformity, and low rates of change, whereas the consequences related to looseness are social disorganisation, deviance, innovation, and openness to change (Gelfand et al. 2006). Although this construct appears similar to the cultural construct of individualism–collectivism, both constructs may have different consequences and origins (Triandis 1989). For example, Japan is considered a collectivist and tight culture whereas Brazil is considered a collectivist and loose culture, and, in addition, wealth is related to collectivism but has no relationship to tightness (Gelfand 2012). The main difference is that tightness–looseness relates to how behaviour is affected by the strength of social norms and sanctioning, whereas individualism–collectivism is related to how behaviour is affected by one's in-group(s) (Gelfand et al. 2006).

Gelfand et al. (2006) theorised that institutions in tight societies will promote socialisation that has more constraints and high monitoring and sanctioning behaviour, while the opposite would be expected of institutions in loose societies. Consequently, this dimension affects individuals, particularly in ways in which they feel accountable towards and engaged with monitoring and sanctioning norms.

What Kind of Culture Is Japan?

Accurately describing Japanese culture is a challenge. Its culture has been described mainly as group-orientated (Sugimoto 2014), 'shame' (Benedict 1946), and collectivist (Triandis 1994). Members of this culture are considered interdependent, afraid of giving negative impressions of themselves in the presence of others, and value group harmony among their in-groups (Kawabata et al. 2010; Martinez 2007). Cross-cultural studies often group Japanese culture alongside other East Asian cultures, noting similar influences from Confucian and Buddhist teachings (Hamamura 2012; Kitayama and Park 2007). These studies often compare the culture of Japan to that of the US (or, more generally, East Asia to that of North America), because these cultures are considered opposites on the Individualism–Collectivism dimension (Hamamura 2012).

Oyserman et al. (2002) conducted several meta-analyses to examine whether, overall, Americans were more individualistic and less collectivistic than other groups. Their results showed inconsistent findings for Japan as a more collectivist culture. For example, most studies that have presented evidence on Japan as a collectivist culture demonstrated low reliability scales for these measures. When the measures were changed so that their scales had high reliability, Americans were actually higher or no different in collectivism than Japanese.

Another problem is the idea of culture as a static phenomenon. In actuality, culture is dynamic. It is able to continue unchanged for centuries, or it can change within a few decades (Hamamura 2012). Judging from scholarly observations on the characteristics of Japanese culture, it would be assumed that collectivism best describes the culture of Japan. Takano and Osaka (1999), however, argued that the assumption that Japan was a collectivist culture was based merely on observations and anecdotes rather than on empirical evidence. They referred to this assumption as the 'common view', which dated back to observations from Ruth Benedict (1946), which noted the prominence of hierarchy and social relationships. To fill this gap in knowledge, they reviewed 15 empirical studies that compared Japan to the US on the individualism–collectivism dimension.

Of the total, only one study supported the notion that Japan was a collectivist culture while nine of the studies found no difference in culture between the two countries. The five remaining studies reported that Japanese culture was more individualistic than American culture. Although the review showed evidence that Japan may not be a collectivist culture, the researchers acknowledged that the results of these studies should be treated with caution, because their samples were from university student populations and changes may have occurred in Japanese culture over time. Evidence has suggested that Japan may have been a collectivist culture at one point in time, but, because of increased modernisation, it may have become more individualistic in recent years. In addition, university students were generally more individualistic than adults, so the use of this population may have obscured the true extent of collectivism in Japan. If anything, the findings may actually reveal lower collectivist tendencies of younger generations (Fukushima et al. 2009; Kobayashi et al. 2009).

That Japanese culture may be individualistic is not an arbitrary proposition. Conformity has declined in contemporary times, and the assumption is that individualism is the cause (Suwa and Suzuki 2013). This seems to be the case, except it may be a new kind of individualism that has prematurely developed among rapid social changes. This individualism does not empower the individual and promote independence, but rather it fosters physical and mental isolation. The rise of digital communication has only encouraged this form of individualism among youth, who attach more weight to online communication in their private world than to building relationships in reality.

Another observation in support of Japanese culture as individualistic is from the economy. Hashimoto and Traphagan (2008) note that, after the economic recession in the nineties, young people realised that traditional ties—educational success, filial obedience, and hard work—no longer guaranteed them financial stability and upward mobility like they had for their parents. As the incentives were not there, young people developed more voluntary and temporary ties, more reminiscent of those found among individualist cultures.

Hamamura (2012) acknowledged the dynamic nature of culture, and investigated the extent to which, culturally, Japan resembled the US after modernisation—in modernisation theory a positive correlation was believed to exist between economic growth and individualism. Twenty-six indicators from different data sources (cross-temporal analysis) were used to evaluate seven areas related to culture (i.e., family relationships, urbanisation, general trust, socialisation, social values, friendship, and the importance of effort). The findings showed that, despite some cultural aspects resembling the US, Japan still persisted in its cultural heritage of collectivism. There was a higher preference for social harmony in Japan, and more importance on social obligations and contributions. Although Japanese culture may eventually resemble that of the US, Hamamura highlighted that the existence of a cultural lag would need to be explained.

Can Culture Explain Crime in Japan?

Few empirical studies exist that test the effects of culture on crime cross-nationally. Karstedt (2006) divided 26 countries into democracies and nondemocratic societies (autocracies) based on previous work that classified countries using elections, number of party systems, and actual regime change upon election results. According to this classification, Japan was classified as a non-Western democracy, but it had low individualism. Two other datasets on lethal violence were used, in which homicide and homicide victimisation were examined between 1968 and 1972, as well as in a longer period from 1960 to 2000. The former time range was used in order for the results to be comparable, as previous work by Hofstede (1983) examined the same time period. Karstedt examined whether two main democratic values (which also formed two of Hofstede's dimensions), individualism and egalitarianism, were able to reduce the level of violent crime. If so, then it would be expected that democracies would have lower levels of violent crime than autocracies, which are characterised as having authoritarian and collectivist values. To some extent, democracies represented individualist cultures whereas autocracies represented collectivist cultures.

Karstedt's findings generally confirmed that democracies had lower rates of lethal violence compared to autocracies, and that the lower levels of lethal violence were also related to high levels of individualist and egalitarian values. Exceptions to this relationship were the US and Japan. The US exhibited high levels of lethal violence as well as high levels of democratic values, whereas Japan exhibited low levels of individualism but also low levels of lethal violence. Karstedt concluded that lower levels of lethal violence were possible because democratic values were translated into practice through institutions.

The US, although highly democratic, experienced higher levels of violence possibly because economic discrimination contradicted egalitarian values, which created a discrepancy between perceived egalitarianism and actual reality, as well as significant structural inequality. For Japan, Karstedt speculated that its unusual low crime and low individualism were attributable to influential traditions. It is unclear what traditions she was specifically referring to, and, because her focus was on the relationship between democratic values and violence, there was not enough scope to delve into the specifics of relevant traditions. Nevertheless, she suggests that culture may be able to explain this relationship between low individualism and low violence.

In her previous paper, Karstedt (2001) outlined ideas for future research using culture to explain crime (see also Karstedt 2012). Her discussion highlighted the limitations of contemporary cultural discourse as well as the advantages of incorporating the study of culture from psychology in understanding crime. She referred to the literature on crime in Japan as an example of how culture had been improperly used to understand overall crime phenomena in East Asian countries by lumping all the cultures together.

Karstedt's (2001) paper is significant because it is the only criminological paper that specifically focuses on culture and how it can be used to explain crime. Borrowing from psychology, Karstedt stated that the purpose of cross-cultural criminology should be to (1) transport criminological theories to other cultures to examine the extent of their applicability; (2) explore and discover variations in crime and different forms of social control; and (3) integrate and widen criminological knowledge to become a more inclusive and universal criminology. She even outlined approaches to the study of culture and crime, such as examining cultural dimensions from cross-cultural psychology and applying them to understand different contexts using either an *extensive* (quantitative and large samples) or *intensive* (qualitative and case studies) approach.

Cultural Theories on Crime in Japan: From Sociological to Psychological

Although it is not very clear whether Japan exhibits more of a collectivist than an individualist culture, theories attempting to elaborate upon the cultural explanation, beyond the 'black box' of culture, suggest collectivist and tight cultural characteristics. The cultural characteristic that has been explored the most seems to be group-orientation.

Hechter and Kanazawa (1993) proposed that dependence and invisibility were key to understanding why Japan had a high level of social order, which referred to members' compliance to norms that the state attempted to enforce. They believed that the combination of dependency and visibility within groups unintentionally created the social order observed in Japan. Hechter and Kanazawa questioned whether explanations that emphasised Confucian values were the real causes of social order.

They argued that, if Confucian values were responsible for lower crime as well as higher social order, then modernisation would be less of an influence. If this was the case, then, compared to Japan, less industrialised East Asian countries would also exhibit lower crime rates. The evidence, however, did not support this notion. Crime rates between 1979 and 1988 were used as proxies for social order to support their theory. Comparatively, Japan had the lowest rates across all major felonies (homicide, violence, and theft) compared with six other major industrialised countries in the West and in East Asia. Hechter and Kanazawa also briefly mentioned that, using a number of indicators, Japan exhibited the lowest rate of 'civil strife'.

According to their solidaristic theory of global order, societal-level social order primarily emerged, not from the state and its institutions, but as a by-product of local-level social order created by individual members and their groups such as in schools and workplaces. In the case of Japan, groups attempted to maintain order by monitoring and sanctioning unwanted behaviours of individual members. In addition, groups also make individual members dependent on them by offering incentives such as exclusive friendship, status, or money.

This dependence was a form of control, which groups used to ensure that their members complied with their intricate rules and behavioural expectations. The attempts to enforce personal social order in these groups created, unintentionally, overall social order.

Subsequently, Nobuo Komiya (1999) set out to explain the precise mechanisms of the cultural explanation for low crime in Japan. First, he explored the history of Western influence on Japan, beginning in the Meiji period when Japan decided to interact with Western powers. Soon, the state prioritised emulating the legal structures of European powers in the hopes of attaining economic growth. This period was referred to as the Meiji Restoration. Komiya made an interesting observation: the Meiji government managed to emulate Western legal systems only in form, but not in spirit. In reality, the government encouraged loyalty to the emperor and restricted Western ideas such as individualism and liberalism. This dual identity was developed to ensure that the government was considered legitimate by its people. As a result, the Japanese viewed formal laws as applicable to strangers and non-members of the out-group, whereas informal laws or traditional duties were applicable to acquaintances and members of their in-group. He referred to the latter as the inner circle, *uchi*, while the former was referred to as the outer circle, or *yoso*. Relationships and their maintenance within uchi are factors that have resulted in low crime.

In order to succeed (and survive) in Japanese culture, one must learn how to be an effective member of in-groups. Unlike in the West, where individual autonomy was encouraged, assimilating and identifying with an in-group was promoted in Japan. The formation of groups was usually based on proximity, in that membership in a group depended on one's location—school, company, or neighbourhood. These groups created numerous rules and norms in order to ensure that members—who were unlikely to be like-minded to each other—conformed. A high level of self-control, honed since childhood and forming an essential part of an individual's socialisation, was needed to effectively conform to group norms and rules. For conformity and loyalty, individual members were rewarded with security, in which they were supported and cared for by the group.

Komiya considered the uchi as an effective means of crime prevention. Unlike in the West, where more socially skilled and confident people succeeded on their own in gaining security in their social environment, the emphasis on group membership in Japan allowed less socially skilled and confident people to be looked after; in particular, people who were vulnerable and in need of group support. Consequently, being a member of an in-group made every individual accountable, and thus, deviating from group norms would be detrimental to remaining as a member.

Setsuo Miyazawa (2012) argued that the Japanese conformed because the cost of not doing so was substantial. He noted that this was why children conformed to their parents' wishes and expectations; not because they were emotionally attached to their parents, but more because they understood that disobeying was a huge cost for living in a social structure that rewarded conformity.

The uchi, however, has its own limitations: in groups where deviance is the established norm, such as criminal organisations or religious cults, conforming also applies. As an example of a deviant in-group, Komiya referred to the religious and doomsday cult, Aum Shinrikyo. In addition to the manufacturing of illegal drugs, abduction, extortion, and murder, the cult carried out sarin gas attacks: one in Tokyo in 1995, as well as a smaller attack in the Nagano Prefecture the year before (Hughes 1998). These attacks killed 18 people and injured almost 4000 others.

Uchi cannot account for victimless crimes, because these do not affect in-groups. What is significant about this is that abiding to norms and following rules are not done for the sake of being a good citizen. Instead, they are done in order to be viewed as a good member of the in-group so that benefits can be continually enjoyed. This may be why white collar crime may be a bigger problem in Japan than in other countries. Pontell and Geis (2007) suspected that the low crime rate in Japan may be inaccurate because it did not account for white collar and corporate offending. It was believed that because of the high level of communitarianism, preservation of the group took the highest priority. Consequently, loyalty and obedience may lead individuals to 'sacrifice' themselves in order to hide corporate crimes.

As Hechter and Kanazawa (1993) had theorised, Komiya's cultural explanation also emphasises that social order and low crime are more the products of in-group expectations of their members than because of state regulations or the desire to be good members of society. Psychological studies support this.

There is ample discussion about the relationship between culturally shared beliefs and behaviour—is behaviour the result of internalised shared beliefs or is behaviour context-specific? The cultural agent perspective proposes that culturally shared beliefs and values are reflected in an individual's personal beliefs and values (Hashimoto et al. 2011). Recently, however, this perspective has been challenged by many studies that suggest a cultural game player perspective. This perspective proposes that individuals adjust their behaviour in light of the expected reactions of others in order to achieve their goals.

Examples are cross-cultural studies by Toshio Yamagishi, which have extensively investigated differences in the notion of trust between Japan and the US. As the common view holds that collectivism defines Japanese culture and individualism defines American culture, trust is thought to be higher in collectivist cultures than in individualist cultures. Observations about Japanese culture, ranging from everyday interactions to business dealings, also comment on the strong level of mutual trust. The assumption about the Japanese is that they inherently are group-orientated, even preferring to be in groups, because of their culture.

Yamagishi and Yamagishi (1994) questioned this, because their previous research provided contradictory findings: Americans had higher levels of general trust than Japanese. They, too, wanted to further examine in what context would the Japanese be more trusting. Their findings from administered surveys to a large student sample (over 1000 students in Japan and 500 in the US) provided additional support for their previous results. They concluded that, while Americans were generally more trusting of others, Japanese sought assurance in their interactions. What this means is that social uncertainty is related to trust in others whereas social certainty is related to assurance. This explains why the Japanese are more likely to prefer socially certain situations interacting with people through their social network and in-groups—it assures them that their security will not be threatened.

In a later study, Yamagishi et al. (1998) built upon previous findings to further their growing theory on trust. They wanted to investigate under what conditions would the Japanese and American participants exhibit general trust or form committed partnerships. Through several experimental designs, the researchers manipulated social uncertainty and general trust.

For example, to test whether Japanese participants differed from their American counterparts in forming committed partnerships, even when their level of trust and the level of social uncertainty were taken into account, they were asked to form part of a buyer–seller simulation. Each participant was given the equivalent of five dollars to buy products from two 'sellers' through a computer. In addition, buyers would sometimes purchase overpriced products, and at other times, they would purchase underpriced products, and this occurred with both sellers. Participants would resell these products to the experimenter, and, depending on the price, would either make a profit or a loss. One seller, however, was considered trustworthy whereas the other was considered untrustworthy. This was determined whenever the seller had a chance to extort money from participants, which the untrustworthy seller always took advantage of, until he was replaced by another seller, of whom the participant had no prior experience.

The results from these studies showed that the Japanese did not differ from the Americans. When social uncertainty was high, as with an expected loss from an untrustworthy partner, committed partnerships were more likely to form; those who had higher levels of general trust, however, were less likely to form committed partnerships than those who had lower levels of general trust.

Yamagishi and colleagues concluded that long-term success in Japan is determined by being a member of these closed in-groups. It is difficult to leave such groups and find new ones. Therefore, having a high level of general trust and leaving uchi in such a society is risky and has high opportunity costs. The perceived high level of trust among Japanese stems from observations of this group formation. Yamagishi and colleagues, however, demonstrate that trust and group-orientation are not consequences of internalised moral values, but develop because they are approaches to succeed in a society that promotes interdependence.

In fact, in a previous study, Japanese were more likely than Americans to behave exploitatively and less cooperatively once opportunities for monitoring and sanctioning were removed (Yamagishi 1988). Based upon earlier work on the solidaristic theory of global order outlined by Hechter and Kanazawa (1993), Miller and Kanazawa (2000) have used Yamagishi's work to support their observations on group-orientation. They make clear that the behaviour of group members is monitored and sanctioned based on whether it promotes group interests, not according to whether it meets social conventions. This is why deviant groups also exist in Japan. One may argue that deviant groups exist in other societies too, and they also use monitoring and sanctioning to control their members' behaviours. An example would be street gangs. It can therefore be argued there is nothing unique about Japan. Miller and Kanazawa, however, argue that what is indeed unique to Japan is that their conventional groups behave similarly to deviant groups in how they treat their members. As a consequence of monitoring and sanctioning of conventional groups—which are the majority in society—they unintentionally promote overall social order while in the pursuit of their group interests.

As the result of a high level of group-orientation, two cultural characteristics are more prominent in Japan and need further study. The first is shame. The concept of shame in criminology received unprecedented attention because of John Braithwaite's (1989) work, *Crime, Shame, and Reintegration*. It was the first major Western criminological theory for which Japan provided the inspiration (Miyazawa 2012). This may not have been a surprise, as Ruth Benedict (1946), in her anthropological study, had referred to Japan as a shame culture whereas the US was referred to as a guilt culture. Braithwaite, however, made no distinction between shame and guilt because he argued that they were part of the same social process—inducing guilt and shaming both depended on criticisms by others.

The theory proposed that societies, like Japan, that have strong familial and community ties, succeed in controlling crime because individual members understood appropriate behaviours and norms. Violations were dealt with through shaming, in which the individual who violated norms was made to feel that he had failed to meet norm and behavioural expectations, and that others have evaluated him negatively. Shame, specifically for the Japanese, is the feeling of realising that one's conduct has deviated from norm expectations and has been exposed to the eyes of others (Komiya 1999).

Being monitored by others is a common occurrence. According to Sugimoto (2014), this phenomenon is called *seken*, and it is an imagined but real entity, 'encompassing a web of people who provide the moral yardsticks that favor the status quo and traditional practices' (p. 301). It is embedded in the Japanese psyche and has the ability to approve or disapprove individual behaviour (Holloway 2010).

Messner's (2014) *relational centrality*, which is similar to Komiya's (1999) conception of uchi and *giri* (traditional duty or indebtedness), is the extent to which interpersonal relationships with accompanying obligations are central to people's everyday lives. It is another theory that has been influenced by psychological research. Inspired by research on the self and agency of cultural psychologists, Shinobu Kitayama and Yukiko Uchida, Messner proposed that the concept of self-control, as understood by Gottfredson and Hirschi (1990), was limited to a self that was prominent among individualist cultures.

Messner proposed that self-control theory would need to be elaborated upon in order to account for collectivist countries like Japan, because self-control was an individual trait and this would be less significant in a collectivist culture than in an individualist culture. He suggested that two forms of self-control should be conceptualised, the original and one that was interdependent whereby others would act as a constraining force. Relational centrality, which was an institutional-level factor, would affect both these forms of self-control by emphasising one over the other.

Although low self-control would lead to offending in both contexts, relational centrality helped to explain how institutional-level-controls influenced the level of self-control in different cultures. Messner (2015) further expanded two other criminological theories, Institutional Anomie and Routine Activities, to explain influences of collectivist cultural elements on these theories. He focused, however, on China and the cultural characteristic, *guanxi*, which is somewhat similar to the Japanese giri, but pertains more to business dealings.

Conclusion

It is debatable whether Japanese culture is collectivist, but most of the evidence suggests that it is. Perhaps this is less true than in the past. Some scholars, however, have suggested that many of the cultural characteristics observed in the Japanese are context-specific and arise at the individual level rather than being enforced by large social institutions. Low crime may just merely be a by-product of maintaining group-order. Qualities of group-maintenance, such as high self-control and social attachment, however, have been shown to be related to low crime. Nevertheless, culture should be considered and included in a framework of possible explanations for crime. Each of these explanations, whether sociological or psychological, are likely to be interlinked. This means that, together, these explanations can contribute to a better understanding of crime than they would individually.

References

Aldous, Christopher, and Frank Leishman. 2000. *Enigma Variations: Reassessing the Kôban.* Oxford: Nissan Institute of Japanese Studies.

Bayley, David H. 1976. *Forces of Order: Policing Modern Japan.* Berkeley: University of California Press.

Benedict, Ruth. 1946. *The Chrysanthemum and the Sword.* Boston: Houghton Mifflin.

Braithwaite, John. 1989. *Crime, Shame and Reintegration.* Cambridge: Cambridge University Press.

Bui, Laura. 2018. "Examining the Academic Achievement–Delinquency Relationship in Southeast Asian Americans." *International Journal of Offender Therapy and Comparative Criminology* 62 (6): 1556–72.

Chan, Darius K. S., Michele J. Gelfand, Harry C. Triandis, and Oliver Tzeng. 1996. "Tightness-Looseness Revisited: Some Preliminary Analyses in Japan and the United States." *International Journal of Psychology* 31 (1): 1–12.

Chol, Hyung, Gilbert C. Gee, and David Takeuchi. 2009. "Discrimination and Health among Asian American Immigrants: Disentangling Racial from Language Discrimination." *Social Science & Medicine* 68 (4): 726–32.

Chu, Rebekah, Craig Rivera, and Colin Loftin. 2000. "Herding and Homicide: An Examination of the Nisbett-Reaves Hypothesis." *Social Forces* 78 (3): 971–87.

Durkheim, Emile. 1924. *Sociology and Philosophy*. New York: Free Press.

Fukushima, Miyuki, Susan F. Sharp, and Emiko Kobayashi. 2009. "Bond to Society, Collectivism, and Conformity: A Comparative Study of Japanese and American College Students." *Deviant Behavior* 30 (5): 434–66.

Gelfand, Michele J. 2012. "Culture's Constraints International Differences in the Strength of Social Norms." *Current Directions in Psychological Science* 21 (6): 420–24.

Gelfand, Michele J., Jana L. Raver, Lisa Nishii, Lisa M. Leslie, Janetta Lun, Beng Chong Lim, Lili Duan, et al. 2011. "Differences Between Tight and Loose Cultures: A 33-Nation Study." *Science* 332 (6033): 1100–1104.

Gelfand, Michele J., Lisa H. Nishii, and Jana L. Raver. 2006. "On the Nature and Importance of Cultural Tightness-Looseness." *The Journal of Applied Psychology* 91 (6): 1225–44.

Goold, Benjamin. 2004. "Idealizing the Other? Western Images of the Japanese Criminal Justice System." *Criminal Justice Ethics* 23 (2): 14–25.

Gottfredson, Michael R., and Travis Hirschi. 1990. *A General Theory of Crime*. Stanford: Stanford University Press.

Hamai, Koichi. 2011. "Review of Dag Leonardsen Crime in Japan: Paradise Lost?" *Social Science Japan Journal* (September): 4–6.

Hamamura, Takeshi. 2012. "Are Cultures Becoming Individualistic? A Cross-Temporal Comparison of Individualism-Collectivism in the United States and Japan." *Personality and Social Psychology Review* 16 (1): 3–24.

Harzing, Anne-Wil. 2006. "Response Styles in Cross-National Survey Research: A 26-Country Study." *International Journal of Cross Cultural Management* 6 (2): 243–66.

Hashimoto, Akiko, and John W. Traphagan. 2008. "Changing Japanese Families." In *Imagined Families, Lived Families: Culture and Kinship in Contemporary Japan*, edited by Akiko Hashimoto and John W. Traphagan, 1–12. New York: SUNY Press.

Hashimoto, Hirofumi, Yang Li, and Toshio Yamagishi. 2011. "Beliefs and Preferences in Cultural Agents and Cultural Game Players." *Asian Journal of Social Psychology* 14 (2): 140–47.

Hechter, Michael, and Satoshi Kanazawa. 1993. "Group Solidarity and Social Order in Japan." *Journal of Theoretical Politics* 5 (4): 455–93.

Hofstede, Geert. 1983. "National Cultures in Four Dimensions: A Research-Based Theory of Cultural Differences among Nations." *International Studies of Management and Organization* Xlll (1): 46–74.

Holloway, Susan D. 2010. *Women and Family in Contemporary Japan.* Cambridge: Cambridge University Press.

Howard, Gregory J., Graeme Newman, and William Alex Pridemore. 2000. "Theory, Method, and Data in Comparative Criminology." *Criminal Justice* 4: 139–211.

Hughes, Christopher W. 1998. "Japan's Aum Shinrikyo, the Changing Nature of Terrorism, and the Post-Cold War Security Agenda." *Pacifica Review: Peace, Security & Global Change* 10 (1): 39–60.

Imada, Toshie. 2012. "Cultural Narratives of Individualism and Collectivism: A Content Analysis of Textbook Stories in the United States and Japan." *Journal of Cross-Cultural Psychology* 43 (4): 576–91.

Johnson, David T. 2006. "The Vanishing Killer: Japan's Postwar Homicide Decline." *Social Science Japan Journal* 9 (1): 73–90.

Karstedt, Susanne. 2001. "Comparing Cultures, Comparing Crime: Challenges, Prospects and Problems for a Global Criminology." *Crime, Law and Social Change* 36 (3): 285–308.

———. 2006. "Democracy, Values, and Violence: Paradoxes, Tensions, and Comparative Advantages of Liberal Inclusion." *The Annals of the American Academy of Political and Social Science* 605 (1): 50–81.

———. 2012. "Comparing Justice and Crime Across Cultures." In *The SAGE Handbook of Criminological Research Methods*, edited by David Gadd, Susanne Karstedt, and Steven F. Messner, 373–90. London: Sage.

Kawabata, Yoshito, Nicki R. Crick, and Yoshikazu Hamaguchi. 2010. "The Role of Culture in Relational Aggression: Associations with Social-Psychological Adjustment Problems in Japanese and US School-Aged Children." *International Journal of Behavioral Development* 34 (4): 354–62.

Kitayama, Shinobu, and Hyekyung Park. 2007. "Cultural Shaping of Self, Emotion, and Well-Being: How Does It Work?" *Social and Personality Psychology Compass* 1 (1): 202–22.

Kluckhohn, Clyde. 1954. "Culture and Behavior." In *Handbook of Social Psychology*, edited by Gardner Lindzey, 921–76. Cambridge: Addison-Wesley.

Kobayashi, Emiko, Harold R. Kerbo, and Susan F. Sharp. 2009. "Differences in Individualistic and Collectivistic Tendencies Among College Students in Japan and the United States." *International Journal of Comparative Sociology* 51 (1–2): 59–84.

Komiya, Nobuo. 1999. "A Cultural Study of the Low Crime Rate in Japan." *British Journal of Criminology* 39 (3): 369–90.

Lewis, Charlie, Masuo Koyasu, Seungmi Oh, Ayako Ogawa, Benjamin Short, and Zhao Huang. 2009. "Culture, Executive Function, and Social Understanding." *New Directions in Child and Adolescent Development* 123: 69–85.

Liu, Jianhong, and Setsuo Miyazawa. 2018. *Crime and Justice in Contemporary Japan*. Cham: Springer.

Martinez, Dolores P. 2007. *Modern Japan Culture and Society*. London: Routledge.

Matsumoto, David, and Linda Juang. 2013. *Culture and Psychology*. Belmont: Wadsworth/Thompson Learning.

Messner, Steven F. 2014. "Social Institutions, Theory Development, and the Promise of Comparative Criminological Research." *Asian Journal of Criminology* 9 (1): 49–63.

Messner, Steven F. 2015. "When West Meets East: Generalizing Theory and Expanding the Conceptual Toolkit of Criminology." *Asian Journal of Criminology* 10 (2): 117–29.

Miller, Alan, and Satoshi Kanazawa. 2000. *Order by Accident: The Origins and Consequences of Conformity in Contemporary Japan*. Boulder: Westview.

Miyazawa, Setsuo. 2012. "The Enigma of Japan as a Testing Ground for Cross-Cultural Criminological Studies." *International Annals of Criminology* 50 (1/2): 153–75.

Nelken, David. 2009. "Comparative Criminal Justice: Beyond Ethnocentrism and Relativism." *European Journal of Criminology* 6 (4): 291–311.

Nisbett, Richard E., and Dov Cohen. 1996. *Culture of Honor: The Psychology of Violence in the South*. Boulder: Westview Press.

Oyserman, Daphna, Heather M. Coon, and Markus Kemmelmeier. 2002. "Rethinking Individualism and Collectivism: Evaluation of Theoretical Assumptions and Meta-Analyses." *Psychological Bulletin* 128 (1): 3–72.

Pontell, Henry N., and Gilbert Geis. 2007. "Black Mist and White Collars: Economic Crime in the United States and Japan." *Asian Journal of Criminology* 2 (2): 111–26.

Rake, Douglas D. E. 1987. "Crime Control and Police-Community Relations: A Cross-Cultural Comparison of Tokyo, Japan, and Santa Ana, California." *The Annals of the American Academy of Political and Social Science* 494: 148–54.

Roberts, Aki, and Gary LaFree. 2004. "Explaining Japan's Postwar Violent Crime Trends." *Criminology* 42 (1): 179–210.

Shiraev, Eric B., and David A. Levy. 2010. *Cross-Cultural Psychology*. Boston: Pearson.

Steinhoff, Patricia. 1993. "Pursuing the Japanese Police." *Law & Society Review* 27 (4): 827–50.

Sugimoto, Yoshio. 2014. *An Introduction to Japanese Society*. 4th ed. Cambridge: Cambridge University Press.

Suwa, Mami, and Kunifumi Suzuki. 2013. "The Phenomenon of 'hikikomori' (Social Withdrawal) and the Socio-Cultural Situation in Japan Today." *Journal of Psychopathology* 19 (3): 191–98.

Takano, Yotaro, and Eiko Osaka. 1999. "An Unsupported Common View: Comparing Japan and the U.S. on Individualism/Collectivism." *Asian Journal of Social Psychology* 2: 311–41.

Thornton, Robert Y., and Katsuya Endo. 1992. *Preventing Crime in America and Japan: A Comparative Study*. Armonk: M.E. Sharpe Inc.

Triandis, Harry C. 1989. "The Self and Social Behavior in Differing Cultural Contexts." *Psychological Review* 96 (3): 506–20.

Triandis, Harry C. 1994. *Individualism and Collectivism*. Boulder: Westview.

Triandis, Harry C. 2001. "Individualism-Collectivism and Personality." *Journal of Personality* 69 (6): 907–24.

Westermann, Ted D., and James W. Burfeind. 1991. *Crime and Justice in Two Societies*. Pacific Grove, CA: Brooks/Cole.

Yamagishi, Toshio. 1988. "The Provision of a Sanctioning System in the United States and Japan." *Social Psychology Quarterly* 51 (3): 265.

Yamagishi, Toshio, Karen S. Cook, and Motoki Watabe. 1998. "Uncertainty, Trust, and Commitment Formation in the United States and Japan." *American Journal of Sociology* 104 (1): 165–94.

Yamagishi, Toshio, and Midori Yamagishi. 1994. "Trust and Commitment in the United States and Japan." *Motivation and Emotion* 18 (2): 129–66.

Zedner, Lucia. 1995. "In Pursuit of the Vernacular: Comparing Law and Order Discourse in Britain and Germany." *Social & Legal Studies* 4: 517–34.

3

Life Course

Explaining the development of antisocial behaviour and offending across the life span of individuals is considered the hallmark of
Developmental and Life Course Criminology (DLC). Studies in this
area developed in the 1980s in regard to understanding criminal careers.
It later incorporated three other relevant areas of study to form DLC:
the risk factor prevention paradigm, Developmental Criminology, and
Life Course Criminology (Farrington 2005).

DLC first emerged from findings from the longitudinal studies developed in Western countries: the classic American longitudinal studies of
husband–wife teams, Sheldon and Eleanor Glueck as well as William
and Joan McCord; then ones from the UK by Israel Kolvin, as well
as Donald West and David Farrington; from Scandinavia by David
Magnusson, Carl-Gunnar Janson, and Lea Pulkkinen; from Canada by
Marc Le Blanc and Richard Tremblay; and New Zealand by Phil Silva
and David Fergusson (Farrington 2013). The 1980s were considered the
golden age because of the establishment of further longitudinal studies,
especially the three Causes and Correlates studies originally funded by
the Office of Juvenile Justice and Delinquency Prevention (OJJDP) in
the American cities of Denver, Pittsburgh, and Rochester (Farrington
2017).

© The Author(s) 2019   **51**
L. Bui and D. P. Farrington, *Crime in Japan*, Palgrave Advances in Criminology
and Criminal Justice in Asia, https://doi.org/10.1007/978-3-030-14097-7_3

For a study to qualify as one of DLC interest, it must be a prospective longitudinal survey: repeated measures on age-based changes and transitions—including information on risk and protective factors—for the same people throughout their lives are required to investigate possible causes of crime, which can best be found by examining what is known as within-individual changes (Farrington 1988). Identifying 'causes' also mean that the factors must be prospective—they must be measured before the outcome, which is most likely offending. The most significant prospective longitudinal studies in the field are concerned with community samples of at least hundreds of people with repeated measures, often interviews, that span five or more years (Farrington and Welsh 2007).

The language of DLC—causes, development, individual differences—highlights that this field of study takes much of its approach from psychology, and indeed, the methodological approach itself often reveals that influence, an influence that is set in scientific empiricism. When the features of DLC are separated, Developmental Criminology is grounded in psychology, and emphasises the study of the onset of offending as well as childhood and adolescent factors that either increase the risk to offend or protect against that risk, whereas Life Course Criminology, grounded in sociology, emphasises the study of desistance and the influence of life events in adulthood (Farrington 2017).

The two approaches overlap and are often used interchangeably in the literature, but the distinction is concerned with particular criticisms: Life Course criminologists criticise Developmental criminologists for their limited consideration of macro-level social changes, whereas the latter criticises the former for their limited consideration of individual and biological factors. Although the two areas differ in their perspectives, they are usually aligned by their use of the scientific method. Both of these types of sociologists and psychologists pay more attention to systematic observation and experimentation; testing quantitative predictions from theories; and replicating key results (Farrington 2012). This is a reflection of general trends in American criminology, whereas the contrast between sociological and psychological perspectives is sharper in British criminology.

According to McAra and McVie (2017), DLC has experienced not only the most fruitful advances in theory and method in the last two decades of the twentieth century (the previously referenced 'golden age'), but it has also received some of the harshest criticism—particularly the psychological elements—chiefly from criminological perspectives dominant in the UK such as the radical and cultural, which are critical of quantitative and developmental approaches generally. They criticise the field of study as failing to adequately acknowledge 'structural contexts and cultural difference' and 'oversimplifying individual experiences'. In spite of these criticisms, the authors find that DLC has been resilient, and its endurance is perhaps attributable to its researchers' disposition to engage with policy; its solutions resonate with policy makers, and McAra and McVie believe that DLC has 'radical' possibilities for innovation and impact that seem to sometimes go unrecognised in British criminology.

A recent paper from Farrington et al. (2015) presented findings on the latest longitudinal research on criminal careers in Japan using data from the National Research Institute of Police Science (NRIPS), the research institute affiliated with the National Police Agency (NPA), and the Ministry of Justice (MoJ) in hopes of encouraging more longitudinal research in Japan. The paper was based on a panel presentation on longitudinal and criminal career research at the sixth annual conference of the Asian Criminological Society in Osaka,[1] and is the most recent publication (in English) to discuss current trends on studies of the life course and offending in Japan.

The study of the life course on offending has not been conducted on Japanese populations as comprehensively outside the NRIPS, if done at all, as the institute has a history of innovative research on birth cohorts and delinquency careers. The two main limitations to the NRIPS's study of DLC, however, are the discontinuation of juvenile criminal records at the age of 20 and the use of police statistics. Linking juvenile and adult criminal records was forbidden by law, even for research,

---

[1]The panel presentation was titled, 'Longitudinal Studies for Developing Criminology in the UK, the US and Japan: Current Efforts and Future Prospects'.

though it seems that now, at the time of writing this chapter, this is no longer the case (T. Mori 2018, personal communication, 6 December). In addition, the NRIPS studies rely solely on police records, which do not have information on possible correlates of offending. The official statistics collected by the police are often restricted to knowledge on the prevalence and frequency of offences, and suffer from limitations of their own, such as the recording of offences, which are only of those reported to the police and whose categorisation depend on definitions that may change from year to year (Farrington et al. 2003).

Recent collaborations and individual projects from NRIPS and the MoJ have resulted in the three studies, presented in the paper, where one is ongoing. We use each of these in Farrington et al. (2015) to highlight issues and findings in DLC, including the study of offending across the life course generally, and their relationship to developments in Japan.

Recidivism

The first study in Farrington et al. (2015) focused on recidivism. It is considered to be the first analysis of such, but it was the findings of the second study on repeat offenders that convinced the government—the Ministerial Meeting created in 2003—to focus more on preventing recidivism. In addition, the White Papers on Crime provided evidence of urgency. For those released either after serving the full-term in prison or on parole in 2012, within five years, 38.3% returned to prison, whereas within a ten-year period of having been released in 2007, 46.4% returned (Ministry of Justice 2018). Within a year of release, however, the numbers for reimprisonment were relatively low: roughly about 5% in both 2007 and 2012. As in other developed countries, Japan has approached the prevention of reoffending with rehabilitation initiatives such as institutional and community-based treatment, including specialised treatment programmes for sex and drug offenders, so identifying factors that contribute to recidivism, ideally causes, to target in intervention programmes has become a subject of interest.

Nine years after its creation, the Ministerial Meeting (the Meeting) developed a framework to address recidivism, whereby prevention initiatives rested on four principles: (1) approaches should be evidence-based; (2) pathways towards reoffending should be better understood; (3) consideration should be focused on repairing the harms caused to larger society by crime, and towards the safety of victims, which seem to refer to ideas from restorative justice; and (4) mid and long-term approaches supported by the public should be continued. The prevention of reoffending would, too, centre on effectively tailoring approaches to the needs of offenders and reintegrating them into society. This is reminiscent of the Risk-Need-Responsivity (RNR) model (Andrews and Bonta 2010) developed in Canadian corrections, whereby factors are targeted that are specific to the offender and that can be changed.

The study on recidivism of former child sex offenders from Farrington et al. (2015) analysed a sample of 733 men who had been imprisoned for child sexual violence.[2] The rearrest rate for sexual offences among this population during a five-year period after release was 24.4%, and one-third of those rearrested had committed their offence within one year of release. Those who had completely served their sentence had a higher prevalence of rearrest within one year of release than those who were released on parole (11.9% versus 4.3%). The authors highlighted the need to identify correlates of recidivism, or in other words, identify reasons for the reoffending, and this information is often nonexistent in police data. As they had matched police data to that obtained from the MoJ, the researchers were able to test four possible correlates: older age and being on parole (compared to those who had served their full sentence upon release and compared to those who had finished their parole) were considered significant factors that predicted a decreased likelihood of rearrest post-release. In response to these findings, as of 2011, police visits have taken place at the homes of former offenders recently released, advising them to have direct contact with officers.

---

[2]The violence comprised indecency through compulsion, forcible rape, rape during the course of robbery, and sexually motivated kidnapping of victims under 13 years old.

Risk and Protective Factors

The study of correlates has a long history in criminology that continues to this day. The use of the term correlates, however, implies the uncertainty of influence—does being on parole, for example, actually have an influence on reoffending, or does it reflect an unmeasured factor or preexisting difference? Another example: does association with delinquent peers have an influence on offending, say, because of peer pressure to commit crime, or is it the other way around because those who offend tend to find and associate with like-minded peers? In DLC, the term 'correlates' is replaced by the terms risk and protective factors to underscore more of a certainty towards temporal ordering and the possibility of identifying causality. These factors deal with the likelihood of offending, and first originated in public health research, in which factors that either enhanced or reduced the odds of substance and alcohol misuse in adolescence and early adulthood were examined (Hawkins et al. 1992).

Past reviews and meta-analyses highlight multiple individual, familial, peer, school, and community risk factors that increase the risk of offending, and there are many: these include low intelligence, impulsiveness, disrupted families, parental conflict, poor child rearing, an unemployed parent, antisocial parents, large families, low socio-economic status, delinquent peers, high delinquency schools, poor academic performance, weak bonding to school, low school aspirations, disorganised neighbourhoods, and neighbourhood disadvantage (Derzon 2010; Hawkins et al. 2000; Jolliffe and Farrington 2009; Lipsey and Derzon 1998).

Protective factors, however, have been less studied, but they are a more positive approach and more attractive to communities than studying only risk factors, which emphasise deficits and problems (Pollard et al. 1999). Protective factors decrease the risk of offending in spite of the risk factor's presence, but there are also promotive factors, a type of protective factor (Lösel and Farrington 2012). The difference is that promotive factors predict a low probability of offending, like the main effect, and are at the desirable end of an explanatory variable's distribution (Stouthamer-Loeber et al. 2002). Most of the research on promotive factors is linked to the study of resilience in developmental psychopathology, and Lösel and Farrington (2012) reviewed the literature and identified 30 promising individual, family, school, peer, and neighbourhood promotive factors. Examples of these were low impulsivity, intensive parental supervision, bonding to school, non-deviant good friends, and cohesion and informal social control.

Some may rightfully question whether there is a point in distinguishing between risk and promotive factors—surely both are merely the opposite ends of the same variable? The variable's relationship to delinquency, however, may be nonlinear (Farrington and Ttofi 2011). Some variables may have effects only on the promotive end and may also increase the probability of desirable development (Lösel and Farrington 2012). Loeber et al. (2008) found many factors that had only promotive effects including low ADHD, low physical punishment by parents, good parental supervision, an older mother, and a good neighbourhood.

Causes

Recidivism as an issue is also reflected in the growing interest of predicting reoffending, as a number of studies on the topic have been published by Japanese scholars and practitioners, particularly studies investigating offender risk assessments, specifically their predictive accuracy and inter-rater reliability. Most of these risk assessments studied were developed outside of Japan such as the Structured Assessment of PROtective Factors for violence risk (SAPROF; Kashiwagi et al. 2018) and the Youth Service List/Case Management Inventory (YLS/CMI; Takahashi et al. 2013). In fact, the MoJ has recently developed its own risk assessment instrument, the Ministry of Justice Case Assessment instrument (MJCA) to help inform assessment and treatment of young offenders (Mori et al. 2017).

Recidivism is of interest to DLC criminologists as part of criminal career research. DLC is concerned with preventing recidivism through individual and social factors found in the community, during developmental stages and life transitions, rather than prevention through extensive experience with the justice process and through the use of related criminal justice agencies in rehabilitation and treatment. The latter type of recidivism research tends to fall within the scope of risk assessment. There are differences between researching recidivism within the framework of risk assessment and researching it within the framework of DLC, but both share the need to investigate and identify causes and causal mechanisms of reoffending.

Establishing causality within the study of risk assessment has relied on identifying dynamic risk factors. These are considered to be factors that change either slowly or quickly, such as attitudes or parenting styles, and their changes are thought to influence changes in offending over time (Hanson and Harris 2000). Rehabilitation programmes and interventions should be able to affect these amenable factors and their changes within individuals monitored (Moore 2015). In order to qualify as causal, the dynamic risk factor needs to fulfil the following: (1) correlate with violence; (2) precede violence; (3) change spontaneously or through intervention; and (4) predict changes in the likelihood of violence when it changes (Kraemer et al. 1997).

Understanding causes is inherent within DLC as its concerns are with why someone starts, progresses, and desists from offending over the life course (Farrington 2003). Akin to the concept of dynamic risk factors, causality is determined by whether a risk factor changes, and if it does, whether it causes a change in the rate of offending (Murray et al. 2009). Most studies, however, are unable to examine causes as they examine between-individual differences, whereby risk factors are compared between offenders and non-offenders, or risk factors are correlated with offending at a single time point. This cannot address change, so that is why longitudinal studies are emphasised because they are able to address within-individual changes, whereby changes in life events of the same person are compared (Kazemian et al. 2009). For example, associating with delinquent peers is a known risk factor for offending, but Farrington and colleagues (2002) found that this factor mattered little within individuals because their risk of offending remained the same during periods of associating and not associating with delinquent peers during the life span. It seems that, when comparing offenders and non-offenders (between-individual change), offenders happen to associate more with delinquent peers, suggesting that this is a symptom rather than a cause of offending. Cross-sectional studies are unable to account for preexisting differences between the two groups and many factors may merely measure the same underlying theoretical construct as offending.

Criminal Careers

Criminal careers refer to the characterisation of the trajectory of offending by an individual over the life course (Blumstein et al. 1986). The study of criminal careers centres on the ages of onset, duration, escalation, and desistance. Generally, criminal careers are not specialised, and individuals engage in a variety of offences, but a minority, such as child sex offenders, tend to be more specialised. The second study in Farrington et al. (2015), whose findings were initially reported in 2009 to the Meeting, focused on criminal careers, and used two datasets from the Research and Training Institute (RTI) of the MoJ: the 'one-million offender data' and '700,000 offender data'. Each individual had to meet three conditions to be included in the datasets: (1) born after 1 January 1930; (2) older than 20 years of age at the time of the trial; and (3) had not died by 30 September 2006. Similar to previous findings on criminal careers, a minority of offenders were responsible for the majority of offences: among the sample of more than one million offenders, 29% were convicted more than once but they contributed to 58% of all convictions, whereas 71% of the sample had been convicted only once and contributed to 42% of all convictions. The most serious and chronic of offenders seemed responsible for the largest number of convictions; 6.4% of all (1,680,495) convictions from this sample were attributed to 0.8% of the sample who had ten or more convictions.

This small minority of offenders, known as chronic offenders, comprise about five to ten per cent of the population but account for more than half of all the crimes committed (Piquero et al. 2003). Chronic offenders were first highlighted by Wolfgang and colleagues (1972) in a large 1945 birth cohort of young males in Philadelphia, USA. Criminal career research is also interested in finding distinct offender groups and their specific offending trajectories in order to facilitate effective identification and prevention. The definition and particular characteristics of chronic offenders, for example, have been refined recently, identifying three possibly distinct groups using data from the Cambridge Study in Delinquent Development (Cambridge study), which is a prospective longitudinal study of 411 London boys: chronic, referring to a group characterised by shorter career spans but higher levels of offences, and who were responsible for many of the total number of convictions; persistent, a group characterised by a slightly later age of onset for conviction and a much longer criminal career; and chronic-persistent, a group that is considered the most problematic as it is a hybrid of the worst characteristics of the previous two (Whitten et al. 2018). The need to identify offender groups and clarify offending trajectories concerns the age-crime curve, a seemingly universal but deceptive established fact in DLC and criminology generally.

The Age-Crime Curve

Probably the most important phenomenon in the study of the development of offending is the age-crime curve (Farrington 2017). The curve shows a remarkably similar pattern across most times and places: a rise of the rate of aggregate offending up to a peak in adolescence, between ages 15 and 18, that then gradually decreases in the twenties and beyond. The age-crime curve is usually more sharply peaked for males than it is for females, whose curve tends to be smoother and has a higher average age of offending. The age-crime curve is essentially visual evidence of the relationship between age and crime: one is more likely to commit crime during the teenage years than in older age. The main drawback is that data usually are not gathered in childhood. There are two possible reasons for this: first, the age of criminal responsibility is later in childhood, at 10 in England and Wales and 14 in Japan, for example; and second, a belief that children are innocent still pervades most societies, and that, perhaps, there is no need to collect offending information on children.

Nagin and Tremblay (1999) traced 1037 Canadian boys in Quebec from ages 6 to 17 and identified a small group of boys who followed a 'chronic physical aggression trajectory', whose level of violence was constant; their physical aggression peaked at around age two and declined slowly up to adolescence. By age 17, these boys, who made up 5% of the sample, were four times more violent than the moderate group, and they were responsible for most of the violent crime. The scholars speculated that, unlike most children, these boys might have failed to learn how to appropriately regulate their violent behaviour. The implication is that children may be inherently violent—there is, perhaps, a reason for the 'terrible twos'—but they are socialised to control their behaviour. The age-crime curve may not completely be accurate because it often excludes very young ages and legal antisocial behaviour; if it included this information, the curve may actually show a peak at much younger ages.

Analyses of birth cohorts in the 'one-million' and '700,000' offender datasets from Farrington et al. (2015) support the existence of a similarly patterned age-crime curve in Japan: there was a rise in overall crime soon after the war, whereby those born in 1935 had higher rates of crimes in their early twenties (1958–1960) compared to those born in 1950 (and in their early twenties in the 1970s). For all birth cohorts, however, offending peaked in the early twenties and abruptly declined after, which conforms to past findings on the age-crime curve.

In the 1980s, one of the fiercest criminological debates occurred over the age-crime curve. It involved the question of whether it was possible to draw valid conclusions about individual criminal careers from aggregate data as displayed in the age-crime curve. As explained by Piquero et al. (2003), Gottfredson and Hirschi, before the publication of their seminal *A General Theory of Crime* (1990), had launched a series of critiques on the study of criminal careers. They argued that, as what was known about crime from longitudinal studies could be replicated in cross-sectional studies as well, there was no need to research criminal careers, and therefore, no need to use longitudinal studies, which were costly financially and in time. As further evidence, they underscored that the relationship between age and crime was invariant, as demonstrated by the age-crime curve, which was found to have similar characteristics across all times and places. They claimed that its invariance applied to all individual offenders and it was unaffected by life events.

The most prominent criminal career scholars at the time, Blumstein et al. (1988), responded, highlighting that two components to the age-crime curve existed: (1) participation, the number of offenders, and (2) frequency, the number of offences. It seemed that Gottfredson and Hirschi interpreted the age-crime curve as merely a display of frequency, but the decline after the curve's peak could also be attributed to desistance from criminal careers. So, what exactly was declining? The number of people participating in their criminal careers, or the number of offences committed by active offenders? It is this question of what was declining, they argued, that could only be addressed by criminal career research. Blumstein et al. (1988) concluded that participation increased to a peak in the teenage years and then decreased, but frequency did not, showing that individual offending curves were different from the aggregate curve.

The claim of the 'invariant age-crime curve' has been challenged by a number of scholars. Johnson (2008) points to a number of past studies in Japan that have found that among murderers, middle-aged males are the most prominent. In addition, the second study in Farrington et al. (2015), found that, from the '700,000 offender data', 75.5% of those who were first convicted (after the age of 20 as this was based only on adult criminal records) when they were 65 years old or older were reconvicted within two years of release. The finding supports current crime trends in Japan that relate to its ageing population.

Elderly Crime

Beginning in the mid-nineties, the country experienced a rise in elderly crime. This has continued to increase, peaking between 2005 and 2009, after which it has somewhat declined, but it remains at a relative plateau at 135.8 crimes per 100,000 persons who are 65 years and older in 2016 (Ministry of Justice Japan 2018). That same year, 72.3% of the elderly cleared for crimes were cleared for theft. Among female elderly offenders, the vast majority of them (80.3%) were cleared for shoplifting. Among the total number of people cleared for theft, 29.4% were identified as elderly. A number of scholars have pointed to social difficulties experienced by the elderly, especially as more live longer. In fact, according to the United Nations (2017), in 2015, Japan had the highest number of centenarians in the world, a rate of 4.8 per 100,000 persons.

Social ties and belonging seem to be seriously challenged as one ages. Loneliness as well as economic hardship, likely attributed to the lack of government and family support, may aggravate situations, making offending an attractive option, or an act of desperation. The MoJ (2009) identified economic anxiety as contributing to elderly crime, as many lived without a stable income. Its RTI (2007, cited in Enoki and Katahira 2014) surveyed a number of elderly offenders about their living circumstances prior to imprisonment and found that financial difficulties occupied many of their responses. Almost a quarter of those who had committed murder responded that 'it was difficult to make ends meet'. Sugie (2017) analysed prefectural-level arrest records to investigate whether the rise in elderly arrests was related to changes in social integration at four time points. Measures of social integration suggested that there was indeed a weakening of an older individual's bond to society: divorce, particularly among elderly women; lack of cash assistance; and increases in the number of workers in the area who commute to other prefectures were all related to the increases in elderly arrests, but mainly for larceny. In such a context, the finding on high elderly recidivism within two years from Farrington et al. (2015) is understandable.

Desistance

The way desistance is approached depends on which group of criminologists one approaches. An obvious definition would be when an individual stops offending, but this would not clarify whether desistance should be viewed as one event or a process. Some researchers view desistance as involving a reduction in offences or seriousness of offences, but others define this as de-escalation or deceleration (see Loeber and Le Blanc 1990). It seems unlikely that desistance should be defined after the commission of short periods of non-offending (Piquero et al. 2003).

Desistance gained prominence with two studies, one in the US and one in the UK (Bonta and Andrews 2017). The first study was that of Robert Sampson and John Laub (1993) who analysed the Gluecks's original study of 500 delinquent males from the 1950s in Boston, USA and conducted a follow-up from about ages 30 to 70. As their approach leaned more towards the sociological, their theory that emerged from their findings emphasised informal social control, and aimed to explain desistance through meaningful jobs and positive marital relationships. The second one, the Liverpool Desistance Study, was conducted by Shadd Maruna (2001) in the UK. He matched a group of 30 former offenders who had not offended for a year to a group of 20 offenders who were still active. Both groups were interviewed about their experiences. Unlike Sampson and Laub's study, Maruna focused more on psychological factors, primarily on self-identity. He found that desistance had a 'redemptive narrative' that highlighted personal responsibility and the impetus to do well. Those who continued to offend had a 'condemnation' story and a feeling of hopelessness over their circumstances as they thought they lacked any control over them.

The significance of desistance is, too, reflected in the third study discussed in Farrington et al. (2015), as it has to do with new initiatives from RTI on recidivism as well as on desistance. Information on individual and social factors that may impact on rehabilitation from more than 800 young ex-offenders released from juvenile training schools between January and March 2013, as well as from a comparison sample, have been gathered repeatedly from mailed questionnaires, and the study aimed to continue until at least 2016.

Similarly, Barry (2017) compared the experiences of onset and desistance of offending among young people in Scotland and Japan. In her paper she noted the difficulty of gaining access to young offenders through official channels, which was not unusual, but that most, if not all, of the research on offending and desistance in Japan was conducted by the MoJ or by psychologists working in Juvenile Training Schools. For both groups of young people, their views on desistance were fairly similar, in that normality and integration into mainstream society were regarded as motivators to desist, and they desisted by self-determination as well as because of social and emotional supports. A major difference, however, was that the Japanese were often inclined to blame themselves for their offending whereas the Scottish were often inclined to attribute structural barriers to their offending such as a lack of employment opportunities that would give them a purpose in life. Barry argued that, although this may be a cultural difference, it may reflect how young people, particularly offenders, are regarded by policy makers and practitioners of criminal justice. Although both groups of young people believed that effective desistance could be achieved by better engagement between justice practitioners and young offenders, it seemed that consultation with offenders and ex-offenders by policy makers was still in its infancy in Japan.

Conclusion

The launch of new longitudinal studies would be particularly rewarding in advancing knowledge about offending, as it would be able to produce new insights into criminal careers and possible causes of crime in Japan. Certain notions from DLC such as criminal careers, desistance, and the age-crime curve have been researched and show fairly similar results in Japan as in other countries. Most research in Japan, however, is carried out by government agencies and related practitioners rather than by academic scholars; access to offending populations is strict and decisions on criminal justice and crime policies seem to be based on research that is exclusively conducted by the government. These may be barriers to conducting prospective longitudinal studies, which require community populations and following individuals from a young age through the life course, in spite of possible criminal justice involvement.

References

Andrews, Donald A., and James Bonta. 2010. "Rehabilitating Criminal Justice Policy and Practice." *Psychology, Public Policy, and Law* 16 (1): 39–55.

Barry, Monica. 2017. "Young Offenders' Views of Desistance in Japan: A Comparison with Scotland." In *Comparative Criminology in Asia*, edited by Jianhong Liu, Max Travers, and Max Chang, 119–29. New York: Springer.

Blumstein, Alfred, Jacqueline Cohen, and David P. Farrington. 1988. "Criminal Career Research: Its Value for Criminology." *Criminology* 26: 1–35.

Blumstein, Alfred, Jacqueline Cohen, Jeffrey A. Roth, and Christy A. Visher. 1986. "Criminal Careers and 'Career Criminals'." Panel on Research on Career Criminals, Committee on Research on Law Enforcement and the Administration of Justice, Commission on Behaviorial and Social Sciences and Education, National Research Council. Washington, DC: National Academy Press.

Bonta, James, and Donald A. Andrews. 2017. *The Psychology of Criminal Conduct*. New York: Routledge.

Derzon, James H. 2010. "The Correspondence of Family Features with Problem, Aggressive, Criminal, and Violent Behavior: A Meta-Analysis." *Journal of Experimental Criminology* 6 (3): 263–92.

Enoki, Hiroaki, and Kiyohiko Katahira. 2014. "Statistical Relationship Between Elderly Crime and the Social Welfare System in Japan: Preventative Welfare Approach for the Deterrence of Elderly Crime." *Niigata Journal of Health and Welfare* 14 (1): 48–57.

Farrington, David P. 1988. "Studying Change Within Individuals: The Causes of Offending." In *Studies of Psychosocial Risk: The Power of Longitudinal Data*, edited by Michael Rutter, 158–83. Cambridge: Cambridge University Press.

———. 2003. "Developmental and Life-Course Criminology: Key Theoretical and Empirical Issues—The 2002 Sutherland Award Address." *Criminology* 41 (2): 221–55.

———. 2005. *Integrated Developmental and Life-Course Theories of Offending*. New Brunswick: Transaction.

———. 2012. "Foreword: Looking Back and Forward." In *The Future of Criminology*, edited by Rolf Loeber and Brandon Welsh, xxii–xxiv. Oxford: Oxford University Press.

———. 2013. "Longitudinal and Experimental Research in Criminology." In *Crime and Justice*, edited by Michael Tonry, Vol. 42 (1), 453–527. Chicago: University of Chicago Press.

———. 2017. "Developmental Criminology." In *The Routledge Companion to Criminological Theory and Concepts*, edited by Avi Brisman, Eamonn Carrabine, and Nigel South, 60–64. London: Routledge.

Farrington, David P., and Brandon C. Welsh. 2007. *Saving Children from a Life of Crime*. New York: Oxford University Press.

Farrington, David P., and Maria M. Ttofi. 2011. "Protective and Promotive Factors in the Development of Offending." In *Antisocial Behavior and Crime: Contributions of Developmental and Evaluation Research to Prevention and Intervention*, edited by Thomas Bliesener, Andreas Beelmann, and Mark Stemmler, 71–88. Cambridge: Hogrefe.

Farrington, David P., Rolf Loeber, Yanming Yin, and Stewart J. Anderson. 2002. "Are Within-Individual Causes of Delinquency the Same as Between-Individual Causes?" *Criminal Behavior and Mental Health* 12 (1): 53–68.

Farrington, David P., Yutaka Harada, Hiroyuki Shinkai, and Tetsuki Moriya. 2015. "Longitudinal and Criminal Career Research in Japan." *Asian Journal of Criminology* 10 (4): 255–76.

Farrington, David P., Darrick Jolliffe, J. David Hawkins, Richard F. Catalano, Karl G. Hill, and Rick Kosterman. 2003. "Comparing Delinquency Careers in Court Records and Self-Reports." *Criminology* 41 (3): 933–58.

Gottfredson, Michael R., and Travis Hirschi. 1990. *A General Theory of Crime*. Stanford: Stanford University Press.

Hanson, Karl R., and Andrew J. R. Harris. 2000. "Where Should We Intervene?: Dynamic Predictors of Sexual Offense Recidivism." *Criminal Justice and Behavior* 27 (1): 6–35.

Hawkins, David J., Richard F. Catalano, and Janet Y. Miller. 1992. "Risk and Protective Factors for Alcohol and Other Drug Problems in Adolescence and Early Adulthood: Implications for Substance Abuse Prevention." *Psychological Bulletin* 112 (1): 64–105.

Hawkins, David J., Todd I. Herrenkohl, David P. Farrington, Devon Brewer, Richard F. Catalano, and Tracy W. Harachi. 2000. *Predictors of Youth Violence*. Washington, DC: Office of Juvenile Justice and Delinquency Prevention.

Johnson, David T. 2008. "The Homicide Drop in Postwar Japan." *Homicide Studies* 12 (1): 146–60.

Jolliffe, Darrick, and David P. Farrington. 2009. "A Systematic Review of the Relationship Between Childhood Impulsiveness and Later Violence." In *Personality, Personality Disorder and Violence*, edited by Mary McMurran and Richard C. Howard, 38–61. Chichester: Wiley.

Kashiwagi, Hiroko, Akiko Kikuchi, Koyama Mayuko, Dalsuke Salto, and Naotsugu Hirabayashi. 2018. "Strength-Based Assessment for Future Violence Risk: A Retrospective Validation Study of the Structured

Assessment of PROtective Factors for Violence Risk (SAPROF) Japanese Version in Forensic Psychiatric Inpatients." *Annals of General Psychiatry* 17 (5): 1–8.

Kazemian, Lila, David P. Farrington, and Marc Le Blanc. 2009. "Can We Make Accurate Long-Term Predictions About Patterns of De-escalation in Offending Behavior?" *Journal of Youth and Adolescence* 38 (3): 384–400.

Kraemer, Helena C., Alan E. Kazdin, David R. Offord, Ronald C. Kessler, Peter S. Jensen, and David J. Kupfer. 1997. "Coming to Terms with the Terms of Risk." *Archives of General Psychiatry* 54 (4): 337–43.

Lipsey, Mark W., and James H. Derzon. 1998. "Predictors of Violent or Serious Delinquency in Adolescence and Early Adulthood: A Synthesis of Longitudinal Research." In *Serious and Violent Juvenile Offenders: Risk Factors and Successful Interventions*, edited by Rolf Loeber and David P. Farrington, 86–106. Thousand Oaks: Sage.

Loeber, Rolf, and Marc Le Blanc. 1990. "Toward a Developmental Criminology." In *Crime and Justice*, edited by Michael Tonry and Norval Morris, 375–473. Chicago: University of Chicago Press.

Loeber, Rolf, David P. Farrington, Magda Stouthamer-Loeber, and Helene Raskin White. 2008. *Violence and Serious Theft: Development and Prediction from Childhood to Adulthood*. New York: Routledge.

Lösel, Friedrich, and David P. Farrington. 2012. "Direct Protective and Buffering Protective Factors in the Development of Youth Violence." *American Journal of Preventive Medicine* 43 (2S1): S8–23.

Maruna, Shadd. 2001. *Making Good: How Ex-Convicts Reform and Rebuld Their Lives*. Washington, DC: American Psychological Association.

McAra, Lesley, and Susan McVie. 2017. "Developmental and Life-Couse Criminology: Innovations, Impacts, and Applications." In *The Oxford Handbook of Criminology*, edited by Alison Liebling, Shadd Maruna, and Lesley McAra, 607–633. Oxford: Oxford University Press.

Ministry of Justice Japan. 2009. *White Paper on Crime 2008—The Circumstances and Attributes of Elderly Offenders and Their Treatment*. Tokyo: Author.

Ministry of Justice Japan. 2018. *White Paper on Crime, 2017*. Tokyo: Author.

Moore, Robin. 2015. *A Compendium of Research and Analysis on the Offender Assessment System (Oasys) 2009–2013*. London: National Offender Management Service.

Mori, Takemi, Masura Takahashi, and Daryl G. Kroner. 2017. "Can Unstructured Clinical Risk Judgment Have Incremental Validity in the

Prediction of Recidivism in a Non-Western Juvenile Context?" *Psycholgical Services* 14 (1): 77–86.

Murray, Joseph, David P. Farrington, and Manuel P. Eisner. 2009. "Drawing Conclusions About Causes from Systematic Reviews of Risk Factors: The Cambridge Quality Checklists." *Journal of Experimental Criminology* 5 (1): 1–23.

Nagin, Daniel, and Richard E. Tremblay. 1999. "Trajectories of Boys' Physical Aggression, Opposition, and Hyperactivity on the Path to Physically Violent and Non-violent Juvenile Delinquency." *Child Development* 70 (5): 1181–96.

Piquero, Alex R., David P. Farrington, and Alfred Blumstein. 2003. "The Criminal Career Paradigm." *Crime and Justice* 30: 359–506.

Pollard, John A., David J. Hawkins, and Michael W. Arthur. 1999. "Risk and Protection: Are Both Necessary to Understand Diverse Behavioral Outcomes in Adolescence?" *Social Work Research* 23 (3): 145–58.

Sampson, Robert J., and John H. Laub. 1993. *Crime in the Making: Pathways and Turning Points Through Life.* Cambridge: Harvard University Press.

Stouthamer-Loeber, Magda, Rolf Loeber, Evelyn Wei, David P. Farrington, and Per-Olof H. Wikström. 2002. "Risk and Promotive Effects in the Explanation of Persistent Serious Delinquency in Boys." *Journal of Consulting and Clinical Psychology* 70 (1): 111–23.

Sugie, Naomi F. 2017. "When the Elderly Turn to Petty Crime: Increasing Elderly Arrest Rates in an Aging Population." *International Criminal Justice Review* 27 (1): 19–39.

Takahashi, Masura, Takemi Mori, and Daryl G. Kroner. 2013. "A Cross-Validation of the Youth Level of Service/Case Management Inventory (YLS/CMI) Among Japanese Juvenile Offenders." *Law and Human Behavior* 37 (6): 389–400.

United Nations, Department of Economic and Social Affairs, Population Division. 2017. *World Population Prospects: The 2017 Revision, Key Findings and Advance Tables.* New York: Author.

Whitten, Tyson, Tara T. McGee, Ross Homel, David P. Farrington, and Maria M. Ttofi. 2018. "Comparing the Criminal Careers and Childhood Risk Factors of Persistent, Chronic, and Persistent-Chronic Offenders." *Australian and New Zealand Journal of Criminology.* https://doi.org/10.1177/0004865818781203.

Wolfgang, Marvin E., Robert M. Figlio, and Thorsten Sellin. 1972. *Delinquency in a Birth Cohort.* Chicago: University of Chicago Press.

4

Family

Family influences have long been considered a prominent and popular explanation for crime. It is thought that the type of family life someone has can largely influence their future behaviour. Adverse early experiences such as parental conflict or neglect (Farrington and Welsh 2007), for example, have been shown to increase the likelihood of later offending. The rationale is that a person's initial socialisation, life experiences, and outlook come from the family, and what is learned is internalised and used as a guide for conduct during life.

An early and comprehensive post-war psychological study on the effect of family processes on delinquency was conducted by Wagatsuma and De Vos (1984). The study was based in Tokyo, in the Arakawa Ward, a low-class area. Their study was distinct because of their choice to study deviance psychologically while being mindful that sociological explanations dominated. They compiled detailed case histories of 50 families, from January 1962 up to November 1966, gathering information on the junior high school boys living in these families as well as on their parents and even grandparents. The rationale for their study was that although a sociological approach could use social patterns to help us to understand why certain areas have higher levels of

© The Author(s) 2019
L. Bui and D. P. Farrington, *Crime in Japan*, Palgrave Advances in Criminology and Criminal Justice in Asia, https://doi.org/10.1007/978-3-030-14097-7_4

crime, it was limited in its explanation of why individuals in those areas were involved in crime, and usually only a minority of them contributed to the bulk of crime. Only a psychological approach, they argued, would be able to explain this. Their interest was in understanding crime through interactions and dynamics among family. Indeed, they found that the parents of delinquent boys were less responsive to their children's emotional needs, tended to use harsh discipline, and had difficulty in accepting their parental roles.

The family in Japan, like many Japanese institutions, has been considered as a model by other nations to aspire towards. Scholars have noted the distinct stability and strength of the Japanese family system compared to other industrialised countries, with its large proportion of extended families living together in the same household (Sugimoto 2014). The state projected an image of the typical Japanese family: husband as primary, and ideally sole, breadwinner; stay-at-home wife responsible for the children's upbringing; and children focused on meeting the family's educational aspirations set for them (Ronald and Alexy 2011). This image does not seem abnormal compared to images of the family in other countries. The distinction, however, derives from the idea that such family dynamics still persist and are the expected norm.

The children's first education comes from their parents. Child-rearing is seen as the parents' duty in Japan, where children are socialised to value and strive towards personal diligence and social harmony (Holloway 2010). The purpose is to develop and cement the traits that are conducive to success in this society. Often the onus of this responsibility falls on the mother (Kadonaga and Fraser 2015). This responsibility is regarded as a central feature of the Japanese family, in which the strong emotional bond between mother and child is often highlighted (Toyama- Bialke 2003). It is, therefore, unsurprising that family life is considered synonymous with 'woman' (White 2002). Yoder (2004) explained that the ideal occupation for mothers, traditionally, had been housewife, because if they tended to their family's needs, they would ensure their children's future success in society. Fathers usually are absent from child-rearing because their foremost duty is to provide, and they may take the employment away from home and live apart from their family. Although women may like to work and raise their children at the same time, employment practices of corporations and societal pressures make it difficult for them to do both (Kadonaga and Fraser 2015).

Perhaps because of the state's historical use of the family as a powerful political tool (Becker 1988; Ronald and Alexy 2011), the family tends to be a major concern in official discourse. To the state, all social issues are considered reflections of current family conditions (White 2002). The declining economy and births and the increase in crime are considered to be the fault of the family. In recent times, official discourse has proclaimed that the Japanese family is in 'crisis' (Ronald and Alexy 2011).

Understanding modern families, though, depends on which discourse is chosen. That is, the family can be viewed through two lenses: public and private. White (2002) argues that the state and the media, in their public, official discourse, portray families differently from the private, unofficial discourse. To the state, the ideal stable and harmonious family is facing severe threat from modernity. This, White (2002) believes, inaccurately depicts the reality of Japanese families, which have always been far from perfect. In actuality, families must find innovative ways to maintain their household while adhering, sometimes minimally, to social norms and expectations. The phrase 'to do as a family' embodies what White observes, in that these families attempt to present a veneer of the expected family ideal (Sugimoto 2014).

Both public and private discourses have consequences for the types of family-related crimes that occur, and for reasons why the family contributes to later offending. Domestic and sexual violence are on the rise, yet the true extent is uncertain, as much of it is still part of the 'dark figure' of crime (Aldous and Leishman 2000; Kitamura et al. 1999). Public discourse seems to have something to do with the continuation and escalation of these hidden crimes towards family members because of traditional and widely held expectations about the role of each family member, particularly wives and mothers. It is only recently, early in the twenty-first century, that public discourse has acknowledged domestic and sexual violence as problems, resulting in the passing of legislation to label them as punishable crimes (Tanaka et al. 2017).

Family Violence

Violence in the family is a rather new issue in Japan. Long considered a private or irrelevant matter, it was only recently identified as an illegal social problem. Most forms of this violence are not recorded in official statistics. The primary reasons for this are enduring social taboos (Kozu 1999) and patriarchy (Sasaki and Ishii-Kuntz 2016). An example of how social taboos affect the under-recording of crime is found for rape cases prior to the introduction of domestic violence legislation: Konishi (2000) highlighted the lack of victim support for those suffering from post-traumatic stress disorder as the result of rape. Many of these women had neither sought treatment nor informed the police, and this seemed to be associated with the negative attitudes society held towards speaking publicly about sex and towards women who exhibited aggression or assertiveness (Kozu 1999). In the past few decades, several forms of family violence have emerged as social issues in need of addressing: filial violence, child maltreatment, filicide, intimate partner violence (IPV), and elder abuse. Progress in preventing family violence is slow, and seems hampered by obdurate traditional social attitudes and cultural beliefs.

Filial Violence

Before the early 1990s, when other forms of family violence surfaced in public consciousness, violence against parents was synonymous with domestic violence (Kozu 1999; Sugimoto 2014). Now, this is referred to as filial violence, in which children verbally or physically assault family members, usually their parents (Okamura 2016). This violence may also include throwing or destroying objects in the home. Kumagai (1983) describes the profile of those who engage in filial violence: outside the home, these children, usually aged 15–16 years and male, are considered 'good boys and girls' who do well at school. The majority come from upper-middle class backgrounds. Their families are small and they usually live only with their mothers as their fathers may be absent because of employment away from the home. Most likely, these children are the eldest of their siblings or they are an only child. They usually lack appropriate social skills and experience because they have not been properly disciplined.

Although parents tend to be victims of filial violence, ironically, the true victims are generally considered to be the children, because family and societal pressures have caused them to act out violently (Kozu 1999). It is difficult to gauge the extent of filial violence because parents are reluctant to report the abuse. Parents will suffer in silence in order to protect their children, but also, they do not want their community to know and risk social disapprobation (Okamura 2016). Their reluctance to report their children also stems from the fear that others will perceive the parents as failures in their responsibility.

Child Maltreatment

The Prevention of Child Abuse Act (PCA), passed in 2000, defined child maltreatment as comprising four types of abuse by parents or guardians: neglect, as well as physical, psychological, and sexual abuse (Kadonaga and Fraser 2015). IPV, in which children witness a parent commit violence towards another parent, may also be considered a form of psychological abuse. One of two spousal abusers, usually the husband, have often been found to physically abuse their children (Kozu 1999). As family matters are viewed as private, non-family members are less likely to intervene and family members are less likely to report child maltreatment. In recent years, however, reports of child abuse have risen and this could be attributed to increased awareness and easier access to Child Guidance Centres or to the police to report cases (Kadonaga and Fraser 2015).

Child sex abuse, in particular, is problematic because many people deny that such harm could exist in a morally upstanding country like Japan (*The Japan Times* 2017). The reality is that sexual abuse has a stigma. Kitamura and colleagues (1999) investigated child abuse in their study but decided not to ask their participants about experiences of sexual abuse, as they understood that the topic would make participants uncomfortable and embarrassed. Although existing legislation acknowledges that child abuse is a problem, when sex abuse does occur by people other than the parents or guardians, the fault is considered to lie with the parents or guardians—it is classified as neglect on their part (Tanaka et al. 2017). Kadonaga and Fraser (2015) list a few risk factors for child maltreatment and they apply only to parents: the decline of extended familial supports, low paternal involvement in childrearing, and demanding work schedules for both parents who seek professional careers.

To gauge the prevalence of child sexual abuse in Japan, Tanaka and colleagues (2017) systematically reviewed publications on child sexual abuse among non-clinical populations. Eight studies met their inclusion criteria. Together, the studies suggested that the prevalence of penetrative child sexual abuse was low compared to the prevalence internationally, but the prevalence of molestation among females was considered fairly high. The authors believed that the prevalence of molestation of female children in Japan was possibly similar to or higher than the prevalence in other countries. They attributed the frequency of child sexual abuse and its underreporting to patriarchy and hierarchy, in which males and elders preside. If a child is sexually abused, doubts about reporting it to someone may arise because the child has been taught to be obedient to authority figures. If a female child is sexually abused, fears about negative social reactions may prevent her from seeking help as she may be held responsible for her victimisation.

If child abuse can be translated into monetary costs, it would be as much as the cost of damage done by the 2011 earthquake and tsunami: Wada and Igarashi (2014) calculated the social cost of child abuse, in which 90% of the data came from 2012 to 2013. They examined direct and indirect costs; direct costs included the costs of child social welfare services and private child abuse prevention groups, while indirect costs included death from the abuse and depression associated with the abuse. The social cost of child abuse for one fiscal year was as much as the cost of damage to the Fukushima prefecture from the Tōhoku earthquake and tsunami (¥1.6 trillion compared to ¥1.9 trillion; equivalent to about £12 trillion and £15 trillion, respectively). The scholars, however, thought that it was highly likely that their calculation underestimated the true cost of child abuse.

Filicide

Filicide received a lot of media attention in the 1970s when dead, abandoned newborn babies, likely to have been asphyxiated and wrapped in plastic, were discovered in coin-operated lockers at train stations (Kouno and Johnson 1995). Almost all of the murderers were the baby's mother (Kozu 1999). These crimes significantly decreased once lockers were moved to more visible places, and education about contraception and the publication of these crimes became widely known. In some cases, filicide–suicides occurred. These types of maternal filicide have a deeper meaning in Japan because they carry a particular interpretation: the parent wanted to escape any shame and burden related to having others know about personal family matters (Kadonaga and Fraser 2015).

Yasumi and Kageyama (2009) investigated trends of filicide from 1994 to 2005 by gathering filicide cases in one of the leading national newspapers, *Asahi Shimbun*. They defined filicide as the killing of children under the age of 15 by their parents or step-parents. Results showed that filicide–suicides and filicide cases where the child was unwanted tended to occur in prefectures located in rural areas, and filicide cases where abuse led to the child's death occurred mostly in areas with the largest populations, which were in Osaka and three suburban areas of Tokyo—Saitama, Chiba, and Ibaraki. Interestingly, annual filicide rates were strongly associated with the rates in the general population of suicide and unemployment, but not homicide; this suggests that filicide may be influenced by socio-economic factors.

Castellini (2014) explored the psychology of maternal filicide through Ribu, a women's liberation movement that emerged at the same time as the coin-locker crimes, who had sided with women who had killed their children. Filicide, in this context, was understood by Ribu as a violent manifestation of the 'female grudge unleashed' towards an oppressive, patriarchal society. The argument was that these women did not kill; they were made to kill. The media portrayed these women as unusually wicked; the enormity of their deed was two-fold: the killing itself and their failure to adhere to social conventions of being female. This is a familiar observation in the West as well. Smart

(1976), in her book *Women, Crime, and Criminology*, argued that women offenders were treated as 'doubly deviant' because they not only offended but they had also strayed from their expected gender roles.

Ribu challenged conventional beliefs that the mother–child relationship was natural and interdependent and that the family was the foundation of Japanese society. The nuclear family was a consistent target of Ribu because it believed that, in the family, male fantasies of 'femininity' were propagated and sustained. The immense societal pressure and expectation of Japanese women to be good wives and mothers forced them to live only to serve their husbands and offspring, denying them a fulfilling existence. Beneath the surface of conventional familial harmony and bonds was the reality: 'to make do as a family'. The extreme would be these cases of violence, which reflected the discrepancy between public and private discourse.

Intimate Partner Violence

Sasaki and Ishii-Kuntz (2016) defined intimate partner violence (IPV) as comprising seven forms: physical, sexual, psychological, economic, social, and dating violence, as well as stalking. The purpose of IPV is control, as the perpetrator views the intimate partner as a mere possession. Likely perpetrators of IPV are medical doctors, business owners, and public servants. Although large-scale studies conducted in the West revealed that IPV was experienced by both men and women (Lussier et al. 2009), the issue is more pertinent to women in Japan. Public discourse treated IPV as a non-issue, with the general public excusing and tolerating husbands' use of violence towards their wives (Yoshihama and Horrocks 2010). In 2001, the Act on the Prevention of Spousal Violence and the Protection of Victims was passed to directly address IPV by identifying victims and providing adequate help such as support centres and hotlines (Kataoka et al. 2010). It is the first law to explicitly make spousal violence a crime (Kita et al. 2014). The law has been revised several times since, in 2004, 2007, and 2013, because it was unclear what exactly composed domestic violence (Nagai 2017).

Public discourse on the sanctity of marriage and role expectations, however, continue to influence societal attitudes, which make it hard for abused spouses to seek help. Women tend to stay in their abusive marriages because of stigmas associated with divorce and public exposure of such private matters (Kozu 1999; Mieko 1999). Nagae and Dancy (2010) confirmed these concerns from their qualitative study of 11 women who, along with their husbands, were born in Japan. These women wanted to leave their violent marriages but they stayed, because of patriarchal cultural beliefs that emphasised male dominance and that the occurrence of IPV was the result of wives' disobedience and inadequacy in meeting traditional gender roles. IPV perpetration may also extend to in-laws, who typically use emotional abuse. These cultural beliefs about gender roles seem stronger in Japan than in other countries. Nguyen et al. (2013) examined perceptions of violence against women among a sample of 943 university students in Japan, China, and the US. The findings showed that Japanese students had more traditional attitudes towards women, followed by China and then the US. Compared to American students, the Japanese were more likely to blame the victim and excuse the domestic violence.

Family registration, known as *koseki*, acts as a further deterrent for women who want to leave their abusive relationships. The system is distinct from other forms of registration in different countries because each household is considered a unit, in which family events such as births, marriages, divorces, and adoptions can be accessed and scrutinised (Sugimoto 2014). Critics have argued that this system disadvantages women as it upholds the patriarchal model of family and traditional gender roles (Castellini 2014). Based on the registration, any family member who does not conform to society norms will be socially ostracised. For women who defy conventions and divorce, the registration documents this, which may affect the job and marriage prospects of their children (Sugimoto 2014).

Elder Abuse

Of all forms of family violence, elder abuse is the least studied, even though it has existed for a while, only recently surfacing in public consciousness and discourse (Kozu 1999; Hayashi 2016). The societal emphasis on hierarchy, in which the older a person is, the more deference that person receives, may have contributed to the slow realisation that this issue was real. In a survey of older (mean age = 70.3 years) people's perceptions of elder abuse, those who reported watching television for longer periods of time were less likely to know of anyone who had experienced elder abuse (Tsukada et al. 2001). They were more likely to know of someone who had experienced this through social contacts, which suggests the discrepancy in presented information between public and private discourses.

Research in the late 1990s on domestic elder abuse revealed that females, those over the age of 75, and those who could not adequately perform activities of daily living (ADL), were more likely to be victims; daughter-in-laws tended to be the main perpetrators; neglect seemed to be the most prominent form of family abuse; victims suffered from multiple incidents of abuse; and the primary reasons for the occurrence of this abuse were pre-existing bad relationships (between victim and perpetrator) and stress related to caregiving (Kozu 1999; Tsukada et al. 2001). These factors continue to be risks found in investigations conducted since 2000 (Anme 2004; Anme et al. 2005; Sasaki et al. 2007).

When the national Long-Term Care Insurance programme was launched in 2000, signs of elder abuse were uncovered through mandatory assessments of the elderly, and a national survey was conducted by the Institute for Health Economics and Policy to establish characteristics of this abuse (Nakanishi et al. 2009). The Elder Abuse Prevention Act was enacted in 2006 and defined elder abuse similar to the four types of child maltreatment, but also included economic abuse in which perpetrators unfairly received benefits or distributed the elderly victim's property (Hayashi 2016). Victims were considered to be anyone aged 65 and over. Major social shifts, along with the introduction of the national insurance programme, have affected the way that caregiving is now handled: caregiving was assumed to be the sole responsibility of the family, where the daughter-in-law was expected to fulfil this duty, but now more formal, community-based services are available and used (Anme et al. 2005). The consequences of this may change risks for elder abuse, although recent publications present findings that have not changed much from previous ones (Hayashi 2016).

The Family as an Explanation for Crime

The family as an explanation for crime, as in a child's later offending, can be divided into six factors according to psychological criminology: one, child-rearing methods; two, large family size; three, child maltreatment; four, disrupted families and parental conflict; five, criminal and antisocial parents and siblings; and six, other parental factors. These divisions serve primarily to organise the vast number of findings and constructs on the relationship between family and crime found in Western, industrialised populations (Farrington 2011). Although findings and constructs on the family are diverse, the fact that family factors consistently relate to and predict crime in empirical studies demonstrates its explanatory importance. Meta-analyses to summarise findings on the relationship between family and crime identify child-rearing methods as the most important family explanation. Specifically, parental coldness such as rejection and hostility and low parental monitoring—either direct or indirect—are important dimensions (Hoeve et al. 2009; Loeber and Stouthamer-Loeber 1986). Many of these family factors that have been identified and established in Western studies also apply to Japan, albeit with differences to consider.

Child-Rearing Methods

Child-rearing methods refer to ways in which parents raise their child: discipline, supervision or monitoring, level of attachment, warmness or coldness of emotional relationships, and level of involvement. Discipline refers to how a parent reacts to their child's behaviour (Farrington and Welsh 2007). Harsh forms, such as hitting, slapping, yelling, and screaming, have been shown to be associated with later offending (Farrington 2005b). There seem to be different views on how Japanese society perceives physical punishment. One view proposes that tolerance towards physical punishment is widespread because it is considered an indication of parental concern (Kadonaga and Fraser 2015). Another view proposes that only 'mild corporal punishment' is acceptable such as 'spanking on the bottom', 'kneeling', or 'staying home after school and studying', but more serious forms of physical punishment can be used only for cases of delinquency, bullying, and dangerous activities (Ishii-Kuntz 2016). Many people, however, believe that child abuse is the result of parental discipline; this reflects the confusion over what constitutes physical discipline and what constitutes child abuse.

Due to the different perceptions of physical punishment in Japan compared to Western industrialised societies, harsh discipline may be relatively unimportant in explaining later offending. This is because findings from Deater-Deckard et al. (1996) concluded that the effects of physical discipline may depend on the meaning ascribed to it: in their study comparing the relationship between maternal physical discipline and children's externalising behaviours in black and white American families, they found that this relationship was only significant for white families. Physical discipline was thought to have a different meaning for black families, indicating parental concern for their children. These children did not think that physical punishment indicated a lack of parental warmth and concern.

In a comparative study of youth violence in the Japanese city of Osaka and the American city of Seattle, harsh discipline was associated with violence in neither city (Bui et al. 2014). A couple of empirical studies, however, have included another form of harsh discipline that is very pertinent to Japanese children: being locked out of the house. Ostracism is a form of punishment, and discipline encompasses ignoring the disobedient child, or threatening that child with abandonment (Lebra 1976). It expresses to children that they risk rejection, social exclusion, and abandonment if they misbehave. Thus, the most severe punishment in Japan is considered to be locking the child out of the house (Bayley 1976). Studies testing this, however, were unable to find a significant relationship between being locked out of the house and serious delinquency (Bui et al. 2016, 2018).

The comparative study between Osaka and Seattle also investigated low parental monitoring, defined as parents who did not know where their children were or who their children were with, and found that it was strongly related to youth violence among Japanese males (Bui et al. 2014). When this relationship for the Japanese was compared to that of Americans, it was weaker. A previous study of Sapporo youth also found the same relationship between low parental monitoring and delinquency (Laser et al. 2007).

In Bui et al. (2014), low attachment had no relationship to violence among Japanese but was strongly related to violence among Americans. The relationship between attachment and offending has its roots in sociologist Travis Hirschi's (1969) *Causes of Delinquency* and psychologists John Bowlby and Mary Ainsworth's (1991) attachment theory. The idea is that children's strong emotional bonds to parents will make them less likely to engage in delinquency because they will consider the expectations of their parents in their decision-making.

A meta-analysis of 74 published and unpublished international studies revealed that poor parental attachment was indeed linked to delinquency, and that stronger effects were found if parent and child were of the same sex (Hoeve et al. 2012). The finding from Bui and colleagues (2014) suggests that parental attachment as a concept is relatively unimportant for explanations for offending among Japanese youth, but it could actually suggest that the concept of attachment may need to be adjusted for different contexts.

As mothers are more likely than fathers to be responsible for their child's socialisation in Japan, it would be expected that the influence of maternal parenting would be stronger than that of paternal parenting. The importance of maternal attachment on later offending can be traced to the early research of John Bowlby in England, which formed the foundations of attachment theory. In a sample of 44 boys who were prone to stealing, Bowlby (1944) discovered that many of them had experienced maternal deprivation and separation. His belief was that if a child suffered from prolonged periods of deprivation during the first five years of life, this would lead to detrimental consequences, notably difficulty in establishing relationships (an 'affectionless character'). Despite significant criticism regarding his methodology, his work generated great interest on the importance of the mother–child relationship in early life.

In Bui (2014), when low attachment and monitoring were compared between parents, poor maternal parenting was more strongly related to high risk-taking and delinquency than was poor paternal parenting for both Japanese female and male youth. For males, however, these types of poor child-rearing from fathers still had some association with their high risk-taking. This finding may be a reflection of gender roles and expectations, in which sons, who would be next in line as head of household, would be affected by their fathers' behaviour towards them. In another study conducted in Sapporo, a poor maternal relationship was found to be related to delinquency, but a poor paternal relationship had no effect (Laser et al. 2007). Distinguishing between maternal and paternal parenting seems necessary when investigating family explanations for crime among Japanese populations.

Questionnaires administered by Hiramura et al. (2010) to 946 children and their parents in a rural prefecture also showed differences in delinquency and parenting styles between mothers and fathers. Both child aggression and delinquency were predicted by low maternal care, characterised by coldness, indifference, and neglect. This is not a surprise when considering the literature on the strong mother–child bond. These externalising behaviours were also predicted by *high* paternal overprotection and *low* maternal overprotection, meaning that fathers who had a more controlling and intrusive parenting style, or mothers who had a more permissive parenting style that encouraged independence, were likely to have aggressive or delinquent children.

Hiramura and colleagues (2010) did caution, however, that their statistical analyses (using structural equation modelling) had failed to confirm the latter result, and that further investigation was required. Nishikawa et al. (2010) addressed this issue in their study of child-rearing, parental attachment, and children's internalising and externalising behaviour. In their study, dysfunctional parenting was related to undesirable behaviours among youth, and overprotection was particularly related to girls' undesirable behaviours. Otani et al. (2013), in a later study, found that parental overprotection was related to children's increased dysfunctional attitudes towards achievement and dependency. These, in turn, may lead to numerous mental health issues in adulthood, such as depression.

Judging from the literature, mothers spend more time with their children than fathers in Japan. It also seems that this may be true cross-nationally. Ishii-Kuntz (1994) compared fathers' and their children's (ages 10–15 years) perceptions of paternal involvement in 1149 Japanese and 1000 American father–child pairs. Compared to American fathers, Japanese fathers spent less time chatting, having dinner, and playing sports with their children, although Japanese fathers had breakfast more often with their children than American fathers did. Sons spent more time with their fathers in America than sons did in Japan, but no differences were found for the amount of father–daughter interaction.

Ishii-Kuntz referred to the knowledge that parents were more protective of daughters than of sons in Japan, particularly because sons would leave to start their own households while daughters may live with the family for longer before they marry. Also, once daughters marry, they are considered a part of someone else's family. An interesting finding concerns children's favourable perceptions of their fathers: American children were more likely to express a favourable assessment of their fathers the more time they spent together, whereas Japanese children's perceptions of their father were largely unaffected by the amount of time spent together. Although the study did not investigate relationships with offending, it does have implications. The less time that Japanese fathers spend with their children could be seen to negatively affect parental discipline and supervision, as only the mother will be responsible for this, but, although Japanese children may not spend as much time with their fathers as other children do, they understand and respect paternal authority and it could be through their mother that they create a positive image of their father. In a way, the father is present in the home, although he may be physically away.

Large Family Size

It is common in Japan for several generations of a family to live together (Sugimoto 2014). Some observers misinterpret this as the persistence of traditional family values, when in actuality this arrangement is more driven by practicality. Property is expensive, so young people live with or near to their parents and provide them with support and care. Living in a multigenerational household produces ambivalence in wives, where they feel a continuous sense of worry and security (Takeda et al. 2004). They worry about caregiving to their ageing in-laws but also feel financially secure. In recent decades, though, the number of multigenerational households has been in decline.

Some wonder: 'what constitutes "large" family size?' In the Cambridge study, it was considered to be four or more siblings by a boy's tenth birthday (West and Farrington 1973). In several studies conducted by Bui and colleagues (2014, 2016) in Japan, large family size was considered to be five or more family members living with the young person. For females, large family size was not related to serious delinquency, whereas it was a risk for violence among Japanese males in the comparative study of Osaka and Seattle. The latter result was attributed to other aspects of large family size such as overcrowding. Farrington and Welsh (2007) proposed a couple of reasons why large family size was linked to delinquency: one was that parental attention was compromised when there were more children in the household, or, second, overcrowding might lead to frustration and conflict, especially in cramped conditions.

It seems that something else—a mediator—contributes to the relationship between large family size and delinquency. Ooki (2013) examined Japanese annual government reports of fatal child maltreatment between 2005 and 2012 and identified 14 cases that involved multiple births. These births tended to be from large-sized families compared to single births or to the general population, and it was suggested that the burden of child-rearing increased the risk of child maltreatment among all children in the family.

Child Maltreatment

Child maltreatment is a crime itself, but the victims are likely to become violent offenders in later life (Widom 1989). Incarcerated Japanese juvenile offenders, both male and female, who met criterion A for post-traumatic stress disorder,[1] have reported physical assault and abuse as the most prevalent traumas experienced (Yoshinaga et al. 2004). The relationship between maltreatment and delinquency

---

[1]Criterion A has to do with exposure to actual or threatened death, serious injury, or sexual violence (American Psychiatric Association 2013).

is consistent enough that, for recommendations on strengthening child guidance centres, Konishi (2014) suggested that resources for child maltreatment and delinquency in each local agency should be combined.

A high prevalence of Japanese children who live in institutional or residential homes, known as Children's Homes, have experienced abuse and neglect (Ohara and Matsuura 2016). Government statistics in 2010 revealed that 42% of these children suffered from physical abuse, 4.1% from sexual abuse, 63.7% from neglect, and 21% from psychological abuse. Prior to arrival to the homes, these children had lived in criminogenic family environments where mental illness, poverty, drug addiction, and divorce were rife. Their behavioural and emotional problems were similar to levels found among inmates in correctional institutions, with a high prevalence of antisocial and delinquent behaviours.

Based on the previous evidence, Ohara and Matsuura (2016) collected records of 809 children from these homes, where over half were male, with a mean age of 10.49 years, and they gathered information from childcare workers using questionnaires. They wanted to identify risk factors for delinquency in these homes, and found that 60% of these children had been abused. The children also came from unstable family backgrounds and exhibited significant internalising and externalising behaviours. Parent–child conflict and neglect were the strongest risk factors for delinquency among this group.

Self-reports of 555 Sapporo 18 to 19-year-old youth, in which 38% were female, revealed that a history of sexual abuse was related to female delinquency (Laser et al. 2007). Although the measure of sexual abuse did not specify the perpetrator or when the abuse occurred, this result is aligned with the literature on the association of sexual abuse with female delinquency in Japan: among detained female juvenile offenders, a high percentage have experienced a traumatic event, in which sexual abuse was the most frequently reported (Ariga et al. 2008).

Matsuura et al. (2013) collected information on the prevalence of child maltreatment in a group of severe offenders detained in a female juvenile correctional facility. They compared the prevalence to that in a group of similarly aged first-year female high school students and found that physical and psychological abuse was much higher for the incarcerated group (mean of 25.35% vs. mean of 2.1%). They had conducted a very similar study previously and found similar results (Matsuura et al. 2009). The prevalence of a history of abuse among juvenile offenders is generally high, but it is greater among females than it is among males (Ando 2004). Takii (1992) highlighted that these girls were not supported when they disclosed their abuse, and this led them to be involved in a variety of delinquent and maladaptive behaviours, as illustrated by a case example from the Sendai Juvenile Classification Home:

> A woman was admitted to the Juvenile Classification Home at age 18.9 years. When she was nine years old her mother left home, leaving her to be cared for by her father and her older brother. Her father was alcoholic and violent, beating and kicking her daily, particularly after he learned that she had been secretly meeting her mother. At age 14 she left home to live with her mother, but the mother's cohabitant forced her to have sex with him. She disclosed this to her mother, who accused her of lying. The sexual abuse continued and the victim attempted suicide, ran away from home, began glue-sniffing, and was finally arrested for working as a prostitute. She did not exhibit delinquent behaviour when she was being physically abused, probably because she was receiving support from her mother, even though they did not live together. She must have felt helpless and desperate when, having fled to her mother from her father's violence, her mother was unable to protect her from sexual abuse or believe that it could be happening. It was only then that the victim became emotionally unstable, depressed, with low self-esteem, and had aggressive, negative feelings towards her mother. (46)

Although this case example is quite dated, it illustrates how child maltreatment puts a child at risk of offending. Women who have a history of child sexual abuse by a known perpetrator also have an increased risk of being future victims of IPV (Yoshihama and Horrocks 2010). These findings on the relationship between child sexual abuse and female delinquency are similar to international results (Chesney-Lind and Sheldon 2014; Siegel and Williams 2003).

Disrupted Families and Parental Conflict

Disrupted Families

The Arakawa study (Wagatsuma and De Vos 1984) mentioned at the beginning of this chapter was unable to examine the relationship between disrupted families and delinquency because their sample comprised intact families. Instead, they managed to gather information on previous marriages. The parents of children who were delinquent were almost twice as likely to have been in a previous marriage than the parents of children who were non-delinquent (58% vs. 26%). Many of these separations for both groups, though, had been caused by deaths from the Second World War.

Early research in Japan on broken and disrupted homes, dating back to the 1920s, was able to replicate findings from Western populations (see Wagatsuma and De Vos 1984). Among youth involved in delinquency, step-parents tended to be present and broken homes tended to be caused by divorce or abandonment. Broken homes caused by death were not related to delinquency. Notable among some of these classic findings are ones by psychiatrists in the 1950s. They presented findings similar to John Bowlby's maternal deprivation thesis, but they also found that children who were five years or older had an increased risk of delinquency if they had no father.

Bowlby's research propagated the notion that broken homes produce delinquency (Farrington and Welsh 2007). The findings on this relationship in Japan and in Western industrialised countries are fairly similar although more progress, it seems, has been made in the latter. Research on this relationship has grown since the 1960s and it coincided with the observation that rates of delinquency and disrupted families were rising in Western industrialised countries (Haas et al. 2004).

Three main classes of theories exist to explain why disrupted families are linked to delinquency (Juby and Farrington 2001): first are trauma theories. Parental attachment is at the heart of these theories, and Bowlby's maternal deprivation thesis and Hirschi's control theory are two influential examples. The trauma from losing a parent is considered the basis of the relationship between disrupted families and delinquency. The loss is more traumatic because of the attachment to the parent. Second, there are life course theories. Separation is viewed as one of a multitude of stressful life experiences, which may include parental conflict, parental loss, changes in parents, reduced income, and poor child-rearing methods. These experiences accumulate and may be very damaging to the child, depending on the child's age and how disruptive the experiences are. Third, are selection theories. These suggest that the relationship between disrupted families and delinquency reflects pre-existing factors that may contribute to child behaviour problems. A notable pre-existing factor is parental conflict, considered to precede and be responsible for both family disruption and delinquency.

Juby and Farrington (2001) tested these three types of theories using the Cambridge study. Before this, investigations of disrupted families were limited to simple factors like the dichotomous broken/intact home or single/two- parent that did not take into account the actual complexities of family disruption. Their findings concluded that life course theories best explained the relationship between disrupted families and delinquency. What happened to the boys after the disruption mattered most: those who stayed with their mothers were involved in delinquency less than those who stayed with their fathers, relatives, or with others. In fact, the propensity to offend for boys who stayed with their mothers was just the same as for boys living in intact and low-conflict families.

The concept of the single-parent household is different from broken homes and disrupted families. It seems that the experience and aftermath of the latter two factors are what contributes to a child's later offending, whereas the former contributes because it is only the absence of another parent that diminishes the probability of receiving good child-rearing. Nevertheless, living with a single parent has been shown to significantly increase the risk of offending (Farrington 2005b; Haas et al. 2004; Hawkins et al. 2000). It is thought that, compared to two parents, one parent will devote less attention to properly monitoring and disciplining the children because of long hours at work, or circumstances surrounding the family break-up (Piquero et al. 2010; Theobald et al. 2013). What the study from Juby and Farrington highlights is that how broken homes are measured may not fully capture the complexities inherent in this concept. This is a particular challenge when conducting a cross-cultural study.

In the previous comparative study between Osaka and Seattle, living in a single-parent household protected against youth violence in Japan, but was a risk in America (Bui et al. 2014). For this study, adolescents were asked if they were currently living with their mother or father,[2] and an absence of one parent (usually the father) was taken to mean that they lived in a single-parent household. Absences, however, could also mean that the parents were still together, but the father was working away from home. This is a common practice among large corporations and national and local governments in Japan, where it is estimated that one in 50 workers live away from home (Sugimoto 2014). The practice is referred to as *tanshin funin* and workers, likely married, are required to relocate without their families for career progress (Nakadaira et al. 2006). Therefore the absence of one parent may not be as damaging as assumed; instead it could be indicative of higher socio-economic status. Nonetheless, government statistics in 2010 revealed that the poverty rate was almost five times higher in one-parent households compared to two-parent households (54.3% vs. 12.2%) (Kadonaga and Fraser 2015), and this is assumed to be based on actual separation.

Parental Conflict

The PCA, the legislative act against child maltreatment in Japan, considers witnessing violence between parents as a form of psychological child abuse. This consideration has merit: children who witness violence between their parents are likely to develop antisocial behaviour themselves (Farrington and Welsh 2007). Widom (1989) called this the 'cycle of violence', in reference to Albert Bandura's (1977) social learning theory, which proposes that exposure to violence teaches children that this behaviour is normal and acceptable; it tells them that in order to get what they want, violence is an effective means. Longitudinal

---

[2]This question was asked slightly differently in the Seattle sample and the parent, whoever the adolescent lived with, answered: 'Did the student live with his or her natural mother/father?'

studies of Western populations have shown that witnessing severe IPV in adolescence is related to IPV and violent crime in adulthood (Ireland and Smith 2009). These behaviours continue well into midlife, likely as a result of living in a high-risk environment where antisocial behaviour and neurological deficits develop and are maintained (Lussier et al. 2009). Laser et al. (2007) found this to be true in their study of Sapporo youth: males who witnessed domestic violence between their parents were more likely to be deviant, and the authors reckon that deviance was a way for the children to cope.

Criminal and Antisocial Parents

Child maltreatment is a form of intergenerational transmission of violence. Abusive parents are influenced by their own experiences of childhood abuse (Fujiwara et al. 2012). In this sense, child maltreatment, parental conflict, and IPV all contribute to this transmission. It is established knowledge that crime runs in families, where criminal and antisocial parents tend to have children who are also criminal and antisocial (Farrington et al. 2001, 2017a). This intergenerational transmission of violence and crime is detected in Western prospective studies of multiple generations (Thornberry et al. 2009). Besemer (2012) describes this type of transmission as a characteristic or behaviour that is observed in both parent and child.

In a community sample of 1186 adults in Japan, Umeda and colleagues (2015) found that adults who had experienced harsh physical discipline in childhood, such as being punched, slapped, shoved, or grabbed, were very likely to do the same to their children, and this was a strong and independent relationship. Physical discipline had a stronger relation to the intergenerational transmission of physical abuse than to any other forms of childhood abuse.

No study in Japan, to our knowledge, has been conducted where parents' criminal behaviour or convictions are examined to see if they influence a child's subsequent criminal behaviour and convictions. The closest studies are ones on child maltreatment and witnessing IPV between parents.

Other Parental Factors

The rise of teenage pregnancy and abortions in Japan prompted the first epidemiological study on early adolescent (under 15 years of age) reproductive health. It confirmed that teenage pregnancy was associated with juvenile victimisation and delinquency (Baba et al. 2014). This finding is slightly different to findings from Western longitudinal studies, in which teenage pregnancy has been shown to predict delinquency and antisocial behaviour of *the children* (Farrington and Welsh 2007). Teenage mothers are thought to reflect a myriad of risks for their child because they tend to use poor child-rearing methods, come from low-income families, and often raise the child without the biological father.

Laser and colleagues (2007) explored cultural-specific parental factors and their relation to delinquency among Japanese youth. One was the mother's involvement in *telekura*, telephone sex, as there had been 'lively' discussions about this by the mainstream media. The other was the frequency of fathers visiting brothels. The children confirmed whether their parents partook in such activities through statements. For example: 'I believe that my mother was involved with *telekura* to meet other people/to make money'. Only the father visiting brothels was related to the child's delinquency, and this had more of an effect on males, possibly because the knowledge threatened their sense of morality.

Family Violence Prevention

Family violence directly relates to the family as an explanation for crime in Japan. Although the two concepts, family violence and family as an explanation for crime, are conceptually different, a psychological perspective links them together. Not only could child maltreatment, parental conflict, and criminal or antisocial parents be crimes themselves, but they sustain the continuity of criminality through the generations. Parents who are violent increase the chances that their child will be violent too. This is supported by evidence that children who are abused or witness violence at home, especially between parents, are likely to offend later in life. Family circumstances also lead to the presence of risks and these in turn may influence other risks as well. For example, in a sample of mothers and children staying in 83 welfare facilities called mother–child homes, Fujiwara et al. (2012) found that IPV was related to child maltreatment and poor maternal parenting, but parental separation (from the father) improved the mother's parenting. From previous evidence, these risks increase the child's chances for future offending and maladaptive behaviours. Family-related crimes and their risk factors are interlinked, creating a web of antisocial behaviour.

Indeed, Farrington (2001) noted a similar observation years ago among Western studies. Offending was considered to be a symptom of a larger syndrome of antisocial behaviour. Those who offended tended to have a variety of other 'symptoms' including heavy drinking, reckless driving, sexual promiscuity, bullying, and truancy. They tended to be more deviant than non-offenders at that age, and to carry these behaviours into the next developmental phase, becoming an antisocial child, then an antisocial adolescent, and then an antisocial adult. These antisocial behaviours are likely to be passed on to their children through socialisation and exposure to similar risks.

Integrating Sociological and Psychological Perspectives on Family Violence

A particular challenge for family prevention and intervention in Japan is that family issues are kept private because of societal attitudes and taboos. This is the consequence of the dichotomy between public and private, evident in attitudes and values that promote a dual nature, and this acts not only as a restraint against discussing private matters openly but as a misrepresentation of reality. Aggravating this problem is the patriarchal social structure that encourages men to view women as inferior and deserving of abuse. Kumagai (2016a), a prominent Japanese sociologist on the family, highlighted, in her co-edited anthology, that sociocultural characteristics contribute to the prevalence of family violence in Japan.

Understanding family violence is also hampered by scholarly limitations. This is noticeable in Kumagai's (2016b) preface when she remarks that her 'stance and views on family violence are not fully appreciated in Japan' (vi). Her ideas on family violence are largely influenced by the pioneering work of Murray Straus, an American sociologist. One obstacle seems to be that family violence is perceived as an individual pathology in Japan rather than as a social issue. Kumagai promotes a life course perspective in understanding this violence because of the observed intergenerational transmission and possible within-individual continuity. She also suggests that studies should consider regional differences and be based on representative samples, instead of based on only problem families. Intriguingly, her recommendations are already being followed in the area of Developmental and Life Course Criminology (DLC).

Recall from the previous chapter that DLC is concerned with the development of offending and antisocial behaviour, risk and protective factors at different developmental stages, and the impact of life events on the life course (Farrington 2005a). Many of its ideas are from psychological findings on human development. DLC findings are based on prospective longitudinal studies, mainly conducted in Western industrialised countries, which follow individuals initially in the community and through different developmental phases. Its theories contribute to knowledge on the overlap between offending and antisocial behaviour, continuity from childhood to adulthood in criminality, and the influence of biological and psychological factors. The risk factor prevention paradigm, one framework that informs DLC, maybe most pertinent to family violence prevention in Japan. There is psychological research aligned to DLC already being conducted by Japanese scholars and practitioners to prevent and reduce family violence.

Identification of Risk Factors and Development of Preventative Measures

Japanese researchers and practitioners have begun using psychological theories to understand the origins of child maltreatment and to design interventions (Kadonaga and Fraser 2015). A criticism had been that many of the theories used to explain maltreatment in Japan had been imported from countries like the US and UK, and they failed to incorporate context-specific insights. This limitation is less of an issue now. Investigations into risk factors for different forms of family violence have appeared in quite a few research articles on Japan. The idea of risk focused-prevention is simple: identify individual and social factors that predict an increase of the probability of offending, and then target them to prevent offending through intervention and prevention programmes (Farrington 2000; Farrington and Ttofi 2011). A major limitation of many studies on risk factors for crime in Japan is that they assess risk and offending at only one time point. Therefore these are not proper studies of risk factors; rather these are studies of correlates for offending.

In order to ensure that family risk factors predict crime and not the other way around, longitudinal studies are needed in Japan. Unlike cross-sectional studies, which measure the family factor and crime at the same time, longitudinal studies would measure the family factor before the crime. This will clarify the temporal ordering of factors and confirm whether correlates should be considered as risk factors (Murray et al. 2009). Repeated measures throughout the life course will also help in understanding the causes and continuity of antisocial behaviour.

Once risk factors are identified, effective programmes must be designed. Examples can be found in the studies of elder abuse and IPV. Based on current research findings on elder abuse at the time, Tsukada et al. (2001) recommended a multi-preventative approach that included counselling, advisory and legal services, and community networks. Most important, though, was empowering the elderly to be independent and to be aware of elder abuse so that the abuse could be detected early. Home visits to investigate reported cases and those resistant to outside support from intervention teams and networks have been recommended, but these initiatives have been slow to progress because of limited funding in smaller municipalities, preventing collaboration between relevant agencies (Nakanishi et al. 2009).

A critical and often overlooked time to assess for IPV is during pregnancy. Pregnant women who had a history of abortion or pregnancy, were over the age of 30, or had a male partner under the age of 30, were more likely to suffer from IPV (Kita et al. 2014). This abuse also affects infants: verbal IPV while pregnant directly predicted later maternal shaking or smothering of the mother's four-month-old babies in the Aichi prefecture (Amemiya and Fujiwara 2016). Because of societal attitudes towards IPV and the cultural values of keeping private matters hidden in Japan, pregnant women may not disclose their abuse. Kataoka and colleagues (2010) tried to find a solution by conducting a randomised controlled trial in which 328 women, initially 14–25 weeks pregnant, were randomly assigned to either an interview or self-administered questionnaire group in a Tokyo prenatal clinic. The women were assessed at three different time points for IPV. Self-administered questionnaires were effective in detecting IPV more so than interviews, likely because women felt more secure in disclosing their abuse through writing.

Usually, family risk factors, such as child-rearing methods and parental conflict, mean that developmental prevention programmes are needed. These focus on at-risk children and their families because of the emphasis on early prevention (Farrington et al. 2017b). Within the Japanese context, it seems that such programmes might not work. Home visiting programmes for new mothers in the Aichi prefecture were examined for their effectiveness in reducing parental stress and increasing social capital (Fujiwara et al. 2012). The results showed that, after being visited once or twice by a public health nurse or community staff member, new mothers reported no reduction in stress and no difference in social capital compared to new mothers who did not participate. More visits, however, could be effective, and more research is clearly needed on this topic.

Conclusion

It seems that family factors that are involved in transmitting violent and criminal behaviour from one generation to the next are important, so the identification of family violence should be given more attention. Findings from the Cambridge study in the UK, for example, have indicated that secondary IPV programmes should be included, as antisocial adolescents with poor verbal skills who lived in high-risk family environments as a child were likely to be involved in IPV later in life (Lussier et al. 2009). For Japan, it seems that scholars and practitioners are identifying effective approaches to detecting and preventing family violence, but longitudinal studies that underline a life course perspective are needed to identify effective prevention programmes.

References

Ainsworth, Mary S., and John Bowlby. 1991. "An Ethological Approach to Personality Development." *American Psychologist* 46 (4): 333–41.

Aldous, Christopher, and Frank Leishman. 2000. *Enigma Variations: Reassessing the Kôban*. Oxford: Nissan Institute of Japanese Studies.

Amemiya, Airi, and Takeo Fujiwara. 2016. "Association Between Maternal Intimate Partner Violence Victimization During Pregnancy and Maternal Abusive Behavior Towards Infants at 4 Months of Age in Japan." *Child Abuse & Neglect* 55: 32–39.

American Psychiatric Association. 2013. *Diagnostic and Statistical Manual of Mental Disorders*. Washington, DC: Author.

Ando, Kumiko. 2004. "Current Adolescent Forensic Psychiatry in Japan." *Current Opinion in Psychiatry* 17 (5): 417–22.

Anme, Tokie. 2004. "A Study of Elder Abuse and Risk Factors in Japanese Families: Focused on the Social Affiliation Model." *Geriatrics and Gerontology International* 4 (s1): S262–63.

Anme, Tokie, Mary McCall, and Toshio Tatara. 2005. "An Exploratory Study of Abuse Among Frail Elders Using Services in a Small Village in Japan." *Journal of Elder Abuse and Neglect* 17 (2): 1–20.

Ariga, Michio, Toru Uehara, Kazuo Takeuchi, Yoko Ishige, Reiko Nakano, and Masahiko Mikuni. 2008. "Trauma Exposure and Posttraumatic Stress Disorder in Delinquent Female Adolescents." *Journal of Child Psychology and Psychiatry* 49 (1): 79–87.

Baba, Sachiko, Aya Goto, and Michael R. Reich. 2014. "Recent Pregnancy Trends Among Early Adolescent Girls in Japan." *Journal of Obstetrics and Gynaecology Research* 40 (1): 125–32.

Bandura, Albert. 1977. *Social Learning Theory*. Oxford: Prentice-Hall.

Bayley, David H. 1976. *Forces of Order: Policing Modern Japan*. Berkeley: University of California Press.

Becker, Carl B. 1988. "Report from Japan: Causes and Controls of Crime in Japan." *Journal of Criminal Justice* 16 (5): 425–35.

Besemer, Sytske. 2012. *Intergenerational Transmission of Criminal and Violent Behaviour*. Leiden: Sidestone Press.

Bowlby, John. 1944. "Forty-Four Juvenile Thieves: Their Characters and Home-Life." *The International Journal of Psycho-Analysis* 25 (107): 19–52.

Bui, Laura. 2014. "Examining the Relationship Between Parenting, Risk-Taking, and Delinquency in Japan: Context and Empirical Applicability." *Asian Journal of Criminology* 9 (3): 171–87.

Bui, Laura, David P. Farrington, and Mitsuaki Ueda. 2016. "Potential Risk and Promotive Factors for Serious Delinquency in Japanese Female Youth." *International Journal of Comparative and Applied Criminal Justice* 40 (3): 209–24.

———. 2018. "Risk and Protective Factors for Serious Delinquency in the Japanese Context: Findings from Osaka Male Youths." In *Crime and Justice in Contemporary Japan*, edited by Jianghong Liu and Setsuo Miyazawa, 119–35. New York: Springer.

Bui, Laura, David P. Farrington, Mitsuaki Ueda, and Karl G. Hill. 2014. "Prevalence and Risk Factors for Self-Reported Violence of Osaka and Seattle Male Youths." *International Journal of Offender Therapy and Comparative Criminology* 58 (12): 1540–57.

Castellini, Alessandro. 2014. "Silent Voices: Mothers Who Kill Their Children and the Women's Liberation Movement in 1970s Japan." *Feminist Review* 106 (1): 9–26.

Chesney-Lind, Meda, and Randall G. Sheldon. 2014. *Girls, Delinquency, and Juvenile Justice*. West Sussex: Wiley.

Deater-Deckard, Kirby, Kenneth A. Dodge, John E. Bates, and Gregory S. Pettit. 1996. "Physical Discipline Among African American and European American Mothers: Links to Children's Externalizing Behaviors." *Developmental Psychology* 32 (6): 1065–72.

Farrington, David P. 2000. "Explaining and Preventing the Globalization of Knowledge—The American Society of Criminology 1999 Presidential Address." *Criminology* 38(1): 1–25.

———. 2001. "Key Results from the First Forty Years of the Cambridge Study in Delinquent Development." In *Taking Stock of Delinquency: An Overview of Findings from Contemporary Longitudinal Studies*, edited by Terence P. Thornberry and Marvin D. Krohn, 137–83. New York: Kluwer/Plenum.

———. 2005a. *Integrated Developmental and Life-Course Theories of Offending*. New Brunswick: Transaction.

————. 2005b. "Childhood Origins of Antisocial Behavior." *Clinical Psychology and Psychotherapy* 12 (3): 177–90.

————. 2011. "Families and Crime." In *Crime and Public Policy*, edited by James Q. Wilson and Joan Petersilia, 130–57. Oxford: Oxford University Press.

————. 2017. "Developmental Criminology." In *The Routledge Companion to Criminological Theory and Concepts*, edited by Avi Brisman, Eamonn Carrabine and Nigel South, 60–64. London: Routledge.

Farrington, David P., and Brandon C. Welsh. 2007. *Saving Children from a Life of Crime*. New York: Oxford University Press.

Farrington, David P., and Maria M. Ttofi. 2011. "Protective and Promotive Factors in the Development of Offending." In *Antisocial Behavior and Crime: Contributions of Developmental and Evaluation Research to Prevention and Intervention*, edited by Thomas Bliesener, Andreas Beelmann, and Mark Stemmler, 71–88. Cambridge: Hogrefe.

Farrington, David P., Darrick Jolliffe, Rolf Loeber, Magda Stouthamer-Loeber, and Larry M. Kalb. 2001. "The Concentration of Offenders in Families, and Family Criminality in the Prediction of Boys' Delinquency." *Journal of Adolescence* 24 (5): 579–96.

Farrington David P., Maria M. Ttofi, and Rebecca V. Crago. 2017a. "Intergenerational Transmission of Convictions for Different Types of Offenses." *Victims and Offenders* 12(1): 1–20.

Farrington, David P., Hannah Gaffney, Friedrich Lösel, and Maria M. Ttofi. 2017b. "Systematic Reviews of the Effectiveness of Development Prevention Programs in Reducing Delinquency, Aggression, and Bullying." *Aggression and Violent Behavior* 33: 91–106.

Fujiwara, Takeo, Makiko Okuyama, and Mayuko Izumi. 2012. "The Impact of Childhood Abuse History, Domestic Violence and Mental Health Symptoms on Parenting Behaviour among Mothers in Japan." *Child: Care, Health and Development* 38 (4): 530–37.

Haas, Henriette, David P. Farrington, Martin Killias, and Ghazala Sattar. 2004. "The Impact of Different Family Configurations on Delinquency." *British Journal of Criminology* 44 (4): 520–32.

Hawkins, David J., Todd I. Herrenkohl, David P. Farrington, Devon Brewer, Richard F. Catalano, and Tracy W. Harachi. 2000. *Predictors of Youth Violence*. Washington, DC: Office of Juvenile Justice and Delinquency Prevention.

Hayashi, Yoko. 2016. "Elder Abuse and Family Transformation." In *Family Violence in Japan: A Life Course Perspective*, edited by Fumie Kumagai and Masako Ishii-Kuntz, 123–51. New York: Springer.

Hiramura, Hidetoshi, Masayo Uji, Noriko Shikai, Zi Chen, Nao Matsuoka, and Toshinori Kitamura. 2010. "Understanding Externalizing Behavior from Children's Personality and Parenting Characteristics." *Psychiatry Research* 175 (1–2): 142–47.

Hirschi, Travis. 1969. *Causes of Delinquency*. Berkeley: University of California Press.

Hoeve, Machteld, Judith Semon Dubas, Veroni I. Eichelsheim, Peter H. van der Laan, Wilma Smeenk, and Jan R. M. Gerris. 2009. "The Relationship Between Parenting and Delinquency: A Meta-Analysis." *Journal of Abnormal Child Psychology* 37 (6): 749–75.

Hoeve, MacHteld, Geert Jan J. M. Stams, Claudia E. Van Der Put, Judith Semon Dubas, Peter H. Van Der Laan, and Jan R. M. Gerris. 2012. "A Meta-Analysis of Attachment to Parents and Delinquency." *Journal of Abnormal Child Psychology* 40 (5): 771–85.

Holloway, Susan D. 2010. *Women and Family in Contemporary Japan*. Cambridge: Cambridge University Press.

Ireland, Timothy O., and Carolyn A. Smith. 2009. "Living in Partner-Violent Families: Developmental Links to Antisocial Behavior and Relationship Violence." *Journal of Youth and Adolescence* 38 (3): 323–39.

Ishii-Kuntz, Masako. 1994. "Paternal Involvement and Perception Towards Fathers' Roles: A Comparison Between Japan and the United States." *Journal of Family Issues* 15 (1): 30–48.

———. 2016. "Child Abuse: History and Current State in Japanese Context." In *Family Violence in Japan: A Life Course Perspective*, edited by Fumie Kumagai and Masako Ishii-Kuntz, 49–78. New York: Springer.

Juby, Heather, and David P. Farrington. 2001. "Disentangling the Link Between Disrupted Families and Delinquency." *British Journal of Criminology* 41 (1): 22–40.

Kadonaga, Tomoko, and Mark W. Fraser. 2015. "Child Maltreatment in Japan." *Journal of Social Work* 15 (3): 233–53.

Kataoka, Yaeko, Yukari Yaju, Hiromi Eto, and Shigeko Horiuchi. 2010. "Self-Administered Questionnaire Versus Interview as a Screening Method for Intimate Partner Violence in the Prenatal Setting in Japan: A Randomised Controlled Trial." *BMC Pregnancy and Childbirth* 10: 84.

Kita, Sachiko, Kataoka Yaeko, and Sarah E. Porter. 2014. "Prevalence and Risk Factors of Intimate Partner Violence Among Pregnant Women in Japan." *Health Care for Women International* 35 (4): 442–57.

Kitamura, Toshinori, Nobuhiko Kijima, Noboru Iwata, Yukiko Senda, Koji Takahashi, and Ikue Hayashi. 1999. "Frequencies of Child Abuse in Japan: Hidden but Prevalent Crime." *International Journal of Offender Therapy and Comparative Criminology* 43 (1): 21–33.

Konishi, Takako. 2000. "Cultural Aspects of Violence Against Women in Japan." *Lancet* 355 (9217): 1810.

Konishi, Tokikazu. 2014. "Strengthening the Child Guidance Functions in the Child Welfare System: Toward Early Solutions for Child Maltreatment and Delinquency Cases." *Waseda Bulletin of Comparative Law* 32: 1–10.

Kouno, Akihisa, and Charles F. Johnson. 1995. "Child Abuse and Neglect in Japan: Coin-Operated-Locker Babies." *Child Abuse and Neglect* 19 (1): 25–31.

Kozu, Junko. 1999. "Domestic Violence in Japan." *American Psychologist* 54 (1): 50–54.

Kumagai, Fumie. 1983. "Filial Violence: A Peculiar Parent-Child Relationship in the Japanese Family Today." *Journal of Comparative Family Studies* 12 (3): 337–49.

———. 2016a. "Conclusion: Prevention and Intervention of Violence in Japan." In *Family Violence in Japan: A Life Course Perspective*, edited by Fumie Kumagai and Masako Ishii-Kuntz, 153–64. New York: Springer.

———. 2016b. "Introduction: Toward a Better Understanding of Family Violence in Japan." In *Family Violence in Japan: A Life Course Perspective*, edited by Fumie Kumagai and Masako Ishii-Kuntz, 1–48. Singapore: Springer.

Laser, Julie, Tom Luster, and Toko Oshio. 2007. "Promotive and Risk Factors Related to Deviant Behavior in Japanese Youth." *Criminal Justice and Behavior* 34 (11): 1463–80.

Lebra, Takie Sugiyama. 1976. *Japanese Patterns of Behavior*. Honolulu: University Press of Hawaii.

Loeber, Rolf, and Magda Stouthamer-Loeber. 1986. "Family Factors as Correlates and Predictors of Juvenile Conduct Problems and Delinquency." In *Crime and Justice*, edited by Michael Tonry and Norval Morris, 29–149. Chicago: University of Chicago Press.

Lussier, Patrick, David P. Farrington, and Terrie E. Moffitt. 2009. "Is the Antisocial Child Father of the Abusive Man? A 40-Year Prospective Longitudinal Study on the Developmental Antecedents of Intimate Partner Violence." *Criminology* 47 (3): 741–80.

Matsuura, Naomi, Toshiaki Hashimoto, and Motomi Toichi. 2009. "Correlations Among Self-Esteem, Aggression, Adverse Childhood Experiences and Depression in Inmates of a Female Juvenile Correctional Facility in Japan." *Psychiatry and Clinical Neurosciences* 63 (4): 478–85.

———. 2013. "Associations Among Adverse Childhood Experiences, Aggression, Depression, and Self-Esteem in Serious Female Juvenile

Offenders in Japan." *Journal of Forensic Psychiatry & Psychology* 24 (1): 111–27.

Mieko, Yoshihama. 1999. "Domestic Violence: Japan's 'hidden Crime'." *Japan Quarterly* 46 (3): 76–82.

Murray, Joseph, David P. Farrington, and Manuel P. Eisner. 2009. "Drawing Conclusions About Causes from Systematic Reviews of Risk Factors: The Cambridge Quality Checklists." *Journal of Experimental Criminology* 5 (1): 1–23.

Nagae, Miyoko, and Barbara L. Dancy. 2010. "Japanese Women's Perceptions of Intimate Partner Violence (IPV)." *Journal of Interpersonal Violence* 25 (4): 753–66.

Nagai, Susumu. 2017. "Status of Victims of Spousal Violence and the Future Tasks: The Case of Japan." In *Domestic Violence in International Context*, edited by Diana Schaff Peterson and Julie A Schroeder, 136–46. Oxon: Routledge.

Nakadaira, Hiroto, Masaharu Yamamoto, and Toh Matsubara. 2006. "Mental and Physical Effects of Tanshin Funin, Posting Without Family, on Married Male Workers in Japan." *Journal of Occupational Health* 48 (2): 113–23.

Nakanishi, Miharu, Yumiko Hoshishiba, Nobuyuki Iwama, Tomoko Okada, Etsuko Kato, and Hiroshi Takahashi. 2009. "Impact of the Elder Abuse Prevention and Caregiver Support Law on System Development Among Municipal Governments in Japan." *Health Policy* 90 (2–3): 254–61.

Nguyen, Toan Thanh, Yasuko Morinaga, Irene Hanson Frieze, Jessica Cheng, Manyu Li, Akiko Doi, Tatsuya Hirai, Eunsun Joo, and Cha Li. 2013. "College Students' Perceptions of Intimate Partner Violence: A Comparative Study of Japan, China, and the United States." *International Journal of Conflict and Violence* 7 (2): 261–73.

Nishikawa, Saori, Elisabet Sundbom, and Bruno Hägglöf. 2010. "Influence of Perceived Parental Rearing on Adolescent Self-Concept and Internalizing and Externalizing Problems in Japan." *Journal of Child and Family Studies* 19 (1): 57–66.

Ohara, Takaharu, and Naomi Matsuura. 2016. "The Characteristics of Delinquent Behavior and Predictive Factors in Japanese Children's Homes." *Children and Youth Services Review* 61: 159–64.

Okamura, Rie. 2016. "Filial Violence: An Unrevealed Problem for Decades." In *Family Violence in Japan: A Life Course Perspective*, edited by Fumie Kumagai and Masako Ishii-Kuntz, 103–22. New York: Springer.

Ooki, Syuichi. 2013. "Characteristics of Fatal Child Maltreatment Associated with Multiple Births in Japan." *Twin Research and Human Genetics* 16 (3): 743–50.

Otani, Koichi, Akihito Suzuki, Yoshihiko Matsumoto, Naoshi Shibuya, Ryoichi Sadahiro, and Masanori Enokido. 2013. "Parental Overprotection Engenders Dysfunctional Attitudes About Achievement and Dependency in a Gender-Specific Manner." *BMC Psychiatry* 13 (1): 345.

Piquero, Alex R., Wesley G. Jennings, and David P. Farrington. 2010. "On the Malleability of Self-Control: Theoretical and Policy Implications Regarding a General Theory of Crime." *Justice Quarterly* 27 (6): 803–34.

Ronald, Richard, and Allison Alexy. 2011. "Continuity and Change in Japanese Homes and Families." In *Home and Family in Japan: Continuity and Transformation*, edited by Richard Ronald and Allison Alexy, 1–24. Oxon: Routledge.

Sasaki, Takayo, and Masako Ishii-Kuntz. 2016. "Intimate Partner Violence: Domestic Violence from Japanese Perspective." In *Family Violence in Japan: A Life Course Perspective*, edited by Fumie Kamagai and Masako Ishii-Kuntz, 79–102. New York: Springer.

Sasaki, Megumi, Yumiko Arai, Keigo Kumamoto, Koji Abe, Asuna Arai, and Yoko Mizuno. 2007. "Factors Related to Potentially Harmful Behaviors Towards Disabled Older People by Family Caregivers in Japan." *International Journal of Geriatric Psychiatry* 22: 250–57.

Siegel, Jane A., and Linda M. Williams. 2003. "The Relationship Between Child Sexual Abuse and Female Delinquency and Crime: A Prospective Study." *Journal of Research in Crime and Delinquency* 40 (1): 71–94.

Smart, Carol. 1976. *Women, Crime, and Criminology: A Feminist Critique*. London: Routledge and Kegan Paul.

Sugimoto, Yoshio. 2014. *An Introduction to Japanese Society*. 4th ed. Cambridge: Cambridge University Press.

Takeda, Yasuhisa, Ichiro Kawachi, Zentaro Yamagata, and Shuji Hashimoto. 2004. "Multigenerational Family Structure in Japanese Society: Impacts on Stress and Health Behaviors Among Women and Men." *Social Science and Medicine* 59: 69–81.

Takii, Yasutaka. 1992. "Sexual Abuse and Juvenile Delinquency." *Child Abuse Review* 1 (1): 43–48.

Tanaka, Masako, Yumi E. Suzuki, Ikuko Aoyama, Kota Takaoka, and Harriet L. MacMillan. 2017. "Child Sexual Abuse in Japan: A Systematic Review and Future Directions." *Child Abuse & Neglect* 66 (April): 31–40.

The Japan Times. 2017. "Waking up to Child Abuse." Accessed 31 May. http://www.japantimes.co.jp/life/2014/09/13/lifestyle/waking-child-abuse/#. WS602BP1DPA.

Theobald, Delphine, David P. Farrington, and Alex R. Piquero. 2013. "Childhood Broken Homes and Adult Violence: An Analysis of Moderators and Mediators." *Journal of Criminal Justice* 41: 44–52.

Thornberry, Terence P., Adrienne Freeman-Gallant, and Peter Lovegrove. 2009. "Intergenerational Linkages in Antisocial Behaviour." *Criminal Behaviour and Mental Health* 93 (19): 80–93.

Toyama-Bialke, Chisaki. 2003. "The 'Japanese Triangle' for Preventing Adolescent Delinquency—Strengths and Weaknesses of the Family-School Adolescent Relationship from a Comparative Perspective." In *Juvenile Delinquency in Japan: Reconsidering the "Crisis"*, edited by Gesine Foljanty-Jost, 19–50. Leiden: Brill.

Tsukada, Noriko, Yasuhiko Saito, and Toshio Tatara. 2001. "Japanese Older People's Perceptions of 'Elder Abuse'." *Journal of Elder Abuse and Neglect* 13 (1): 71–89.

Umeda, Maki, Norito Kawakami, Ronald C. Kessler, and Elizabeth Miller. 2015. "Childhood Adversities and Adult Use of Potentially Injurious Physical Discipline in Japan." *Journal of Family Violence* 30 (4): 515–27.

Wada, Ichiro, and Ataru Igarashi. 2014. "The Social Costs of Child Abuse in Japan." *Children and Youth Services Review* 46: 72–77.

Wagatsuma, Hiroshi, and George De Vos. 1984. *Heritage of Endurance: Family Patterns and Delinquency Formation in Japan*. Berkeley: University of California Press.

West, Donald J., and David P. Farrington. 1973. *Who Becomes Delinquent?* London: Heinemann.

White, Merry I. 2002. *Perfectly Japanese: Making Families in an Era of Upheaval*. Berkeley, CA: University of California Press.

Widom, Cathy S. 1989. "Child Abuse, Neglect, and Violent Criminal Behavior." *Criminology* 27 (2): 251–71.

Yasumi, Katsuhiro, and Jinsuke Kageyama. 2009. "Filicide and Fatal Abuse in Japan, 1994–2005: Temporal Trends and Regional Distribution." *Journal of Forensic and Legal Medicine* 16 (2): 70–75.

Yoder, Robert S. 2004. *Youth Deviance in Japan: Class Reproduction of Non-conformity*. Melbourne, VIC: Trans-Pacific Press.

Yoshihama, Mieko, and Julie Horrocks. 2010. "Risk of Intimate Partner Violence: Role of Childhood Sexual Abuse and Sexual Initiation in Women in Japan." *Children and Youth Services Review* 32 (1): 28–37.

Yoshinaga, Chieko, Izumi Kadomoto, Toshiyuki Otani, Tsukasa Sasaki, and Nobumasa Kato. 2004. "Prevalence of Post-traumatic Stress Disorder in Incarcerated Juvenile Delinquents in Japan." *Psychiatry and Clinical Neurosciences* 58 (4): 383–88.

5

Youth

In 1997, police received a letter from someone claiming to be the murderer of eleven-year-old Jun Hase. The letter was found stuffed in the
mouth of the victim's severed head, placed on the front gate of a junior
high school in Kobe (Hamai and Ellis 2008). Similar to the suspicions
of police involved in investigating the previous murder of two-year-
old James Bulger in Liverpool, England, police in Japan suspected
an adult male, only to discover that the killer was a child (Smith and
Sueda 2008). The fourteen-year-old boy, known only by his alias—Seito
Sakakibara—was arrested. He confessed to killing the eleven-year-old
boy as well as a ten-year-old girl with a hammer several months before
(Smith and Sueda 2008). The significance of this case not only lay in its
gruesome violence and shocking nature but triggered important changes
in the way the Japanese justice system perceived young offenders, as well
as the way Japanese society viewed young people.

From a comparative perspective, Japan's juvenile justice system has
been considered welfare-oriented: the reliance on informal social controls and the emphasis on maternal protectionism meant that the justice system was seen as only one of many social institutions that were
responsible for the proper socialisation of children (Lewis et al. 2009;

© The Author(s) 2019
L. Bui and D. P. Farrington, *Crime in Japan*, Palgrave Advances in Criminology
and Criminal Justice in Asia, https://doi.org/10.1007/978-3-030-14097-7_5

Muncie 2015) until they reached adulthood at age 20 (Yokoyama 2015). The Kobe murders led to significant amendments to the juvenile justice system: the minimum age for criminal responsibility was lowered from 16 to 14; juvenile murder suspects over the age of 16 were to be tried as adults in criminal court; discretionary power was given to the Family Court to decide whether to allow prosecutors to attend any hearing, and victims' rights were strengthened (Fenwick 2013).

These changes arose from debates over the leniency of the juvenile justice system towards serious juvenile offenders. Some perceived that young people committed crime because they were unafraid of the likely sanctions (Ryan 2005). The system, too, seemed based on obsolete understandings about youth crime (Smith and Sueda 2008)—the background of the murderer contradicted the widespread view that youth crime was the consequence of a bad environment. The belief that serious delinquency could be committed by an average child was astonishing. No longer were delinquents only children from a bad environment, it could be ones who excelled in school with no antisocial or criminal history (Okabe 2016). Any child from any social class or home environment was thought to be 'at-risk' (Foljanty-Jost and Metzler 2003). In actuality, the 'popularisation of delinquency' was first introduced in the 1970s by the government in their White Paper on Crime, and the subsequent 'average child' theory appeared in newspaper articles in the 1980s (Okabe 2016). Combined, these theories were the accepted understanding of delinquency among social and professional circles.

The Kobe murders intensified existing fears that society was on the brink of collapse; it was another addition to recent tragedies, the Kobe earthquake and the Tokyo subway sarin attack by doomsday cult Aum Shinrikyo. There was also the prolonged slump when the economic bubble burst, where the stock market crashed and prices stagnated (Hino et al. 2018). Gradually more young men and women postponed marriage and parenthood, resulting in a society with the highest proportion of elderly people in the world (Muramatsu and Akiyama 2011). A number of police scandals emerged (Hamai and Ellis 2008). The loss of security became a major social issue. Then the child became the subsequent focus of these national discourses on a 'society in crisis'.

The surge in youth crime, including vicious youth-on-youth murders, led to increased scrutiny of young people. Commentators observed that contemporary youth lacked discipline (Smith and Sueda 2008). They dressed oddly, stole from their parents, and joined street gangs (Laser et al. 2007). For thrills, they involved themselves in 'playful delinquency' and stole bicycles and shoplifted (White 1994). They beat the homeless and older salarymen (Ambaras 2006). They 'daddy-hunted' in casual groups and attacked middle-aged men for money (Yokoyama 2015). High school and middle school girls engaged in sex work and 'compensated dating' with older men (Ambaras 2006). The breakdown of traditional culture was considered to be the fault of these delinquent youth and their families who provided them with inadequate parenting (Yoder 2011).

Youth Crimes

Today, youth crime is no longer regarded as a pressing social problem (Yokoyama 2015). Yet the 'average child' theory endures and the public is led to believe that youth crimes are increasingly becoming more brutal and juvenile offenders are getting younger (Okabe 2016). Professionals, such as lawyers, academics, and probation officers, have expressed their preference for the former, more welfare-oriented juvenile justice system, whereas the public prefers the recent, more punitive approach (Yokoyama 2015). The disagreement on approaches to youth justice between the two groups likely stems from the source each group receives their information. Sensationalist media reports of youth crimes have only elevated public anxiety (Schwarzenegger 2003), while, for professionals, empirical evidence reveals a less exciting but more accurate narrative.

Trends and Prevalence

The trend of juvenile offending rates in Japan is cyclical, where peaks are attributed to social and economic changes (Lewis et al. 2009). After amendments to the juvenile law were implemented, the juvenile crime rate dipped after 2003 (Yokoyama 2015). The latest numbers from the 2015 White Paper on Crime confirm that the (non-traffic) offence rate has continued to sharply drop since 2003, from 165,973 to 60,251 offences in 2014 (Ministry of Justice Japan 2015).

To examine the impact of revisions to the juvenile law, Oka (2009) was able to conduct a natural experiment using panel data on juvenile arrests (excluding arrests for traffic offences) between 1999 and 2002. He compared the effects of deterrence on youth crime between several age groups: ages 13 and younger; ages 16–19; and ages 14–15. The latter group was considered the treatment group because they would have been the most affected by the lowering of the age of criminal responsibility. His results showed that, in spite of the consideration of other factors, arrests of juveniles ages 14–15 decreased significantly following the revision to the juvenile law in 2001. The decrease was even observed for the arrests of youth ages 13 or younger. Oka concluded that changes to the juvenile law did act as a deterrent for youth crime.

The juvenile crime rate in Japan is lower than in other countries, but among late adolescents, the crime rate is five to six times higher than that of the older generations (Ohbuchi and Kondo 2015). Recent numbers show that 90% of criminal juvenile offences are categorised as either brutal crimes (homicide, robbery, arson, and rape), violence (unlawful assembly with weapons, assault, bodily injury, threats, and extortion), or theft (Okabe 2016). The most common youth offence continues to be theft (Yokoyama 2015), where in 2015, it contributed to 60% of the total penal code offences cleared[1] (Ministry of Justice Japan 2016). The number of brutal crimes has been declining since the early 1960s (Ishida and Miwa 2012).

A fairly new crime that has increased significantly in the last few years, especially since police started to record it, is bank transfer fraud (Ellis and Kyo 2017). Youths, sometimes as part of a gang or initiated by an adult, phone elderly persons and pretend to be their child or

---

[1]Penal code offences exclude negligent driving offences causing death or injury; it has the second highest number of juveniles cleared after theft.

grandchild (known as the 'It's me! It's me!' fraud). They plead with the victim to transfer them money to a bank account to help them out of an emergency. Since the crime has been officially recorded in 2009, it has risen eight times higher in 2013 (Ellis and Kyo 2017).

Of course, all these observations are based on official statistics, and an agreed understanding in criminology is that such numbers have limitations. Recall that official records may suffer from underreporting and inconsistent recording, but they generally include more of the worst offenders and offences (Farrington et al. 2003). Self-reports seem to be the apparent solution because they are able to better capture the actual number of crimes committed, but limitations are the possibility that people may conceal their offences or not remember accurately. The best approach seems to be to compare official records with self-reports (Jolliffe et al. 2003). Babinski et al. (2001) found that both measures of offending for different offence types were fairly similar—they showed good statistical agreement. The different measures were useful in their own way, so it depended more on what the researcher wanted to accomplish. High frequency, less serious crimes are better captured by self-reports while the most serious crimes, like interpersonal violence, will be better identified by official records. The exception, however, would be domestic or sexual violence. Public anxiety towards growing serious and brutal youth crime in Japan, though, seems unsupported by the official statistics.

Cross-cultural studies on self-reports of youth crime have given some indication of the true prevalence of different juvenile offences in Japan. The first study of self-reported delinquency on a representative sample was in 1988, and it revealed that high school adolescent males and females in Osaka had a lower prevalence of violence and theft compared to adolescents in the American cities of Seattle and Richmond (Tanioka and Glaser 1991). Theft and joyriding of bicycles and motorbikes, however, were higher for Japanese than for American youth. This is mainly attributable to different contexts, as motor vehicle theft is rare in Japan—most people there ride bicycles or motorcycles.

A study using similar cities compared youth violence in Osaka and Seattle males in 2011 (mean age = 16.1) (Bui et al. 2014). Violence in this and the previous study concerned hitting and hurting someone.

For this recent study, Japanese youth self-reported a significantly higher prevalence of violence than American youth. The higher prevalence seemed unusual as it contradicted international official statistics, but it may reflect the 'dark figure' of crime. Further comparisons of self-reported delinquency and deviance between these two groups appear in Bui's (2012) unpublished dissertation: the Japanese males also self-reported more aggression and property crime than American males, but these numbers were not significantly different. American males, though, ran away from home more and this was significantly higher than for Japanese males (39.8% vs. 18.6%).

Self-reports of deviance from university students, close to the age of adulthood (about 19 years old), show that deviance is lower among Japan compared to that of Western industrialised countries (Kobayashi et al. 2010, 2018; Vazsonyi and Belliston 2007). In a comparison between Japan and America, Japanese students reported lower deviance than American ones (Kobayashi et al. 2010). Over 70% were male in the Japanese group whereas 43% were male among the American sample (mean age = 19.5 years). If the deviance was disaggregated, Japanese students self-reported a higher mean prevalence of destroying property, hurting someone physically (just barely though), and cheating in school. It is uncertain whether these numbers are significantly different between the university students.

Why Is Youth Crime an Issue?

Focus on the younger generation in Japan reflects societal anxiety towards the future (White 1994). Hence, minor deviations cause Japanese society to fear for the worse (Erbe 2003). It seems that not much has changed in the public discourse regarding youth and crime in the last few decades. This is likely because generations born post-war were already viewed as alien. The Prosperity Generation, born between the late 1950s and early 1970s, directly benefitted from Japan's economic success (Sugimoto 2014). They had opportunities to be picky with job prospects, jumping from one employer to another. Their hesitation to make long-term decisions or life plans markedly differentiated them from previous generations. Their children, the Global Generation, born in the late 1970s and onwards, retained much of the same characteristics except that globalisation, high unemployment rates, and rigid educational structures made them more worldly, pessimistic, and outwardly conformist. Intergenerational conflict mainly lies in priorities: older generations placed the public good before self-interest whereas recent generations give most precedence to individual comfort and private interests. It is this lack of loyalty and commitment to the collective that may have something to do with the perceived societal breakdown and crime in Japan.

Current numbers from the 2015 White Paper on Crime confirm that adolescents between ages 14–19 commit the most non-traffic offences compared with any other age group (Ministry of Justice Japan 2009). Likewise, the rate of crime among adolescents in Western countries has been higher than any other age group, as the age-crime curve reveals. Recall that the curve shows a rise of crime during early adolescence, a peak in mid to late adolescence, and then a decline in early adulthood (Piquero and Moffitt 2014).

So what? Someone may wonder: is this merely young people messing about, vandalising walls and shoplifting? The age-crime curve shows that adolescent offending is only a passing phase. Surely this is more trivial than, say, white-collar crime, which drains away more resources and significant sums of money from society? To some extent this is true, but not entirely. In 1980s Japan, and even recently, the optimistic view towards young people and crime noted that increases in delinquency were found for petty offences, not for serious ones (Murai 1988). Most young people who offended had no serious familial or individual issues, and delinquency was a temporary phase for them. Fast forward to the Kobe murders, where the perpetrator was deemed to also have no serious issues, and yet he was likely to be violent again. Serious and violent juvenile offenders may be masked by the age-crime curve.

American psychologist Terrie Moffitt (1993) wanted to know why a high rate of offending was observed during adolescence, yet the rate of crime did not disappear entirely after the decline in early adulthood. In her theory, the developmental taxonomy, young offenders comprised two distinct groups: adolescence-limited (ALs) and life-course persistent (LCPs). (Only later were abstainers included as a typology.) For ALs, delinquency is the result of wanting adult privileges and responsibilities, but being denied them because they are still considered adolescents. Peer influences are strong during this period, and because peers experience similar strain, they seek role models in older peers who may be delinquent. ALs achieve their goals by engaging in delinquent acts that resemble adult status such as drinking, smoking, and theft (Piquero and Moffitt 2014). Once ALs reach adulthood, most will cease their antisocial behaviour.

It is the LCPs that are of most concern. For LCPs, delinquency is only one symptom of their antisocial behaviour, evident from early in life. They will have suffered from a host of undesirable influences, including neurodevelopmental problems worsened by an adverse familial environment and background. Their antisocial behaviour, consequently, becomes part of their overall personality. Compared to ALs, they are a small group of individuals who will persist in offending and antisocial behaviour after adolescence and throughout the life course. It may be difficult to identify LCPs in advance because they may seem similar to their AL peers during adolescence.

This small number of young offenders, typically less than 10%, contributes to more than 50% of offences during those peak years (DeLisi and Piquero 2011; Wolfgang et al. 1972). Continuity in offending and antisocial behaviour from one developmental phase to the next is evident, so it is no wonder that a small portion of the population—chronic offenders—also commit a large portion of all crimes (Farrington 2005). Wolfgang et al. (1972) proposed that these chronic offenders made up 6% of the overall population but made up 18% of the offender population.

A strong link exists between serious delinquency and a variety of problems in substance use, mental health, low self-control, problems at school, and victimisation histories (Baglivio et al. 2014). West and Farrington (1977) referred to it as 'the delinquent way of life,' which was also the title of their third report on the Cambridge study, while Glenn Walker (1990) called it 'the criminal lifestyle'. Serious juvenile offending, however, also produces substantial costs in accessing health, mental health, child welfare, and special education (de Ruiter and

Augimeri 2012). In other words, this small group of juveniles are at high risk of developing poor educational and occupational adjustment and of becoming public health burdens, suffering from major problems in mental and physical health (Skeem et al. 2014).

Moffitt's typologies of ALs and LCPs seem to fit profiles of youth offending in Japan, but only to a certain extent. Neither typology would adequately explain the Kobe murderer, for example. He did not suffer from any obvious adverse life experience or multiple risks that may have propelled him to violence. If the notion of the 'average child' offender is true, that any young person from any background is at risk to offend, even violently and persistently, then Moffitt's theory is less applicable to the Japanese context. The proposed 'maturity gap' in the theory, whereby adolescents feel strain because they want adult independence may not particularly hold true as well: Yamada and Miyashita (2007, cited in Okamura 2016) argue that Japanese adolescents have neither psychological, financial, nor physical autonomy because of cultural expectations for filial piety—complete respect and obedience to parents and elders through life. To better understand the causes of serious youth violence in Japan, other typologies may be needed.

Understanding Serious Youth Violence: Typologies

Early work in criminal typologies can be traced to Cesare Lombroso and Sigmund Freud, in which psychological types of offender were prevalent (Francis et al. 2004). The purpose of typologies was to try to understand the causes of crime and criminal behaviour based on offending patterns (Elliott et al. 2017). Ohbuchi and Kondo (2015) noticed that the use of typologies to understand juvenile crime in Western countries has not advanced in recent years. This may mainly be due to investigations of 'pathways' as proposed by Sampson and Laub (1993) in their landmark research of the Gluecks's data in America, which, has to some degree, replaced investigations of typologies generally in criminology (Francis et al. 2004). Nowadays, however, there is a great emphasis on criminal trajectories (see Piquero 2008).

Ohbuchi and Kondo (2015) reviewed nine studies in Japan that addressed serious juvenile violence since 2000, including offences of murder, death from injury, or death because of robbery. Of those nine, they focused on three studies, two by the authors and one by the Research and Training Institute for Family Court Probation Officers. From the three studies, they developed three psychological typologies of serious juvenile violent offenders: antisocial, pathological, and poor coping.

The antisocial type has a long and diverse history of violence, aggression, and antisocial behaviour dating from early childhood. A host of family risk factors existed in their home environment, and they were likely to have been abused. They did poorly in school and were driven to associate with like-minded peers who were also antisocial. Their personality did not help either, as it is characterised by low self-control, selfishness, aggressiveness, and a need to dominate others. In some cases their violence was the result of committing other offences or in order to avoid detection.

The pathological type appears to be the most common characterisation of serious juvenile violent offenders. They suffered from either maladjustment or mental illness. There was little to no history of delinquent and antisocial behaviours, and family members did not understand the young person's suffering because of their own mental problems or superficial interactions. These young people either stopped attending school and became violent towards their family or they appeared fine on the outside, but developed a fascination for violence and indulged in horror films and violent video games.

Last, the poor coping type commit a serious violent offence because they feel threatened. Most of these types were violent towards family members who subjected them to domestic abuse, such as witnessing their father beat their mother, or forcing upon them immense educational pressure. This type reacted violently out of desperation, fear, immaturity, or a hot temper. In other cases, they have overly indulgent parents who stunted their development. The assumption is that their violence stemmed from significant personality flaws. They tend to be self-centred and immature, while lacking independence and resilience. When obstacles arise and they are unsuccessful, they become easily discouraged and respond with desperation and frustration. Their violence is reactive.

The Kobe murderer could be classed as the pathological type: psychiatrists had suggested that he could be suffering from psychosis. Although his mental state was eventually deemed normal, he had been described as living in a world populated by animated characters from cartoons and video games (Smith and Sueda 2008). The details of his attacks were intimately shared with his imaginary friend (Maruyama and Ascione 2008). Unbeknown to his parents, he was preoccupied with violence and death, and began torturing and killing animals—frogs, pigeons, and cats—after the passing of his grandmother. Initially, in school, he excelled and was popular, but gradually he became withdrawn as academic pressures mounted in junior high school. He developed problem behaviour whereby he threatened and bullied other students (Smith and Sueda 2008; Maruyama and Ascione 2008). This case may fit the poor coping typology, but his serious violence was the direct result of morbid preoccupations.

These typologies overlap with prominent Western findings on antisocial youth development. The antisocial type, as the scholars noted, was similar to well-replicated findings that many serious and violent juvenile offenders have a myriad of adverse developmental and background factors (Loeber and Farrington 1998); this type is also similar to Moffitt's LCP typology. The other two, pathological and poor coping types, expand the understanding of serious and violent juveniles in Japan. Ohbuchi and Kondo (2015) found that their typology was most similar to ones developed by Elliott, Huizinga, and Morse in 1986, and Cornell, Benedek, and Benedek a year later. Both American typologies proposed types of juvenile offenders who were characterised by committing many acts of antisocial behaviour and offending, or suffered from mental illness or emotional confusion, or were influenced by situational factors.

It is uncertain to what extent the types of Ohbuchi and Kondo were influenced by these American typologies of youth offenders. The Japanese types seem to be derived organically from previous studies, based on Japanese cases. Though similar to the American types, Ohbuchi and Kondo's types are distinct. They imply that the dynamics in the home are responsible for the serious violence of youth. These perpetrators either suffer from adverse familial factors, or some negative form of parenting style—suffocating, overly indulgent, or neglectful. In each typology, family members—particularly parents—contribute to their child's violence. Again, the family and the home seem to play prominent roles in increasing a young person's likelihood of later offending.

Explanations

Many reasons have been proposed by critics of modern-day young Japanese to explain youth crime: urbanisation and low social cohesion; the breakdown of the family and poor parenting; an intense focus on examinations and admissions to prestigious schools; materialism; more opportunities for illicit sexual activity; and popular culture (Ambaras 2006). This shows that not only may a diverse range of factors contribute to youth crime, but all of these seem to serve as a confirmation to the public that, yes, society is in crisis.

Yoder (2004), however, was sceptical of these explanations for Japanese youth crime. Popular explanations tended to focus on child–parent relations and dysfunctional parental socialisation methods. He included the wider context in which he highlighted that many official explanations for youth crime were conservative, in saying that the fault lay in the individual and the immediate environment. After all, why would the state blame itself? Also, governmental organisations like the NPA, with their assessments of youth crime, never seemed to contradict the discourse of those in power.

These dynamics, where official discourse may misuse micro-level, psychological explanations, are possibly a reason why psychological perspectives might be dismissed in criminology—they may be perceived as uncritical towards and allied with self-interested authority, perpetuating social inequality.

Yoder gave a more sociological understanding on antisocial behaviour and crime among youth: although he did not deny that the family may contribute to such behaviour among young people, the continuation of youth crime and deviancy, he argued, lay in the social control of young people by adults, even outside the family context as well. Based on his longitudinal study comparing the impact of deviance on the lives of lower and middle-class youth, he argued that this control seemed to be concentrated among the lower class, and consequently, it replicated social disadvantage and inequality and increases deviance.

Class is often neglected in studies of youth crime in Japan and this is intriguing. It may come down to the proliferation of that 'average child' theory because the theory proposes that class cannot matter in the explanation of crime if all children have similar likelihoods of offending. To those who study likelihoods of offending, particularly DLC researchers, this theory may seem obviously incorrect and an oversimplification, as their overall research findings show that, while any child has some likelihood to offend, some children are much more likely to do so than others. According to Okabe (2016), the 'average child' theory assumes that if every child has an equal risk of offending, then it is useless to even propose or investigate explanations for youth crime. He contends that empirical research on youth crime has been inadequate in Japan, viewing research as an opportunity to have a continuous discussion that challenges status quo assumptions about youth and crime. Many related policies have an unclear basis for their implementation. They seem to be based on popular discourse, such as the average child theory, that is prone to containing unreliable and incorrect information.

Okabe debunks the average child theory by looking at the relationship between poverty and crime. Proponents of the average child theory base their argument on court statistics that show a decrease in juvenile offenders coming from a lower social class background. Okabe argues that this observation is inaccurate: if the majority of young people in Japan are born into a middle-class background, of course, there would be a noticeable rate of offending from this group. Whatever time period is studied, however, lower class youth have been found to have a higher likelihood of offending. There may be more young offenders from middle-class backgrounds than in the past, but the highest prevalence continues to be found among lower class young people.

To some, however, national interventions for young people appear extensive, and appear to be so for over thirty years (Hiroyuki 2005).

According to Yokoyama (2015), prevention measures of the juvenile justice system may have contributed to social stability but has also resulted in apparently many docile youth because of over-supervision and over-protection. Whether these observations are valid, it seems that these centre on how best to prevent crime among young people, especially serious violence—crime prevention or crime control? How distinct are these two in Japan?

Crime Prevention and Crime Control

It is correct that crime control is a form of crime prevention, but there are differences. Typically, crime control operates within the boundaries of the justice system (Welsh and Farrington 2012a). Examples are a police officer making an arrest because of a street gang problem or a probation officer assessing an offender about to be released into the community for risks to be targeted. Crime prevention, in its 'pure' form, involves efforts to prevent crime or criminal offending before they arise (Welsh and Farrington 2010). Essentially, crime control applies when an offence has occurred and society is galvanised to action, whereas crime prevention applies when the offence is only anticipated (Welsh and Farrington 2012a).

Ellis and Kyo (2017), in their overview of Japanese juvenile justice, posed a relevant question in reference to Yoder's (2011) later work that argued that all community and agency activities towards young people are forms of control: what activities are considered prevention and diversion, and what activities are considered punitive? Many community and agency activities can be interpreted as either one of these. For example, any child who engages in drinking, smoking, late-night roaming in adult entertainment districts, or in other kinds of misconduct—any behaviour that causes moral degradation to the self or others—may be labelled a 'misconduct juvenile' (Nawa 2006). When such a young person is identified, police officers give guidance, comprising a caution and advice on preventing future delinquent behaviour. If necessary, officers will notify parents or guardians, and even the school or workplace. Advice and guidance to young people 'at risk' of offending is seen by the NPA as necessary because any problematic behaviour that is left unchecked may give rise to actual offences (Lewis et al. 2009). Prevention is the intention of the NPA, but it could also be seen as intrusive, targeting young people who are involved in some innocuous deviance and fun, and implicating other aspects of their life. This may have unintended negative consequences, such as increases in deviance, as Yoder (2004) had previously concluded regarding the social controls of lower class youth.

In several studies based on the same sample in Osaka, Bui and colleagues (Bui et al. 2014, 2016, 2018) found that a consistent and significant factor for serious delinquency and violence was having many close friends who have been picked up by the police. Compared to American youth in one study, the prevalence of this characteristic was five times higher for Japanese youth (71.2% vs. 14.2%). This may be indicative of how common it is for young people to interact with police officers in Japan because of these activities. This may also indicate that these strategies are not working: peer delinquency is associated with one's own delinquency, and offending tends to increase after detection (Farrington 1977). Using news reports from 2008 to 2009, Sakiyama et al. (2011) identified 448 individual offenders to address their research questions on the juvenile justice process. Most of these youths (age range = 9–19), they found, had co-offended (83%).

The relationship between peers and delinquency is strong among adolescents in Japan. In fact, juvenile delinquency is often characterised by group offending (Yamamiya 2003). Like many studies supporting this relationship in the West (e.g., Reiss and Farrington 1991), frequent and serious delinquents in Japan attribute their antisocial behaviour to their peers, and they commit more delinquent acts when they are with peers than when alone (Yamamiya 2003).

Effectiveness of Interventions

Japanese policies relating to the prevention of crime and deviance among young people seem to blur crime control and prevention. Yokoyama (2015) describes some of these activities: juvenile guidance centres are responsible for sending authority to patrol entertainment areas and counsel juveniles and their parents; neighbourhood associations have members patrol their neighbourhood to catch any youth deviance; junior high schools are required to have a teacher in charge of guiding students, and teachers carry out joint patrols with police; police boxes and police houses are common in communities and neighbourhoods; within most police stations there are specific officers in charge of juvenile policing as well as volunteer guidance officers who patrol entertainment areas to guide juveniles and prevent them from offending or being victimised; and increased concern towards children's safety has resulted in the rise of the children security industry where students can have ID cards with a GPS tracking device.

In much of the scholarly work on youth crime in Japan, however, the word 'control'—from informal to formal—rather than 'prevention', is often used to describe measures implemented to prevent deviance and crime among young people. Yoder (2011) argues that a net-widening effect of social control on youth can be observed, whereby in addition to the justice system, schools, social workers, and child protection commissioners are involved. Many anti-delinquency organisations exist. Because of these, it is easy for young people to be drawn into the justice system. According to him, these institutions perceive antisocial behaviour as anything that falls short of middle-class norms and expectations.

As with all social phenomena, whether strategies against delinquency are preventive or punitive is complex. Ellis and Kyo (2017) conclude that, comparatively, it is difficult to categorise Japan as completely welfare-oriented towards potential or actual young offenders. A range of non-criminal justice agencies exist alongside the justice system that pulls in youth and label them as pre-delinquents. In addition to this, however, many young people who would have been classed as offenders in other countries are diverted to child welfare routes. Although it is clear that the Japanese youth justice system has become more punitive, like systems in other countries, it is still a more welfare-based model than others in advanced democracies. A close examination of the system shows that few young people are tried as adults, and many social welfare components continue to operate and predominate. Therefore, it seems to be more crime prevention than crime control.

As Ellis and Kyo (2017) state, it is unclear what the outcomes are for youth who make contact with the police as the result of intervention involvement. No convincing evidence can be found on this. The lack of hard evidence on the effectiveness of juvenile justice policies or why such policies should exist in the first place is echoed by Okabe (2016). He does not believe that any of the fears and concerns about young people, that subsequently influence policies in Japan, are based on empirical evidence.

In some cases, policies are 'evidence-informed' but do not consider the nuances of research findings; the primary issue is that research often does not take centre stage in the policy decision-making process (Welsh and Farrington 2012b). Lewis et al. (2009), in their comparison of English and Japanese youth justice, observe that English policy makers tend to be reactive to specific events or to media pressure and swiftly implement policies without full consultation from experts, giving little time and resources for adequate training. In contrast, Japanese policy makers rely more on social control and make relatively few changes to the justice system; they also give time to test the effects of the newly implemented measures.

Crime prevention programmes can be classified into four strategies (Welsh and Farrington 2012a): one, criminal justice prevention (also known as crime control) involves strategies operated by law enforcement and agencies from the criminal justice system; two, situational prevention reduces crime opportunities and increases the risk of being caught, usually by manipulating the physical environment; three, community prevention aims to prevent changing the social conditions and institutions in communities that may influence offending; four, developmental prevention thwarts the development of criminal potential by reducing the impact of risk factors and increasing the impact of protective factors identified from studies of human development. Much of Japan's juvenile crime prevention seems to be a mixture of criminal justice and community prevention. Criminal justice agencies seem to play a sizeable role in the community aspects, however. This is possibly why Yoder (2011) claimed that these community strategies are forms of control because of their connection to law enforcement.

Strengthening Social Relationships

An underlying theme among the majority of the youth discourse is inadequate social connection. Because of significant social changes, security is a concern—the shrinking family, neighbourhoods, and communities; startling media reports of juvenile violence that cause the public to question if it even knows its youth any more; an official discourse that is quick to blame young people for all societal problems without adequately investigating; young people feeling constrained and pessimistic toward their future prospects. It is hard to feel secure if concerns are unheard and unmet, and if the future seems very uncertain.

Scholars recognise that deviant and delinquent behaviour are related to a multitude of factors that span different aspects of a young person's life. An area that should be focused on is building strong social relationships, not just personally but also with the community and local institutions. An example of a strategy that combines developmental and community prevention was implemented by clinical psychologists Ryushima and Kaji (2006). They believed that, because of weakening community and social ties in Japan, collaboration among many local public sector organisations to form support teams was needed. Although not completely prevention, because the intervention began after the violence, they presented an example of a typical case that confronted support teams:

> The only child from a single mother family had often been absent from school since fourth-grade of elementary school, and the child counselling centre was providing counselling through a family and child commissioner in the community. Isolated from both her former husband and relatives, the mother was on welfare. Soon after enrolling in junior high school, the girl withdrew to her room, and the mother began visiting the psychiatric department of a hospital. Around that time, severe domestic violence started, and the mother, at the end of her tether, rushed to the police for help. (In this case, the school, family and child commissioner, child counselling centre, hospital and police worked together.) (1)

Psychotherapeutic methods and family therapy were used to combat youth crime by the support teams, comprising community organisations. The hope was that the support teams might enrich parent–child relationships and, with the received support, families would be encouraged to develop positive community relationships with local agencies as well. In addition, bringing together leaders and key stakeholders from these agencies gave them the opportunity to combine efforts to most efficiently and effectively solve a case. The use of support teams, the psychologists suggested, was not limited to delinquency. It could also be applied and should work just as well for other problems such as mental disorder or school withdrawal. The idea of forming partnerships among local agencies to help families is good, but making the outcomes broader to not only focus on problems would be better—focus on protective factors should, too, be a priority.

Young people, according to Kadowaki (2003), should not be perceived as asocial. Rather, they want to become active social participants, but substantial changes in urbanisation and pressures to conform via education have in some sense hindered their personal social development and belonging. Likewise, based on their findings, Bui et al. (2018) suggested that offending is indicative of the broader context that young people are confronted with and they should be encouraged to pursue alternative options other than what is based on societal expectations, which may be at odds with contemporary circumstances.

Social connection and relationships may matter most in Japan because relations traditionally are interdependent and strong—they last for life. The decline of these characteristics in interpersonal and societal relations would have more of an impact than, say, a society whose relations are more characterised as independent and fleeting, such as that of the UK. Leonardsen (2003) described Japanese social life immediately after World War II as uncertain and disorganised. The significant loss of life meant that many families were directly affected, and stability in norms was absent. For a society that was integrated, the defeat and subsequent aftermath was a massive blow to mental and physical security as well as to social belonging. This is not to say that poor social relations caused crime increases, but the two factors may have been related: the crime rate immediately after the war peaked up to 1959 (Tsushima 1996). Again, many of these issues, such as low social connection and crime, form part of a broader context indicative of the health of a society and its members.

Prevention should be community and developmental-focused, but perhaps should be independent of criminal justice agencies. This would mean that the attention is also directed towards achieving favourable developmental social outcomes, rather than merely anti-social behaviour. Developmental prevention focuses on behavioural and attitudinal patterns learned during an individual's development (Welsh and Farrington 2010); early childhood is the ideal time for these interventions. For example, early childhood intellectual enrichment programmes that concentrate on cognitive processes, behaviour problems, and executive functioning have had success in improving children's life outcomes (Welsh and Farrington 2012a). With community prevention, changes in social conditions and institutions that influence antisocial behaviour in neighbourhoods are the focus. One example is developing and maintaining partnerships between stakeholder agencies and individuals. But there is little solid evidence that community interventions are effective, except for *Communities That Care*, first developed in the US, and has been implemented widely in many other countries (Farrington 1997; Kuklinski et al. 2015).

One challenge in evaluating the effectiveness of community and developmental prevention is that the effects are not immediately noticeable (Welsh and Farrington 2012b). The 'crime-reducing' effects may take a number of years to become apparent. If prevention occurred in childhood, not until adolescence would the outcomes be observed. This is probably one reason why no substantial evidence may exist in Japan on prevention effects. Interventions should be based on high-quality empirical evidence about 'what works'. Such evidence has shown that preschool intellectual enrichment programmes, child skills training, mentoring, home visiting programmes, parent training, functional family therapy, treatment foster care, and multi-systemic therapy are effective (Farrington 2015).

Conclusion

Official discourse on youth tends to blame them for societal problems, although crime among this group continues to decrease, and is now at its lowest in Japan since the late 1960s (Ellis and Kyo 2017). Strategies for youth crime prevention have been criticised for their perceived punitive and extensive control of young people, and these criticisms reflect the difficulty of implementing research findings in practice. Even though they may be well-intentioned, strategies may not be ideal and may have unintended consequences, but that does not mean idleness should be a virtue. Early intervention, using developmental and community approaches, appears to be most effective to combat not only future offending, but also declining social and community relations. Compared with other countries, it does not seem that crime among young people is too much of an issue, but prevention outside criminal justice would be helpful in reducing negative outcomes from stigma and labelling, and providing support and strengthening of social ties and belonging, an issue that seems more urgent than that of offending among young people. At the same time, addressing the social aspect may not only positively contribute to better relations at the local level, but also the prevention of possible later serious and violent youth crimes.

References

Ambaras, David R. 2006. *Bad Youth: Juvenile Delinquency and the Politics of Everyday Life in Modern Japan.* Berkeley: University of California Press.

Babinski, Leslie M., Carolyn S. Hartsough, and Nadine M. Lambert. 2001. "A Comparison of Self-Report of Criminal Involvement and Official Arrest Records." *Aggressive Behavior* 27: 44–54.

Baglivio, Michael T., Katherine Jackowski, Mark A. Greenwald, and James C. Howell. 2014. "Serious, Violent, and Chronic Juvenile Offenders: A Statewide Analysis of Prevalence and Prediction of Subsequent Recidivism Using Risk and Protective Factors." *Criminology and Public Policy* 13 (1): 1–34.

Bui, Laura. 2012. "Youth Offending in Japan: Context, Applicability and Risk Factors." Doctoral Dissertation, University of Cambridge.

Bui, Laura, David P. Farrington, and Mitsuaki Ueda. 2016. "Potential Risk and Promotive Factors for Serious Delinquency in Japanese Female Youth." *International Journal of Comparative and Applied Criminal Justice* 40 (3): 209–24.

———. 2018. "Risk and Protective Factors for Serious Delinquency in the Japanese Context: Findings from Osaka Male Youths." In *Crime and Justice in Contemporary Japan*, edited by Jianghong Liu and Setsuo Miyazawa, 119–35. New York: Springer.

Bui, Laura, David P. Farrington, Mitsuaki Ueda, and Karl G. Hill. 2014. "Prevalence and Risk Factors for Self-Reported Violence of Osaka and Seattle Male Youths." *International Journal of Offender Therapy and Comparative Criminology* 58 (12): 1540–57.

de Ruiter, Corine, and Leena K. Augimeri. 2012. "Making Delinquency Prevention Work with Children and Adolescents: From Risk Assessment to Effective Interventions." In *Managing Clinical Risk*, edited by C. Logan and L. Johnstone, 199–223. London: Routledge.

DeLisi, Matt, and Alex R. Piquero. 2011. "New Frontiers in Criminal Careers Research, 2000–2011: A State-of-the-Art Review." *Journal of Criminal Justice* 39 (4): 289–301.

Elliott, Amy, Brian Francis, Keith Soothill, and Arjan Blokland. 2017. "Changing Crime Mix Patterns of Offending Over the Life Course: A Comparative Study in England and Wales and the Netherlands." In *The Routledge International Handbook of Life-Course Criminology*, edited by Arjan Blokland and Victor van der Geest, 89–111. New York: Routledge.

Ellis, Tom, and Akira Kyo. 2017. "Youth Justice in Japan." In *Oxford Handbook of Crime and Criminal Justice*, edited by Michael Tonry. Oxford: Oxford University Press.

Erbe, Annette. 2003. "Youth in Crisis: Public Perceptions and Discourse on Deviance and Juvenile Problem Behavior in Japan." In *Juvenile Delinquency in Japan: Reconsidering the "Crisis"*, edited by Gesine Foljanty-Jost, 51–74. Leiden: Brill.

Farrington, David P. 1977. "The Effects of Public Labeling." *British Journal of Criminology* 17: 112–25.

———. 1997. "Evaluating a Community Crime Prevention Program." *Evaluation* 3 (2): 157–173.

———. 2005. *Integrated Developmental and Life-Course Theories of Offending*. New Brunswick: Transaction.

———. 2015. "The Developmental Evidence Base: Prevention." In *Forensic Psychology*, edited by David A. Crighton and Graham J. Towl, 141–159. West Sussex: Wiley.

Farrington, David P., Darrick Jolliffe, J. David Hawkins, Richard F. Catalano, Karl G. Hill, and Rick Kosterman. 2003. "Comparing Delinquency Careers in Court Records and Self-Reports." *Criminology* 41 (3): 933–58.

Fenwick, Mark. 2013. "'Penal Populism' and Penological Change in Contemporary Japan." *Theoretical Criminology* 17 (2): 215–31.

Foljanty-Jost, Gesine, and Manuel Metzler. 2003. "Juvenile Delinquency in Japan: Reconsidering the Crisis." In *Juvenile Delinquency in Japan: Reconsidering the "Crisis"*, edited by Gesine Foljanty-Jost, 1–17. Leiden: Brill.

Francis, Brian, Keith Soothill, and Rachel Fligelstone. 2004. "Identifying Patterns and Pathways of Offending Behaviour A New Approach to Typologies of Crime." *European Journal of Criminology* 1 (1): 47–87.

Hamai, Koichi, and Thomas Ellis. 2008. "Japanese Criminal Justice: Was Reintegrative Shaming a Chimera?" *Punishment & Society* 10 (1): 25–46.

Hino, Kimihiro, Masaya Uesugi, and Yasushi Asami. 2018. "Official Crime Rates and Residents' Sense of Security Across Neighborhoods in Tokyo, Japan." *Urban Affairs Review* 54 (1): 165–89.

Hiroyuki, Kuzuno. 2005. "Juvenile Diversion and the Get-Tough Movement in Japan." *Ryukoku Law Review*, 22: 1–21.

Ishida, Hiroshi, and Satoshi Miwa. 2012. "School Discipline and Academic Acheivement in Japan." In *Improving Learning Environments: School Discipline and Student Achievement in Comparative Perspective*, edited by Richard Arum and Melissa Velez. Stanford: Stanford University Press.

Jolliffe, Darrick, David P. Farrington, David J. Hawkins, Richard F. Catalano, Karl G. Hill, and Rick Kosterman. 2003. "Predictive, Concurrent, Prospective and Retrospective Validity of Self-Reported Delinquency." *Criminal Behaviour and Mental Health* 13: 179–97.

Kadowaki, Atsushi. 2003. "Changes in Values and Life Orientation Among Japanese Youth." In *Juvenile Delinquency in Japan: Reconsidering the "crisis"*, edited by Gesine Foljanty-Jost, 75–90. Leiden: Brill.

Kobayashi, Emiko, Alexander T. Vazsonyi, Pan Chen, and Susan F. Sharp. 2010. "A Culturally Nuanced Test of Gottfredson and Hirschi's 'General Theory': Dimensionality and Generalizability in Japan and the United States." *International Criminal Justice Review* 20 (2): 112–31.

Kobayashi, Emiko, David P. Farrington, and Molly Buchanan. 2018. "Peer Reactions, Peer Behavior, Student Attitudes, and Student Deviance: A Comparison of College Students in Japan and the USA." *Asian Journal of Criminology*. https://doi.org/10.1007/s11417-018-9276-y.

Kuklinski, Margaret R., Abigail A. Fagan, David J. Hawkins, John S. Briney, and Richard F. Catalano. 2015. "Benefit-cost Analysis of a Randomized Evaluation of Communities That Care: Monetizing Intervention Effects on the Initiation of Delinquency and Substance Use Through Grade 12." *Jounral of Experimental Criminology* 11: 165–92.

Laser, Julie, Tom Luster, and Toko Oshio. 2007. "Promotive and Risk Factors Related to Deviant Behavior in Japanese Youth." *Criminal Justice and Behavior* 34 (11): 1463–80.

Leonardsen, Dag. 2003. "Crime in Japan—A Lesson for Criminological Theory? The Cultural Dimension in Crime—What Can the Japanese Experience Tell Us?" Accessed 10 June 2011. http://www.britsoccrim.org/volume6/008.pdf.

Lewis, Charlie, Masuo Koyasu, Seungmi Oh, Ayako Ogawa, Benjamin Short, and Zhao Huang. 2009. "Culture, Executive Function, and Social Understanding." *New Directions in Child and Adolescent Development* 123: 69–85.

Loeber, Rolf, and David P. Farrington. 1998. *Serious and Violent Juvenile Offenders: Risk Factors and Successful Interventions.* Thousand Oaks: Sage.

Maruyama, Mika, and Frank R. Ascione. 2008. "Animal Abuse: An Evolving Issue in Japanese Society." In *The International Handbook of Animal Abuse and Cruelty: Theory, Research, and Practice*, edited by Frank R. Ascione, 269–304. West Lafayette: Purdue University Press.

Ministry of Justice Japan. 2009. "White Paper on Crime 2008—The Circumstances and Attributes of Elderly Offenders and Their Treatment." Tokyo: Author.

Ministry of Justice Japan. 2015. "White Paper on Crime, 2014." Tokyo: Author.

Ministry of Justice Japan. 2016. "White Paper on Crime, 2015." Tokyo: Author.

Moffitt, Terrie E. 1993. "Adolescence-Limited and Life-Course-Persistent Antisocial Behavior: A Developmental Taxonomy." *Psychological Review* 100 (4): 674–701.

Muncie, John. 2015. *Youth and Crime.* London: Sage.

Murai, Toshikuni. 1988. "Current Problems of Juvenile Delinquency in Japan." *Hitotsubashi Journal of Law and Politics* 16: 1–10.

Muramatsu, Naoko, and Hiroko Akiyama. 2011. "Japan: Super-Aging Society Preparing for the Future." *The Gerontologist* 51 (4): 425–32.

Nawa, Shinpei. 2006. "Postwar Fourth Wave of Juvenile Delinquency and Tasks of Juvenile Police." In *Current Juvenile Police Policy in Japan*, edited by Police Policy Research Center National Police Academy of Japan, 1–19. Tokyo: Research Foundation for Safe Society.

Ohbuchi, Ken-ichi, and Hideo Kondo. 2015. "Psychological Analysis of Serious Juvenile Violence in Japan." *Asian Journal of Criminology* 10: 149–62.

Oka, Tatsushi. 2009. "Juvenile Crime and Punishment: Evidence from Japan." *Applied Economics* 41 (24): 3103–15.

Okabe, Takeshi. 2016. "The Quantitative Analysis of Juvenile Delinquency in Contemporary Japan (Part 1)." *Journal of the Literary Society of Yamaguchi University* 66: 121–60.

Okamura, Rie. 2016. "Filial Violence: An Unrevealed Problem for Decades." In *Family Violence in Japan: A Life Course Perspective*, edited by Fumie Kumagai and Masako Ishii-Kuntz, 103–22. New York: Springer.

Piquero, Alex R. 2008. "Taking Stock of Developmental Trajectories of Criminal Activity Over the Life Course." In *The Long View of Crime: A Synthesis of Longitudinal Research*, edited by Akiva M. Liberman, 23–78. New York: Springer.

Piquero, Alex R., and Terrie E. Moffitt. 2014. "Moffitt's Developmental Taxonomy of Antisocial Behavior." In *Encyclopedia of Criminology and Criminal Justice*, edited by Gerben Bruinsma and David Weisburd, 3121–27. New York: Springer.

Reiss, Albert J., and David P. Farrington. 1991. "Advancing Knowledge About Co-Offending: Results from a Prospective Longitudinal Survey of London Males." *Journal of Criminal Law and Criminology* 82 (2): 360–95.

Ryan, Trevor. 2005. "Creating 'Problem Kids': Juvenile Crime in Japan and Revisions to the Juvenile Act." *Journal of Japanese Law* 10 (19): 153–88.

Ryushima, Hidehiro, and Yuji Kaji. 2006. "Clinical Psychology-Based Community Support for Delinquency." *Japanese Journal of Clinical Psychology* 2 (2): 1–14.

Sakiyama, Mari, Hong Lu, and Bin Liang. 2011. "Reintegrative Shaming and Juvenile Delinquency in Japan." *Asian Journal of Criminology* 6 (2): 161–75.

Sampson, Robert J., and John H. Laub. 1993. *Crime in the Making: Pathways and Turning Points Through Life*. Cambridge: Harvard University Press.

Schwarzenegger, Christian. 2003. "The Debate About the Reform of the Juvenile Law in Japan." In *Juvenile Delinquency in Japan: Reconsidering the "Crisis"*, edited by Gesine Foljanty-Jost, 173–98. Leiden: Brill.

Skeem, Jennifer L., Elizabeth Scott, and Edward P. Mulvey. 2014. "Justice Policy Reform for High-Risk Juveniles: Using Science to Achieve Large-Scale Crime Reduction." *Annual Review of Clinical Psychology* 10 (January): 709–39.

Smith, David, and Kiyoko Sueda. 2008. "The Killing of Children by Children as a Symptom of National Crisis: Reactions in Britain and Japan." *Criminology and Criminal Justice* 8 (1): 5–25.

Sugimoto, Yoshio. 2014. *An Introduction to Japanese Society*. 4th ed. Cambridge: Cambridge University Press.

Tanioka, Ichiro, and Daniel Glaser. 1991. "School Uniforms, Routine Activities, and the Social Control of Delinquency in Japan." *Youth & Society* 23 (1): 50–75.

Tsushima, Masahiro. 1996. "Economic Structure and Crime: The Case of Japan." *Journal of Socio-Economics* 25 (4): 497–515.

Vazsonyi, Alexander T., and Lara M. Belliston. 2007. "The Family → Low Self-Control → Deviance: A Cross-Cultural and Cross-National Test of Self-Control Theory." *Criminal Justice and Behavior* 34 (4): 505–30.

Walter, Glenn D. 1990. *The Crimina Lifestyle: Patterns of Serious Criminal Conduct*. Newbury Park: Sage.

Welsh, Brandon C., and David P. Farrington. 2010. *The Future of Crime Prevention: Developmental and Situational Strategies*. Bethesda: National Institute of Justice.

———. 2012a. "Crime Prevention and Public Policy." In *Oxford Handbooks Online*, edited by B. C. Welsh and D. P. Farrington, 1–19. New York: Oxford University Press.

———. 2012b. "Science, Politics, and Crime Prevention: Toward a New Crime Policy." *Journal of Criminal Justice* 40 (2): 128–33.

West, Donald J., and David P. Farrington. 1977. *The Delinquent Way of Life*. London: Heinemann.

White, Merry I. 1994. *The Material Child: Coming of Age in Japan and America*. Berkeley: University of California Press.

Wolfgang, Marvin E., Robert M. Figlio, and Thorsten Sellin. 1972. *Delinquency in a Birth Cohort*. Chicago: University of Chicago Press.

Yamamiya, Yuko. 2003. "Juvenile Delinquency in Japan." *Journal of Prevention & Intervention in The Community* 25 (2): 27–46.

Yoder, Robert S. 2004. *Youth Deviance in Japan: Class Reproduction of Non-conformity*. Melbourne, VIC: Trans-Pacific Press.

———. 2011. *Deviance and Inequality in Japan: Japanese Youth and Foreign Migrants*. Bristol: The Policy Press.

Yokoyama, Minoru. 2015. "Juvenile Justice and Juvenile Crime: An Overview of Japan." In *Juvenile Justice: International Perspectives, Models, and Trends*, edited by John A. Winterdyk, 179–208. London: CRC Press.

6

School

Yamaguchi Kayo, aged 13:

> What is 'normal'? What is 'abnormal'? … What most people call 'normal' is what most people do. That is, they go to school properly and get a respectable job. People seem to see someone like myself who does not go to school as being not normal, as being strange. But I think that it is wrong to think that way. I think that to go to school and to get a job is the easiest way to live… I do not want to run on fixed rails but on rails created by myself. It is a difficult and painful way, but I believe that it will be good for me.
>
> —Ishikawa et al., *Tōkōkyohi as Discussed by Children: 402 accounts*, 1993

Education in Japan served as evidence of its cultural uniqueness and low crime. It was hailed by foreign researchers who perceived it to be successfully shaping children to become harmonious and conforming adult citizens (Yoder 2004). The Japanese school system comprises six years for elementary (ages 6–11), three years for middle (ages 12–14), and three years for senior high (ages 15–17) schools, whereby elementary and middle school education are mandatory (Harada 1995). It is the middle school years where children must work hard to gain entrance to

© The Author(s) 2019
L. Bui and D. P. Farrington, *Crime in Japan*, Palgrave Advances in Criminology and Criminal Justice in Asia, https://doi.org/10.1007/978-3-030-14097-7_6

the best high schools. During this time, children are expected to achieve high academic performance, and the school aims to provide them with the needed social skills to become prosocial members of society.

The high school entrance exam, which determines the quality of high school that students will enter and, hence, the subsequent quality of university and career, looms heavily over the middle school years (Fukuzawa 1994). Children's lives during this time become a tight schedule of many extracurricular activities and cram schools—if their families can afford them. In the mid-1990s, the perceived decline in conformity among young people became a pressing concern (Folijanty-Jost and Metzler 2003). This was part of the larger discourse on young people, but focused on violence related to schools: drug abuse, knife attacks, and suicides of bullying victims.

The Relationship Between School Factors and Offending

The relationship between school factors and offending is among the best-documented in criminological research literature. A meta-analysis concluded that those with low academic achievement have twice the odds of committing delinquency than those with high academic achievement (Maguin and Loeber 1996). From Developmental and Life Course Criminology, being older than their grade level, weak bonding to school, low educational aspirations, low school motivation, and poorly organised and functioning schools are shown to increase young people's risk for delinquency and later serious and violent offending (Farrington and Loeber 2000). Meanwhile, in addition to high intelligence, high academic achievement is the most replicable characteristic that protects against later offending (Jolliffe et al. 2016). Many of these are applicable to Japan. Why these are pertinent factors relate to expectations during the middle school years.

In recent times, youth violence and offending in Japan have been attributed to extreme competition for further education at the best high schools and universities (Ishida and Miwa 2012). Before then, it was thought that lack of education was the culprit. The chances of attending better quality and higher ranked schools significantly dwindle if a child is from a poor social background or is involved in delinquency during their time in middle school. This may only increase the chances of later and continued offending.

The onset of delinquency and offending begins in middle school, where numbers of deviant behaviours seem to also be at their peak (Metzler and Folijanty-Jost 2003). The majority of youth who are involved in delinquency experience academic failure first before becoming delinquent (Yamamiya 2003). In a sample of 518 male youth arrested by police, Harada (1992) found that most began offending in middle school and were the lowest achievers in their class (Yamamiya 2003). In a later study, Harada (1995) used arrest records for 4194 juveniles (77% males) up to age 19 who were in middle school at the time of their first arrest. Those who showed school maladjustment (where delinquency was related to disliking school or poor academic achievement) at the time of their first arrest had a higher probability of being rearrested during their middle school years compared to those with no school maladjustment.

After these juveniles graduated from middle school, however, there was no significant difference in rearrests between students with school maladjustment and those with no maladjustment. Harada's findings suggest that, for those who do poorly in school, this gives them little incentive to try to do better, and delinquency may be a way to relieve stress—high academic achievement can only be given to a few, and results from tests and overall school performance are made visible to everyone. When students continue on to high school—and 98% of them do (Sugimoto 2014)—low academic achieving students attend schools with similarly performing students, so competition is hardly an issue.

Quite a few school characteristics that have been identified in Western studies apply to Japan, but it is the middle school years where these become more pronounced. Some students may have low school bonding, motivation, or educational aspirations. This may be a function of poor academic achievement, and these feelings may be aggravated by the visibility of students' performance compared to others. Yoder (2004) argues that the dichotomy between low and high academic achieving students is also a dichotomy between low and middle-upper class students—low academic achieving youth tend to also come from lower-working class backgrounds. These students who did poorly in middle school were likely to misbehave and less likely to conform. They are then separated into different high schools based on their academic performance, where Yoder contends it is more likely that lower-working class youth will attend lower ranking schools. They are further labelled as deviants and are at increased risk for later offending. These findings show how sociological and psychological factors interact to increase the likelihood of antisocial behaviour and offending. Those who are from lower-working class backgrounds are likely to have difficulty doing well in middle school, because rules and norms favour those from middle-class backgrounds. Their poor performance may lead them to develop low motivation, and low attachment to school, as well as low educational aspirations that heighten the probability of antisocial behaviour and offending.

Conformity

Imposing conformity in schools takes many forms: teachers in middle school submit a report about students to the high school that students wish to enter. This report details information about the student at school and at home, so they are under pressure to be on their best behaviour all the time (Yamamiya 2003). Students are expected to clean their classrooms each day after school and are taught to attend to details by learning correct behaviour (Sugimoto 2014). Attention to detail is part of 'lifestyle guidance' in which disciplinary practices are meant to shape students' lifestyles inside and outside of the school (Fukuzawa 1994). It is middle school where this learning and mastering of conformity takes place. The ideal student is one who follows a well-organised and disciplined lifestyle as the result of internalising social norms that are learned from school (Martinez 2007).

The emphasis on equality and mainstreaming is evident in the public education system (Borovoy 2008). Students are expected to absorb shared values and internalise lessons on character formation, social capacities, and moral education. The implication is that all children are capable of being socialised the same way in order to acquire, to some extent, similar patterns of thought and behaviour. The inclusive approach to schooling, where all students are treated equally, also reveals the assumption that the environment has a large impact on behaviour.

Critics of the education system perceive it as a negative force on children's well-being, enforcing rigid and strict rules to control them (Yamamiya 2003). Folijanty-Host and Metzler (2003) examined activities that were conducive to conformity that middle school students took part in. They wanted to evaluate whether criticisms of the schools were accurate. They chose three middle schools in Niigata prefecture to visit during lessons and to interview educational staff, such as administrators, headmasters, and teachers, as well as parents and students. Their methodology was unclear as little information was given, and their report mainly comprised a detailed description of the school regimen. Their study, however, provides some insight into middle school regimens.

The school curriculum was found to be packed with social activities five days a week and consumed a lot of students' mental energy and time. How to properly interact and behave were clearly defined and were even self-imposed by students. Any behaviour that did not follow norms was classed as delinquency, but the most severe cases were reported to the police. This was usually if a student had seriously assaulted others, but this was rare. Students generally accepted these imposed norms, although the researchers questioned whether students developed a veneer of good behaviour and hid their true feelings.

Folijanty-Host and Metzler concluded that the responses from interviews did not support the notion that students were overly regulated and oppressed in schools. Rules and regulations, though many and detailed, were decided in advance and consistently implemented with students' knowledge. These regulations offered teachers flexibility in responding to misbehaviour, and their responses were generally characterised by reintegration rather than punishment. Deviant and antisocial behaviour, though low compared to other countries, were highlighted by schools as a way of raising awareness, and was meant to justify the use of these controls as prevention. Harada (1995) also finds fault with the interpretation that middle schools excessively control students and, as a result, more delinquency is detected. The reality is that teachers are unlikely to report delinquency to the police.

Yoder (2004), though, views the controls differently. Conformity, he believes, is middle-class in nature. Those who do not conform are blocked from obtaining better career prospects, whereas those who do conform, help to preserve the status quo. This, however, does not prevent many students from valuing educational prestige. Whether these opportunities are accessible to all is another issue, but the notion of 'educational credentialism' is pervasive in Japanese society (Sugimoto 2014). Educational background is considered important for social mobility. Even the average level of formal education in Japan is one of the highest in the world. It is commonly believed that a positive correlation exists between well-being and academic achievement, and that good grades are directly linked to having a happy family life in the future (Yoneyama 2000). These aspirations seem to legitimise conformity in school, and this is probably why the Japanese are considered to have high self-control.

Education and Self-Control

The admiration of the Japanese school system, particularly by foreign researchers, is in respect of perceived ability to shape students to be of a certain agreeable disposition—the kind who will not deviate from societal expectations and norms. It is apparent, then, why these researchers have pointed to the school as an important explanation for Japan's relatively low crime rates: its regulated environment instils proper behaviour in students. To some extent this is true.

Miller and Kanazawa (2000) argue that the school is one component of a large network of informal social control that supports the societal order. Informal social control comprises group monitoring and sanctioning as well as the teaching and reinforcement of appropriate behaviour. Through this control, social norms are internalised. The product of this internalisation is termed *seken*, and recall from previously, that it refers to a web of people whom the individual considers before acting or behaving. These people act as a 'moral yardstick', helping the individual meet their expectations (Sugimoto 2014). This is an everyday psychological force, ensuring that the individual behaves correctly. This form of self-regulation is related to self-control concepts developed in criminology.

Remember that, based on previous studies drawing from cross-cultural psychology, Messner (2015) proposed that self-control theory, when applied to East Asian cultures, should include interpersonal relationships with their associated obligations. This observation referred to the idea that the meaning of 'self', understood in the West as only something motivated by internal attributes and autonomous of others, was different in East Asian cultures: the self was constructed to be interdependent where others' motivations were just as important as one's own. Self-control theory in Japan would need to consider the extent to which goals, desires, and needs of close others—the degree of relational centrality—impact self-control. In other words, the extent of social bonding mediates the relationship between self-control and offending.

This is similar to what Travis Hirschi proposed. Instead of self-control and others' influence as two separate concepts, Hirschi (2004) combined his two control theories, whereby social and self-control were the same. Before, social control theory proposed that bonding to social institutions, such as family, school, and community, prevented young people from being involved in delinquency. Self-control theory, as proposed by Gottfredson and Hirschi (1990), resembling personality, comprised six traits. This revised self-control was thought to be relatively stable over the life course and encompass internal inhibitions of an individual. Therefore, attachments to others act as an individual inhibitor. The revised self-control theory seems to propose that the idea of the 'self', as identified in East Asian cultures, may be just as pertinent in Western cultures. Support for this new conception of self-control in Western populations, however, has been mixed (Ward et al. 2012; Bouffard et al. 2015).

Self-Control as Personality

The question is whether self-control, in the case of Japan, is a personality factor or a survival tactic. To succeed in Japanese society, where group solidarity is important, it is thought that exercising self-control in everyday life will preserve close social relationships. Many sanctions and opportunities to be monitored exist in the close groups with which one is affiliated, so maintaining vigilance in behaviour and fulfilling obligations guarantee access to group benefits like reliability and security (Hechter and Kanazawa 1993). Self-control in this context is seen as a strategy to remain part of in-groups. Towards others in out-groups, self-control may not be so important. Here, Messner's revision is applicable because, depending on who is considered, the relationship between self-control and offending may be strong or weak. Then again, perhaps self-control is both a personality factor and a survival tactic.

Through socialisation from the family and then from the school, norms are internalised. It is these norms that are used as strategies to conform. This process—repeated lessons on conformity—to some extent becomes part of one's personality in Japan. Even self-control theory, in original and revised versions, describes personality. The original version proposed that self-control was developed from parental socialisation, while the revised version states that its levels remain stable through the life course.

In the criminological literature, there are many studies on self-control and its influence on antisocial behaviour and offending. Criminologists, though, disagree about whether self-control should be viewed as a personality factor. Jones et al. (2011), in their meta-analysis, argue that it should be: traits that describe self-control are very similar to those found in psychological models of personality.

Low self-control, the poor ability to control behaviour, is considered an important dimension of personality that is related to later offending (Jolliffe and Farrington 2009). Overwhelming are the number of constructs that refer to it though (Farrington 2007): impulsivity, hyperactivity, restlessness, sensation-seeking, risk-taking, a poor ability to plan ahead, short-term thinking, and a poor ability to delay gratification. The effect of low self-control on offending may be indirect or direct (Jolliffe and Farrington 2009). An example of an indirect effect is through low academic achievement. Children who have low self-control find it difficult, because of poor concentration, to be in the school setting, where a number of rules must be followed (Farrington and Jolliffe 2015). They may achieve low marks and are likely to drop out of school and have poor career prospects. This in turn may lead to few opportunities to succeed conventionally, so they may turn to crime to obtain money or status.

Several studies have shown that low self-control (and similar measures) is related to deviance and crime in Japan. Vazsonyi et al. (2004) compared 335 Japanese university students (mean age = 19.7 years) to 1285 American university students (mean age = 20.0 years) on 24 items measuring low self-control, and found support for this relationship in Japan. This study was later expanded to include a number of other countries with comparable demographics—Hungary, the Netherlands, and Switzerland—and similar results were found in all countries. Kobayashi and colleagues (2010) replicated the 2004 study and found that, although the relationship between low self-control and deviance was significant in both Japan and the US, the relationship was stronger in the US than it is in Japan, meaning that conceptualisations of self-control need to be reconsidered as to how they may apply to other cultures like Japan. Risk-taking has been found to be related to violence and serious delinquency in several studies of high-school aged Osaka youth (Bui et al. 2014, 2018, 2016; Bui 2014).

The link between personality and crime is robust, and several personality traits have been found to be especially apt: temperament, empathy, and low self-control (Farrington and Jolliffe 2015). Personality is seen as stable, as the product of the interaction between the environment and the individual to produce patterns of thinking, feeling, and behaving that are relatively consistent over time (Jones, Miller, and Lynam 2011). Although relatively stable, personality traits can change in absolute terms in different developmental phases. For example, most individuals become more conscientious as they age. In other words, there is relative stability (in the ordering of individuals) but absolute change (in mean scores). One of the most influential personality theories for crime in psychology is Eysenck's theory. It highlights the importance of childhood socialisation in developing self-control.

Hans Eysenck (1977) developed what was known as the most complete psychological theory of crime, because it attempted to explain crime through an interaction between biological, social, and individual factors. He believed that everyone developed a conscience in childhood. This conscience comprised guilt that had accumulated from being punished for misbehaviour, and it prevented individuals from misbehaving in the future. People who committed offences either did not develop a strong conscience (because they were not disciplined properly) or their personality hindered that development. The dimensions of personality that prevented the successful development of the conscience were psychoticism (P; aggressive, cold, and egocentric); extraversion (E; sociable, sensation-seeking, and assertive); and neuroticism (N; anxiety, depression, and irrationality).

As Eysenck's theory evolved, it reached the conclusion that a combination of high E and N scores would be overrepresented in offender populations because such personality traits would produce low self-control, whereas a high P score was directly related to criminal behaviour because these individuals exhibited egocentricity related to testosterone levels (Hollin 2002). Later, the FFM or 'Big Five' personality dimensions replaced Eysenck's theory as the main personality theory of crime (Farrington and Jolliffe 2015). This, too, includes E and N, but also agreeableness (A; altruism, modesty), openness (O; imagination, aesthetic sensitivity), and conscientiousness (C; self-discipline, competence).

Among the 'Big Five' personality dimensions, A and C are considered two of the most relevant traits for self-control (Jensen-Campbell et al. 2007). They also are most strongly and negatively related to offending (Farrington and Jolliffe 2015). Moffitt et al. (2011) investigated the effect of self-control on various life outcomes, including criminal convictions. Conscientiousness was used as a measure to represent the self-control skills of responsibility, industriousness, and orderliness. They followed 1037 individuals from birth to age 32 in New Zealand, and found that childhood self-control was a strong predictor of outcomes in adulthood, and it continued to predict so even after controlling for family influences. Self-control predicted positive adult functioning through better decision-making during adolescence. Improving self-control of children should not only improve their individual functioning but could improve societal well-being through savings in many social costs such as crime control and mental health.

In a study of 56 countries on the 'Big Five' personality dimensions, however, Japan rated unexpectedly on some of the dimensions (Schmitt et al. 2007). On A, it scored lowest next to Lithuania, and on C, it scored lowest next to South Korea. The authors of this study noted that this was unusual considering that countries like Japan are assumed to be high on these personality traits; most people would not think that the Japanese are undisciplined and immodest. They speculated that perhaps different cultural standards of personality traits may be responsible. For example, a culture where C characteristics of being organised and disciplined are set at a very high standard may make anyone's efforts fall short.

Not all agree that high self-control personalities are good for society. After decades of conformity-focused education, and concerns about the stress and pressure of schools on children, school reforms in Japan have started to promote education focused on building individuality and risk-taking among youth (Aspinall 2016). According to reformers, risk-taking in students needs to be nurtured in order to increase economic growth and the quality of life. In light of substantial domestic and international social and economic changes, reformers have questioned the suitability of the current Japanese education system to help students to adapt to modern times. The implementation of more risk-taking and autonomy into Japanese schools, however, seems very difficult, because risk-aversion appears engrained within the mindset of the state and society. Although the notion of the risk society has made its way to Japan, it is not as influential as it is in the West, where social problems are considered to be the fault of the individual; these problems are still seen as a group responsibility in Japan.

Teaching conformity and self-control may contribute to reduced delinquency and crime, but as Harada (1995) notes, such developments may have contributed to reduced street crime while creating new sources of crime in schools. Two problems have emerged from schools to become the centre of societal focus: bullying and school phobia (Ishida and Miwa 2012). The former has been linked with a growing number of suicides while the latter has been attributed to family violence. Sociological explanations have been proposed to explain these phenomena, but their effects are elaborated by a psychological perspective.

Bullying

Bullying gained national attention in 1986, in Japan, when a 13-year old boy hanged himself in the restroom of a department store near his grandparents' residence (Toda 2016). He had left the names of his bullies, who had repeatedly beaten and threatened him in the previous six months (Treml 2001). Before his suicide, he had arrived to his classroom to find a condolence card filled with good-bye messages on his desk, with a vase of flowers from classmates and teachers who had organised his mock funeral. At this time, international attention was given to bullying in Japan (Tam and Taki 2007) but it was not until 2013 that the government passed legislation requiring schools to prepare adequately for bullying incidents. This was after another bullying-related suicide and a violent attack on an education superintendent for the perceived incompetence of schools in dealing with bullying.

Bullying in Japan is referred to as *ijime*, defined as 'a type of aggressive behaviour by which someone who holds a dominant position in a group-interaction process, by intentional or collective acts, causes mental and/or physical suffering to others inside a group' (Yoneyama 2015). This definition is similar to that used in the West whereby bullying is characterised by an imbalance of power between the bully (or bullies) and the victim(s), and the victimisation is deliberate and repeated over time (Farrington 1993; Olweus 1993). Bullying in Japan tends to be directed more to the psychological suffering of victims rather than to their physical suffering (Kanetsuna et al. 2006).

Literature on bullying reveals two types (Yoneyama 2015). Type I bullying is what is usually found in Western countries. This type is committed by a problem student or a group of problem students towards students who are often outside their friendship circle. This bullying tends to be physical and the bully role is fixed, though bullies may be victimised by others. Reasons for bullying usually are unconnected to the school, such as personality or family problems. Type II bullying is based on observations of ijime. Bullies are mainly students who are deemed non-problematic—ordinary, good students. The dynamics of this group-bullying are fluid, in that bullies may become victims and vice versa at any given time. There is a process of social inclusion and exclusion. Because many 'good' students are involved in this type of bullying, it is thought to stem from the educational structure and institution itself. Relationships among classmates, even between friends, are shallow, so classmates will be apathetic towards others being bullied. Among friendship groups, classmates will either ignore their friend being bullied or join in with the bullying. This form of violence tends to happen within the confines of school, and not outside of it.

The most prevalent theory of ijime was proposed by Morita and Kiyonaga, in the 1980s, based on a study of over 1700 primary and middle school students (Yoneyama 2015). The four-tiered structural theory grouped bullying interactions into four typologies: victim, aggressor, bystander, and spectator. These interactions make up four layers of circles where the victim is in the innermost circle surrounded by 'aggressors', who are surrounded by 'spectators', who are surrounded by 'bystanders'. Spectators and bystanders contribute to these interactions because spectators encourage bullies by their interest while bystanders indirectly condone bullies' actions by doing nothing.

This group bullying tends to involve the whole class and is encouraged to continue as it becomes more frequent and persistent (Yoneyama and Naito 2003). This form of bullying thrives on a large audience. Though it is not unique to Japan, it is the most prevalent form of bullying in the country and often occurs within classrooms instead of on schoolyards. If not the whole class, ijime may occur in small friendship circles, aggravating the situation for the victim who will have difficulty belonging to another group. Friendships are more permanent in Japan, and the victim will likely risk being bullied just to stay in the group.

Reasons for Bullying

The manifestation of ijime and its characteristics seem to point to sociological causes, namely, the structure of the school and educational system. Yoneyama and Naito (2003) reviewed the literature on bullying in Japan and proposed the following reasons: bullying can stem from pressure to do well in school, or from classrooms of lower academic-achieving students who believe that studies are pointless for them. Students are socialised to believe that bullying is acceptable towards those who are different, because of the school's focus on conformity and its intolerance towards individuality. Students mimic the power relations of teacher–student relationships towards each other—they submit towards those who have power and oppress those who they consider more socially weak. These reasons may create an uncomfortable and damaging environment where students might find it difficult to keep their distance from bullies and bullying interactions. This may be aggravated by the organisation of the classroom into small groups for various activities such as eating lunch, cleaning, and learning (Yoneyama 2015). Yoneyama and Naito (2003) recommended improvements within the school structure, focusing on teacher–student relations, learner-centred teaching, less stress from the school environment, less school-wide harassment, discrimination awareness, and the abolition of the homeroom system so that students were not bound to the same classmates.

Two psychological theories, however, are used to understand the thinking behind why students resort to and propagate ijime. The first theory proposes that bullying is a way to reduce anxiety in times of stress and frustration. This frustration-aggression thesis suggests that bullying can be reduced by prevention concentrating on stress management and therapy. A couple of studies have found that this theory applies to Japan, South Korea, Australia, Canada, and Hong Kong (Tam and Taki 2007). It focuses on the competitive nature of schools. This theory would be most applicable to the middle school years.

Hara (2002) examined justifications given by children involved in bullying in two middle schools in the Chiba prefecture. He divided the children into six groups, representing different roles within bullying interactions based on classmate nominations. Surprisingly, among each of the six groups, even among the victim group, the majority justified the bullying by blaming the victim (60% and higher). They thought that something about the victim's personality or behaviour made the bullying deserved. Hara connected this to Lerner's just world hypothesis, where people believe that misfortune befalls those who deserve it. According to this, justice prevails: good people are rewarded whereas bad people are punished. The belief that victims deserve the bullying also attests to the bully's abilities of persuasion. Even compared to Australians, Japanese students were more likely to bully and were less likely to help the victim (Nesdale and Naito 2005).

Interviews with Japanese ($n=61$) and English ($n=60$) students (mean age $=13$ years) revealed opinions about reacting appropriately towards bullying. In the study, Kanetsuna et al. (2006) cautioned that though Japanese children knew what to do, they may not necessarily act on it because of mistrust and lack of confidence about the abilities of schools and teachers to resolve bullying issues. This was in contrast to the English students who had more confidence and trust in school-based interventions.

Toda (2016) recently reviewed major research findings on ijime, presented as a process. From a developmental perspective, behaviours similar to bullying may begin in primary school. The reason for the focus on ijime in middle school is that negative emotions seem to peak during early adolescence. In addition, changes in ijime behaviour as well as conceptualisations of it when transitioning from primary to middle school may also contribute to the focus during middle school. Justifications for bullying, as well as inter-group relationships, can escalate the bullying. Victims generally show negative affect, such as irritation, anger, and feelings of helplessness.

Impact of Bullying: Psychological Consequences

Systematic reviews and meta-analyses of longitudinal studies examining the relationship between school bullying and later offending demonstrate the strength of bullying as a predictor even when other childhood risk factors are considered (Ttofi and Farrington 2011). Meta-analyses show that perpetrators of school bullying have twice the odds of committing later violence as non-perpetrators, whereas victims have a lower, but nonetheless increased odds of committing later violence compared to non-victims (Ttofi et al. 2012). A dose-response effect exists, in that the more involved children are in bullying, the greater risk they have for later adverse outcomes. All of these studies have been conducted elsewhere, and it is not clear to what extent the relationship between bullying and later criminality applies in Japan. A descriptive comparison between bullying in the US and Japan discussed criminal consequences, but none of its studies were directly about Japan (see Hilton et al. 2010).

Not only is bullying linked to long-term antisocial behaviour and offending, it is also linked to mental illness and suicidal behaviour. Bullying is considered to be a symptom of conduct disorder, so a combination of mental illness and criminality is possible (Klomek et al. 2015). Those who are involved in bullying have an increased risk of developing undesirable life outcomes: internalising disorders for victims; criminality and externalising disorders for bullies, particularly violent crime and illicit drug misuse; and internalising or externalising disorders and criminality for bully-victims. Among those who are involved in bullying, the bully-victim seems particularly likely to develop various adverse outcomes. They are at increased risk for self-harming behaviour, known as non-suicidal self-injury, regardless of gender (Hamada et al. 2018). Examples are pulling out hair, cutting, hitting, burning, and scratching skin. This type of self-harm is used to regulate negative emotions and to avoid situations that self-harmers dislike. Among self-harming behaviour, bully-victims are likely to self-cut, especially when they perceive that their school is unsafe.

A danger is that those in most need of help will be identified too late. In a sample of 9484 high school students (52% female) in Kochi prefecture, Kitagawa et al. (2014) found that bully-victims were likely to seek help compared to those who were bullies or uninvolved. If, however, they developed suicidal feelings, they did not seek help, and the more serious the feelings were, the less likely it was that they would seek help. Toda (2016) reviewed the Japanese literature and also found adverse outcomes for victims. As adults, these former victims have tended to be more fearful, anxious, detached, and mistrusting of others than non-victims.

Several studies indicate a relationship between bullying and childhood maltreatment. Using a retrospective study design using data from the Japanese Study of Stratification, Health, Income, and Neighbourhood (J-SHINE), Oshio et al. (2013) investigated the impact of childhood maltreatment and school bullying on adult well-being. Being subjected to either one of these experiences prior to graduating from middle school was significantly related to poor adult subjective well-being. Compared to experiencing childhood physical abuse and bullying victimisation, neglect had the strongest relationship to feeling unhappy and unhealthy in adulthood. In another retrospective study, this one of Japanese, South African, and American university students, childhood physical abuse was associated with bullying behaviours in all countries (Dussich and Maekoya 2007). The Japanese were shown to have the highest prevalence of bullying behaviours and to be more likely to make use of false and damaging rumours compared to South Africans and Americans. Prevention may need to be implemented in early childhood, with attention to family dynamics. Indeed, the literature in Japanese raises similar concerns (Toda 2016).

Klomek et al. (2015), after reviewing all published longitudinal studies on bullying between 1960 and 2015 that used large population-based community samples, concluded that tackling bullying requires early childhood intervention. Comorbidities need to be examined, as it is suspected that bullying does not operate alone to produce adverse life outcomes.

Yoneyama (2015) speculates that ijime may indicate a profound sense of disconnect among students towards their schools. Bullying interactions may serve as a substitute for connectedness in school. The lack of longitudinal studies in Japan, especially studies that investigate bullying among young children, has hindered progress in understanding ijime research (Toda 2016). Knowledge about long-term effects is uncertain, as case studies are mostly used, with no attempt to summarise findings using systematic reviews or meta-analyses.

Ijime came to national and international attention because of the number of bullied students who committed suicide (Kawabata 2001), but in less tragic cases, but nonetheless serious, bullied children will refuse to attend school and develop a condition where staying away from school becomes permanent. These cases have been treated as individual pathologies in need of clinical intervention.

School Refusal

Tōkōkyohi, also known as school refusal or school phobia, refers to the condition in which children cannot or refuse to go to school (Yoneyama 2000). Usually, onset is characterised by excessive fatigue. Somatic symptoms such as stomach aches, headaches, breathing difficulties, nausea, and dizziness may also appear. School phobia is considered to be one end of the tôkôkyohi spectrum, whereas school refusal is at the other end, so this condition is seen as a continuum from somatic symptoms to intentional refusal as time progresses. The first reported cases of tôkôkyohi appeared in 1964 when many good students, urban children, and then rural ones, reported wanting to go to school but finding that they could not (Kameguchi and Murphy-Shigematsu 2001). It was not until the 1980s when, coupled with a perceived epidemic of school bullying and youth violence, tôkôkyohi was considered to be a serious issue.

Unlike school truancy, tôkôkyohi limits children to their home. Children who are diagnosed with this condition withdraw from social contact and live reclusively. Other differences are also observed: truant children rarely display any physical problems; parents of truants are usually unaware of their truancy; and truants are likely to be involved in delinquency and antisocial behaviour. Comparing school refusal in Japan and the UK shows a fairly similar prevalence, but it is treated more seriously in Japan because it is a common form of school non-attendance whereas, in other countries like the UK, it is viewed as truancy or dropout (Yoneyama 2000). Tôkôkyohi is particularly challenging because it runs counter to two fundamental ideologies in contemporary Japan: the school as a key institution in learning 'Japaneseness' and acquiring the quality of an upstanding citizen. In light of these ideas, how can staying away from school be a Japanese quality? Other reasons than bullying have been given as to why tôkôkyohi occurs: laziness, school burnout, an act of resistance and protest towards school, or mental illness.

Yoneyama (2000) reviewed the literature on tôkôkyohi and included psychological theories about it. The condition was seen as social maladjustment, so personality traits thought to be problematic would need to be corrected through behavioural therapy and routine group activities. The problem with this proscription is its regimented schedule, resembling the school, which children diagnosed with tôkôkyohi were trying to avoid. Other scholars have criticised this approach, cautioning that the condition should not be referred to as psychosomatic. Although many of the children with tôkôkyohi share somatic symptoms, the use of the term 'psychosomatic' implies that it is all in the child's head and can be cured through changes in mental processes. Therefore, the problem lies in the individual sufferer.

Parents who refuse to believe that their child is suffering from such a condition risk becoming victims of violence. In some cases, parents try to force the child with tôkôkyohi to attend school. They could not comprehend that their child was too fatigued to leave the house. Out of anger, these children attack their parents or develop daydreams of killing them, or both.

Yoneyama (2000) argued that tôkôkyohi can be seen as a process of empowerment stemming from school burnout. Children are in a state of alienation when they attempt to figure out what is truly wrong with them, and once they understand, they feel healed. They feel better not because they are ready to fulfil their societal expectations, but because they recover their individuality. Children who undergo this process question the normality of the school. They find conformity and aspiring to fulfil roles prescribed by society disdainful. Often these children are critical of the school and extend this view towards Japanese society. Yoneyama further argues that although tôkôkyohi is a process to find oneself, the outcome will vary between individuals: some outcomes may be positive, but others may result in violence such as suicide or murder.

Kameguchi and Murphy-Shigematsu (2001) introduced the use of family therapy in tackling tôkôkyohi. In fact, the development of family psychology and family therapy was primarily a response to the emergence of tôkôkyohi as a social issue. Meanwhile, violence from children towards their teachers at school and their parents at home became a serious concern. From this family perspective, tôkôkyohi is not entirely a problem with the school, but more concerned with unhealthy family dynamics.

Earlier reports of tôkôkyohi focused on the school—bullying, academic pressure—as explanations but these were replaced by the realisation that the problem may indicate a broader issue with social relations due to significant socioeconomic changes. This perspective took into account the isolation of shrinking families. Kameguchi and Murphy-Shigematsu (2001) describe the typical observed family dynamics that contributed to the development of tôkôkyohi and subsequent filial violence: mothers derive their identity from the educational attainment of their children, so they invest a lot of their energy and time in their children's lives to the point of overprotection and interference. As the father is not as involved because of his work commitments, mothers have close relationships with their children to compensate for the nonexistence of relationships with their husbands. Consequently, the mother and child are distant towards the father, who becomes isolated within his own family. Children then feel ambivalent; they desire to be autonomous but also want to please their mothers. Tôkôkyohi is the result of being uneasy in the family situation but also is a form of rebelling against the mother. It, too, involves resentment at not being able to develop a self-identity.

Psychologists in Japan believe that the school's narrow focus on conformity to produce ideal members of society is detrimental to the development of individuality (Kameguchi and Murphy-Shigematsu 2001). Children suffering from tôkôkyohi have reported feeling upset by their teachers' lack of personal involvement with them; this is more problematic if the student is having learning problems or does not have adequate social skills. These children also observe that teachers will only appreciate students who are doing well, resulting in the alienation of low academic achievers.

Conclusion

The school is a significant agent of socialisation, further instilling children with the necessary values to succeed in society. As it is an important part of children's lives, even determining their futures, it has a huge influence on their well-being. Part of the reason for the observed high level of self-control in Japan may be attributed to socialisation during education. If children care about future success, they must conform to the ways of the school. In the last few decades, however, the educational system has been criticised for its supposed rigidity, which has been blamed for the rise in school refusal and bullying. Later criminal and poor mental health outcomes are related to bullying, whereas school refusal contributes to the prevalence of family violence. The violence in and as a by-product of schools echoes a previous observation by the criminologist Yutaka Harada (1995): violence has not disappeared; although it may have gone from the streets, it has manifested somewhere else. In this case, perhaps in the schools.

References

Aspinall, Robert W. 2016. "Children's Rights in a Risk Society: The Case of Schooling in Japan." *Japan Forum* 28 (2): 135–54.

Borovoy, Amy. 2008. "Japan's Hidden Youths: Mainstreaming the Emotionally Distressed in Japan." *Culture, Medicine, and Psychiatry* 32: 552–76.

Bouffard, Jeff A., Jessica M. Craig, and Alex R. Piquero. 2015. "Comparing Attitudinal and Situational Measures of Self-Control Among Felony Offenders." *Criminal Behavior and Mental Health* 25: 112–25.

Bui, Laura. 2014. "Examining the Relationship Between Parenting, Risk-Taking, and Delinquency in Japan: Context and Empirical Applicability." *Asian Journal of Criminology* 9 (3): 171–87.

Bui, Laura, David P. Farrington, Mitsuaki Ueda, and Karl G. Hill. 2014. "Prevalence and Risk Factors for Self-Reported Violence of Osaka and Seattle Male Youths." *International Journal of Offender Therapy and Comparative Criminology* 58 (12): 1540–57.

Bui, Laura, David P. Farrington, and Mitsuaki Ueda. 2016. "Potential Risk and Promotive Factors for Serious Delinquency in Japanese Female Youth." *International Journal of Comparative and Applied Criminal Justice* 40 (3): 209–24.

———. 2018. "Risk and Protective Factors for Serious Delinquency in the Japanese Context: Findings from Osaka Male Youths." In *Crime and Justice in Contemporary Japan*, edited by Jianghong Liu and Setsuo Miyazawa, 119–35. New York: Springer.

Dussich, John P. J., and Chie Maekoya. 2007. "Physical Child Harm and Bullying-Related Behaviors in Japan, South Africa, and the United States." *International Journal of Offender Therapy and Comparative Criminology* 51 (5): 495–509.

Eysenck, Hans J. 1977. *Crime and Personality*. London: Routledge.

Farrington, David P. 1993. "Understanding and Preventing Bullying." In *Crime and Justice, Vol. 17*, edited by Michael Tonry, 381–458. Chicago: University of Chicago Press.

———. 2007. "Childhood Risk Factors and Risk-Focussed Prevention." In *The Oxford Handbook of Criminology*, edited by Mike Maguire, Rodney Morgan, and Robert Reiner, 4th ed., 602–40. Oxford: Oxford University Press.

Farrington, David P., and Darrick Jolliffe. 2015. "Personality and Crime." In *International Encyclopedia of the Social and Behavioral Sciences*, edited by James D Wright, Vol. 17, 774–79. Oxford: Elsevier.

Farrington, David P., and Rolf Loeber. 2000. "Epidemiology of Juvenile Violence." *Child and Adolescent Psychiatric Clinics of North America* 9 (4): 733–48.

Folijanty-Jost, Gesine, and Manuel Metzler. 2003. "Juvenile Delinquency in Japan: A Self-Preventing Prophecy." *Social Science Japan* 25: 39–43.

Fukuzawa, Rebecca Erwin. 1994. "The Path to Adulthood According to Japanese Middle Schools." *Journal of Japanese Studies* 20 (1): 61–86.

Gottfredson, Michael R., and Travis Hirschi. 1990. *A General Theory of Crime*. Stanford: Stanford University Press.

Hamada, Shoko, Hitoshi Kaneko, Masayoshi Ogura, Aya Yamawaki, Andre Sourander, Shuji Honjo, Junko Maezono, and Lauri Sillanm. 2018. "Association Between Bullying Behavior, Perceived School Safety, and Self-Cutting: A Japanese Population-Based School Survey." *Child and Adolescent Mental Health* 23 (3): 141–47.

Hara, Hideki. 2002. "Justifications for Bullying Among Japanese Schoolchildren." *Asian Journal of Social Psychology* 5: 197–204.

Harada, Yutaka. 1992. "A Retrospective Study on the Relationship of Delinquent History in Junior High School to Later School and Employment Careers." *Reports of the National Research Institute of Police Science* 33: 1–13.

———. 1995. "Adjustment to School, Life Course Transitions, and Changes in Delinquent Behavior in Japan." In *Current Perspectives on Aging and the Life Cycle: Delinquency and Disrepute in the Life Course, Vol. 4*, edited by Zena Smith Blau and John Hagan, Vol. 33, 35–60. Greenwich: JAI Press.

Hechter, Michael, and Satoshi Kanazawa. 1993. "Group Solidarity and Social Order in Japan." *Journal of Theoretical Politics* 5 (4): 455–93.

Hilton, Jeanne. M., Linda Anngela-Cole, and Juri Wakita. 2010. "A Cross-Cultural Comparison of Factors Associated with School Bullying in Japan and the United States." *The Family Journal* 18 (4): 413–22.

Hirschi, Travis. 2004. "Self-Control and Crime." In *Handbook of Self-Regulation*, edited by Roy Baumeister and Kathleen Vohs, 537–52. New York: Guilford Press.

Hollin, Clive R. 2002. "Criminological Psychology." In *The Oxford Handbook in Criminology and Criminal Justice*, edited by Mike Maguire, Rod Morgan, and Robert Reiner, 144–74. Oxford: Oxford University Press.

Ishida, Hiroshi, and Satoshi Miwa. 2012. "School Discipline and Academic Achievement in Japan." In *Improving Learning Environments: School Discipline and Student Achievement in Comparative Perspective*, edited by Richard Arum and Melissa Velez. Stanford: Stanford University Press.

Jensen-Campbell, Lauri A., Jennifer M. Knack, Amy M. Waldrip, and Shaun D. Campbell. 2007. "Do Big Five Personality Traits Associated with Self-Control in Influence the Regulation of Anger and Aggression?" *Journal of Research in Personality* 41 (2): 403–24.

Jolliffe, Darrick, and David P. Farrington. 2009. "A Systematic Review of the Relationship Between Childhood Impulsiveness and Later Violence." In *Personality, Personality Disorder and Violence*, edited by Mary McMurran and Richard C Howard, 38–61. Chichester: Wiley.

Jones, Shayne E., Joshua D. Miller, and Donald R. Lynam. 2011. "Personality, Antisocial Behavior, and Aggression: A Meta-Analytic Review." *Journal of Criminal Justice* 39 (4): 329–37.

Jolliffe, Darrick, David P. Farrington, Rolf Loeber, and Dustin Pardini. 2016. "Protective Factors for Violence: Results from the Pittsburgh Youth Study." *Journal of Criminal Justice* 45: 32–40.

Kameguchi, Kenji, and Stephen Murphy-Shigematsu. 2001. "Family Psychology and Family Therapy in Japan." *The American Psychologist* 56 (1): 65–70.

Kanetsuna, Tomoyuki, Peter K. Smith, and Yohji Morita. 2006. "Coping with Bullying at School: Children's Recommended Strategies and Attitudes to School-Based Interventions in England and Japan." *Aggressive Behaviour* 32 (3): 570–80.

Kawabata, Naoto. 2001. "Adolescent Trauma in Japanese Schools: Two Case Studies of Ijime (Bullying) and School Refusal." *The Journal of the American Academy of Psychoanalysis* 29 (1): 85–103.

Kitagawa, Yuko, Shinji Shimodera, Yuji Okazaki, and Atsushi Nishida. 2014. "Suicidal Feelings Interferes with Help-Seeking in Bullied Adolescents." *PLOS ONE* 9 (9): 1–7.

Klomek, Anat Brunstein, Andre Sourander, and Henrik Elonheimo. 2015. "Bullying by Peers in Childhood and Effects on Psychopathology, Suicidality, and Criminality in Adulthood." *Lancet Psychiatry* 2: 930–41.

Kobayashi, Emiko, Alexander T. Vazsonyi, Pan Chen, and Susan F. Sharp. 2010. "A Culturally Nuanced Test of Gottfredson and Hirschi's "General Theory": Dimensionality and Generalizability in Japan and the United States." *International Criminal Justice Review* 20 (2): 112–31.

Maguin, Eugene, and Rolf Loeber. 1996. "Academic Performance and Delinquency." *Crime and Justice* 20: 145–264.

Martinez, Dolores P. 2007. *Modern Japan Culture and Society*. London: Routledge.

Messner, Steven F. 2015. "When West Meets East: Generalizing Theory and Expanding the Conceptual Toolkit of Criminology." *Asian Journal of Criminology* 10 (2): 117–29.

Metzler, Manuel, and Gesine Folijanty-Jost. 2003. "Problem Behavior and Social Control in Japan's Junior High Schools." In *Juvenile Delinquency in Japan: Reconsidering the "Crisis,"* edited by Gesine Folijanty-Jost, 253–66. Leiden: Brill.

Miller, Alan, and Satoshi Kanazawa. 2000. *Order by Accident: The Origins and Consequences of Conformity in Contemporary Japan.* Boulder: Westview.

Moffitt, Terrie E., Louise Arseneault, Daniel Belsky, Nigel Dickson, Robert J. Hancox, and Honalee Harrington. 2011. "A Gradient of Childhood Self-Control Predicts Health, Wealth, and Public Safety." *Proceedings of the National Academy of Sciences of the United States of America* 108 (7): 2693–98.

Nesdale, Drew, and Mikako Naito. 2005. "Individualism-Collectivism and the Attitudes to School Bullying of Japanese and Australian Students." *Journal of Cross-Cultural Psychology* 36 (5): 537–56.

Olweus, Dan. 1993. *Bullying at School: What We Know and What We Can Do.* Oxford: Basil Blackwell.

Oshio, Takashi, Maki Umeda, and Norito Kawakami. 2013. "Childhood Adversity and Adulthood Subjective Well-Being: Evidence from Japan." *Journal of Happiness Studies* 14 (3): 843–60.

Schmitt, David P., Robert R. Mccrae, Kevin L. Bennett, and Karl Grammer. 2007. "The Geographic Distribution of Big Five Personality Traits: Patterns and Profiles of Human Self-Description Across 56 Nations." *Journal of Cross-Cultural Psychology* 38 (2): 173–212.

Sugimoto, Yoshio. 2014. *An Introduction to Japanese Society.* 4th ed. Cambridge: Cambridge University Press.

Tam, Frank Wai-ming, and Mitsuru Taki. 2007. "Bullying Among Girls in Japan and Hong Kong: An Examination of the Frustration-Aggression Model." *Educational Research and Evaluation* 13 (4): 373–99.

Toda, Yuichi. 2016. "Bullying (Ijime) and Related Problems in Japan: History and Research." In *School Bullying in Different Cultures: Eastern and Western Perspectives*, edited by Peter K. Smith, Keumjoo Kwak, and Yuichi Toda, 73–92. Cambridge: Cambridge University Press.

Treml, Jacqueline Noel. 2001. "Bullying as a Social Malady in Contemporary Japan." *International Social Work* 44 (1): 107–17.

Ttofi, Maria M., and David P. Farrington. 2011. "Effectiveness of School-Based Programs to Reduce Bullying: A Systematic and Meta-Analytic Review." *Journal of Experimental Criminology* 7 (1): 27–56.

Ttofi, Maria M., David P. Farrington, and Friedrich Lösel. 2012. "School Bullying as a Predictor of Violence Later in Life: A Systematic Review and Meta-Analysis of Prospective Longitudinal Studies." *Aggression and Violent Behavior* 17: 405–18.

Vazsonyi, Alexander T., Janice E. Clifford Wittekind, Lara M. Belliston, and Timothy D. Van Loh. 2004. "Extending the General Theory of Crime to 'The East:' Low Self-Control in Japanese Late Adolescents." *Journal of Quantitative Criminology* 20 (3): 189–216.

Ward, Jeffrey T., John H. Boman, and Shayne Jones. 2012. "Hirschi's Redefined Self Control: Assessing the Implications of the Merger Between Social- and Self-Control Theories." *Crime and Delinquency* 61 (9): 1206–33.

Yamamiya, Yuko. 2003. "Juvenile Delinquency in Japan." *Journal of Prevention & Intervention in the Community* 25 (2): 27–46.

Yoder, Robert S. 2004. *Youth Deviance in Japan: Class Reproduction of Nonconformity.* Melbourne, VIC: Trans-Pacific Press.

Yoneyama, Shoko. 2000. "Student Discourse on Tokokyohi (School Phobia/Refusal) in Japan: Burnout or Empowerment?" *British Journal of Sociology of Education* 21 (1): 77–94.

———. 2015. "Theorizing School Bullying: Insights from Japan." *Confero* 3 (2): 1–37.

Yoneyama, Shoko, and Asao Naito. 2003. "Problems with the Paradigm: The School as a Factor in Understanding Bullying (with Special Reference to Japan)." *British Journal of Sociology of Education* 24 (3): 315–30.

7

Mental Disorders

The relationship between mental disorder and offending is not without controversy. A common misperception is that those suffering from a mental disorder are violent and dangerous. Globally, stigmatising attitudes towards mental disorders are a key barrier to help-seeking and successful reintegration of those with a mental illness (Griffiths et al. 2006). In Japan, many people hold negative attitudes about those who are suffering from a mental disorder, believing that these people are also dangerous and unpredictable (Ando et al. 2013).

The MacArthur Violence Risk Assessment Study, conducted between 1992 and 1995 in the US, was the first comprehensive investigation that linked mental disorder and violence, using a sophisticated longitudinal research design with multiple measures (Stuart 2003; Monahan 2002). Subsequent research from many different countries suggests that most people with a mental disorder are not violent and that most violent offences are committed by people who are not mentally ill (Van Dorn et al. 2012). There is, however, a consensus among findings that the risk of violence does moderately increase for those who suffer from severe mental illness, which refers specifically to schizophrenia, schizo-affective disorder, major depression, bipolar disorder, and psychoses (Bruce et al. 2014), although the reasons for this relationship are complicated. For

© The Author(s) 2019
L. Bui and D. P. Farrington, *Crime in Japan*, Palgrave Advances in Criminology and Criminal Justice in Asia, https://doi.org/10.1007/978-3-030-14097-7_7

example, substance abuse, which is more common among those with a mental disorder, is considered to be an important factor that contributes to the significant relationship between mental disorder and offending (Van Dorn et al. 2012).

Media reports of serious violent youth crimes in Japan sometimes include the term 'conduct disorder', assuming that it has direct relevance to crime (Nakane and Nakane 2002). There is some truth to this. Conduct disorder is a repetitive and persistent pattern of behaviour by a child or adolescent, for at least six months or longer, that causes clinically significant impairment in social, academic, or occupational functioning, whereby age-appropriate social norms and basic rights of others are disregarded (Farrington 2004). Literature from Western industrialised countries indicates that adolescents with conduct disorder tend to be aggressive and delinquent (Farrington 2004). Conduct disorder, aggression, and delinquency are viewed as overlapping problems because they share individual, family, peer, and school risk factors, such as impulsiveness, parental conflict, antisocial peers, and low academic achievement (Murray and Farrington 2010).

Relating to recidivism, a meta-analysis of 20 qualifying international studies showed that young people with externalising disorders, specifically attention-deficit/hyperactivity disorder, substance use disorder, or conduct disorder, were at elevated risk for recidivism compared to young people without any of the main internalising or externalising mental disorders (Wibbelink et al. 2017).

Among adults, synthesised research findings from international systematic reviews and meta-analyses provide support for the association between mental disorder and reoffending: those with a psychotic disorder had almost twice the odds of reoffending as those without any psychiatric disorders (Fazel and Yu 2011). A comparison of the likelihood of antisocial and violent behaviours between those with and without a personality disorder (PD; among general and offender populations), from a synthesis of 14 studies, show that those with PD had three times the odds of violence than those without PD in the general population (Yu et al. 2012). A summary of 25 studies in the same meta-analysis found that those released from prison and diagnosed with a PD had two to three times the odds of reoffending compared to those released who either had another or no mental illness.

Comorbidity in offenders, in which more than one mental disorder coexists, is likely to increase the risk of violence, substance misuse, and recidivism (Chandler et al. 2004). In addition, among prison populations, the prevalence of mental illness is high. Based on 62 surveys from 66 relevant publications, those who were incarcerated were two to four times more likely to have psychosis or major depression and about 10 times more likely to have a PD than those in the general population (Fazel and Danesh 2002). Of all PDs, antisocial personality disorder (ASPD) substantially increased the odds of antisocial and violent behaviours, but only among non-offenders (Yu et al. 2012); to have a diagnosis of ASPD, a previous diagnosis of conduct disorder is required.

Often, other terms are used interchangeably with mental disorder: psychiatric disorder, mental illness, and mental health condition. The term mental disorder, however, is used by two established classification systems, the International Classification of Diseases (ICD), published by the World Health Organization (WHO), and the Diagnostic and Statistical Manual of Mental Disorders (DSM), published by the American Psychiatric Association. The ICD acknowledges that, although 'disorder' is not an exact term, using it avoids issues related to the use of 'disease' or 'illness', which implies that there is a clear cause or basis, probably biological (World Health Organization 1992). In contrast, the DSM views the term mental disorder as an 'umbrella' term, and mental illness refers to diagnosable mental disorders that involve significant changes in thinking, emotion, and behaviour as well as distress and problems functioning in daily life.

Both recent versions of the ICD and DSM (numbers 10 and 5, respectively) consider mental disorders as repetitions of behaviours and psychological states related to distress, disability, risk of suffering, or significant loss of freedom (Banner 2013). In Japan, the majority of medical schools and universities use both the ICD and DSM in their regular clinical work, based on a survey of 67 educational institutions (Nakane and Nakane 2002). The DSM, however, is used more for research purposes than the ICD, and this may be attributable to its wide acceptance since the publication of the Japanese version in 1983.

Findings from Japan

Prevalence of Mental Disorders

Initiated by WHO, a coordinated series of World Mental Health surveys were conducted in 28 countries to advance knowledge on the unmet needs for treatment of mental disorders (Ishikawa et al. 2016). The results from the complete data of the Japan survey, conducted between 2002 and 2006 in 11 urban and rural communities ($n = 4130$), revealed that the prevalence of mental disorder was 20.3% for the lifetime and 7.6% for one year. Among lifetime prevalence, anxiety disorders ranked highest, followed by substance, mood, and then impulse control disorders. The most prevalent individual disorders were alcohol abuse/dependence, major depressive disorder, specific phobias, and generalised anxiety disorder. The prevalence of mental disorders in Japan was lower than in participating Western countries, but its pattern of disorders, risk factors, and unmet needs for treatment were similar to those found in these other countries. A distinct finding was a greater lifetime prevalence among males and greater persistence[1] among females. The authors attributed the higher prevalence of persistence among women to gender discrimination. It was estimated that 2.6 million people in Japan suffered from severe role impairment because of mental disorder.

Watanabe (2016), commenting on the WHO-initiated study of Ishikawa et al. (2016), proposes that the prevalence of common mental disorders in Japan may be impacted by recent widespread natural and social changes. The 2011 Tōhoku earthquake may have increased the prevalence of post-traumatic stress disorder but decreased the prevalence of suicide in the following two years. Changes in the lifestyle of young people—a greater preoccupation with being online and video games—in the last decade may also have had an impact on the types of mental disorder that are most prevalent.

---

[1]Proportion of 12-month cases among lifetime cases.

The Medical Treatment and Supervision Act

Prior to 2005, in Japan, major limitations were identified in the treatment of those with a mental disorder who had offended. Often these individuals were diverted to general psychiatric hospitals after being arrested and assessed in court or in a prosecutor's office (Yoshikawa et al. 2007). There, they were treated as civil patients and were released into the community once the psychiatrist deemed it appropriate, regardless of offence seriousness. No community follow-up existed; no one was responsible to reassess or monitor these individuals so that their treatment could be stopped if they wanted. In other situations, these individuals could be confined to hospital for life without any review.

These limitations were addressed when the first forensic mental health law was implemented in 2005 called the Medical Treatment and Supervision (MTS) Act (Ando et al. 2016). This was passed in response to the 2001 incident where a former psychiatric inpatient entered a primary school and stabbed eight children to death (Nakatani et al. 2010). The perpetrator was diagnosed with a PD and was deemed to be not fully responsible for his crime. Fear of crime committed by those with mental disorders subsequently surged nationwide, and this galvanised the government to respond.

Initially, the government focused on the risk of reoffending among those with a mental disorder (Nakatani et al. 2010). It proposed a hospital treatment order for those who were diagnosed with a mental disorder and deemed likely to commit a similar offence. Critics indicated that multiple offences could not be accurately predicted and, eventually, 'risk' was deleted from the legislation. This was after the government justified its actions by explaining that offenders with a mental disorder suffered from 'double handicaps': not only were they offenders, but they were also suffering from a mental disorder. The intensive care that these offenders would receive was less about them being a danger to the public and more concerned with their successful reintegration into society.

The Act was based on ideas from contemporary psychiatry, which promoted community-based care and normalisation (Nakatani 2012). It introduced a tribunal of judge, psychiatrist, and psychiatric social worker to evaluate guilt, sentencing, and treatment orders of offenders who had a mental disorder, as well as an independent review process that would, in the future, consider release. The Act was primarily aimed at those who had seriously harmed others in a 'state of insanity or diminished responsibility' (Nakatani 2012). The majority of offences that qualified for the MTS treatment order have been bodily injury, followed by homicide and arson and these are primarily committed by those diagnosed with schizophrenia (Nakatani et al. 2010). Although the MTS Act was a reaction to offenders with a PD, such offenders are excluded from this treatment order because they are considered to have full criminal responsibility.

Thirty specialist facilities and almost 800 beds were designated for use by forensic patients (Nagata et al. 2016). The process prioritises reintegrating these individuals into society by offering continued, appropriate medical care and monitoring in local communities, and probation plays a primary role in this. The head of the probation office develops a treatment plan for each forensic patient and assigns a rehabilitation coordinator who will assure continuous treatment for their clients (Nakatani 2012).

Relationship to Reoffending

Yoshikawa and colleagues (2007) speculated that it would be many years before any effects could be observed as a result of the MTS Act. They traced 489 individuals, starting in 1980, from discharge to either their initial violent reoffending or until the end of 1991, whichever occurred first. Many identified factors for violent reoffending were generally consistent with the international literature, with the exception of being male. The prevalence of violent reoffending, however, was low at 10%. Because of the low base rate, future evaluations of services from the MTS Act may be problematic. The authors suggested that targeting and reducing risk factors, such as desistance from substance use and compliance with treatment, may be better indicators of success.

Certainly, a number of risk factors have been identified to explain the occurrence of offending and violence among those with a mental disorder. We now consider several disorders in more detail, and the related risk factors for violence.

Developmental Disorders and Comorbidity

Several studies have emphasised the link between pervasive developmental disorders (PDD) and criminal behaviour (Ono and Pumariega 2008). PDD, however, has now been replaced by autism spectrum disorders (ASD) by the American Psychiatric Association (Shin et al. 2014). The National Institute of Mental Health (2015) in the US defines ASD as a group of developmental disorders that can be characterised by repetitive and persistent behaviours; enduring problems in social interaction and communication; and symptoms appearing in the first two years of life that cause the person to require help in daily living.

The link between PDD/ASD and crime has raised the issue of involving child and adolescent psychiatry in preventing youth violence in Japan (Ono and Pumariega 2008). Several high profile cases of violence have been attributed to young people suffering from ASD, which led to Kumagami and Matsuura (2009) describing characteristics of juvenile offenders with ASD from a sample of 28 cases: many of these cases were middle or high school male students with normal intellectual abilities. The majority, however, were diagnosed with PDD/ASD at a juvenile classification home only after they had offended. It seemed that, because these boys attended school and had relatively high IQs, they were overlooked. Over half (57.2%) had one or more adverse childhood experiences, including 30% who had experienced maltreatment.

One reason why ASD may be linked to offending is that it may be comorbid with conduct disorder. A diagnosis of ASD is sometimes overlooked when conduct disorder is present. Harada and colleagues (2009) found that the comorbidity of conduct disorder and ASD among 64 children who were resident in correctional institutions was relatively high compared to previously reported numbers. Those with comorbid conduct disorder and ASD had an early onset, suggesting that their poor prognosis may be attributable to ASD features. Previous research in Japanese has suggested that those with Asperger's Disorder may be violent in personal relationships because of their difficulty in distinguishing between fantasy and reality (Harada et al. 2002).

Research evidence suggests that, often, missed opportunities for accurate diagnosis and treatment may increase a person's likelihood of offending. The young person may be unaware of their troubling behaviour, but by then, it will be too late for early prevention. It seems that proper diagnosis is only prescribed after the young person offends. Treatment is tricky because other childhood risk factors, such as maltreatment, that interact with mental disorder will need to be considered. For example, among adult male repeat offenders diagnosed with ASPD in Fuchu Prison, Tokyo, the prevalence of alcohol dependence was much higher than in the male general population (53% vs. 7%) (Yoshino et al. 2000). This dependence started earlier than that of male inpatients with alcohol dependence but with no diagnosis of ASPD, and the main risk factors were severe childhood conduct disorder and a family history of alcohol dependence.

Schizophrenia

Individuals with severe mental illness are likely to live with and be supported by their families because of the lack of alternative residential options. Approximately between 60 and 85% of those with mental disorders live with family members (Kageyama et al. 2016b). These findings, where violence tends to be experienced by family members and not the general public, are concordant with literature in other countries (Kageyama et al. 2015). Of all severe mental illnesses, schizophrenia has the highest risk of violence against family members.

Schizophrenia is a chronic brain disorder where the individual has trouble differentiating between real and unreal experiences. The symptoms include delusions, hallucinations, trouble in thinking and concentration, and lack of motivation (American Psychiatric Association 2013). From a larger study entitled, 'Japanese Family Violence and Mental Illness', among 302 households that were sampled from the Saitama Prefecture Family Group Association of Persons with Mental Disorders, violence towards a family member was 60.9% over the life course and 27.2% in the past year (Kageyama et al. 2015). From the same larger study, it was found that parents tended to be the caregivers; 58.1% had experienced psychological violence, and 34.8% had experienced physical violence in the past year (Kageyama et al. 2016a). Parents who were rated as highly distressed had almost twice the odds of psychological violence[2] and almost five times the odds of physical violence than parents with low distress. Other risks for distress among parents included low household income, family stigma, and patient's increasing age. It was recommended these risks be considered in hospital discharge and community treatment plans.

Mothers were attacked slightly more often than fathers (51% vs. 47% in the lifetime), but lifetime violence towards fathers and older male siblings were significantly higher from male patients than from female patients (Kageyama et al. 2015). This is likely because male family members were protecting female family members. Compared to other siblings, younger sisters were attacked the most, possibly out of jealousy and because younger sisters may be viewed as the weakest siblings.

Imai and colleagues (2014) conducted a case-control study of Tokyo patients, matching those diagnosed with schizophrenia who had been non-violent to those who had been similarly diagnosed but who had committed violence immediately before emergency hospitalisation. Predictors of violence among those with schizophrenia were auditory hallucinations, incoherence of speech, delusions of reference, the systematisation of delusions, threat/control override symptoms, a long duration of the illness, gross excitement, living with others, and prior violence. Violent acts among those with schizophrenia, they concluded, seemed more associated with elements of the disorder itself, rather than with antisocial traits such as substance abuse and antisocial episodes, which were non-significantly associated with violence.

These findings are different from mainstream understandings of violence, but the difference may be attributable to the comparatively low prevalence of drug use in Japan and to differences in diagnosing patients with psychotic symptoms persisting more than six months from substance use.

---

[2]Verbal or non-verbal communication to cause another person mental or emotional harm.

Gender Differences

Among Japanese female offenders, the prevalence of depression seems high. Their relationship between mental disorder and crime seems to stem from their family circumstances and home life. Previous research on female adolescent inmates (mean age = 17 years) shows high levels of severe depressive symptoms compared to non-incarcerated females (Matsuura et al. 2013). Most of these female inmates were incarcerated for drug or larceny-related crimes. Almost half of these inmates were classified as depressed, possibly having depressive conduct disorder, characterised by loss of interest, hopelessness, sleep disturbances, and altered appetite. Their depression seemed to be related to their prior adverse childhood experiences, aggression, and low self-esteem (Matsuura et al. 2009). Having one or no biological parents (48.1%) was the most reported childhood adverse experience, followed by recurrent physical abuse (27.2%) and having a substance abuser living in the household (24.7%) (Matsuura et al. 2013).

Themes of depressive disorder and family factors are identified for female offenders in gender comparisons: Xie (2000) provided a description of Japanese male and female offenders who had a mental disorder using a population of 2094 official registered mentally ill offenders collected from nationwide surveys in 1980 and 1994. She excluded those with ASPD to reduce confounding and tautological results. This population included not only those convicted, but also those who were acquitted, never charged, or had their sentences reduced.

Compared to males, females were likely to be older at the time of arrest, more educated, married, and socially stable; they were likely to be diagnosed with depression; they tended to have committed fewer crimes previously, but were likely to have been involved in a violent crime, homicide in particular, and their victims were usually family members, often their children. Based on prior criminal records, however, males still committed a larger proportion of violent crimes because they were likely to reoffend.

The enactment of the MTS Act resulted in better access to clinical data for research. Nagata et al. (2016) compared similar characteristics to Xie (2000) between males and females among a sample of 235 offenders, aged 42 years on average, admitted to one specialist forensic mental health facility between July 2005 and October 2013 (13.7% of all MTS inpatients), after the Act went into effect. The female sample comprised 15.4% of the total sample, but the results were consistent with Xie's (2000) previous findings prior to the Act. Women were more likely to be married, have children, and be diagnosed with a mood disorder, compared to men. They had fewer custodial sentences, but were more likely to have committed homicide. Almost half (41.7%) had attempted suicide before their index crime.

Culturally Specific Mental Health Issues

As the norm, prioritising in-groups has its benefits of relative order and safety, as reflected in the low crime rates of official statistics, but it too has its costs. Expectations of conformity in Japan pressure everyone to be like everyone else—a nail that sticks out will be hammered down. To conform is to be rewarded with a social network guaranteed to reciprocate favours and to provide security. In some cases, individuals cannot meet these expectations and the outcome can be devastating. Two prevalent negative outcomes are suicide and social withdrawal, the latter known as *hikikomori*. Both of these relate to violence: suicide questions the traditional definition of violence and hikikomori may increase the risk of family violence.

Suicide

Although Japan is one of the lowest-rated countries for violent crime, it is among the highest in the world for suicide. Among the Organisation for Economic Cooperation and Development (OECD) countries, Japan is the highest (Andrés et al. 2011). Its lethal violence rate, combining homicide and suicide, is higher than that of all industrialised countries (Johnson 2006). As of 2015, suicide was the leading cause of death among people aged 15–29 years (Ministry of Health and Welfare 2016). By gender, suicide is the leading cause of death for males aged 10–44 years and for females aged 15–29 years (Ministry of Health and Welfare 2016).

It was no coincidence that suicide rates spiked from 1997 to 1998, which was the time of the Asian Financial Crisis (Fukuchi et al. 2013). Since 1998, the suicide rate has remained around 25 suicides per 100,000 persons (Tanji et al. 2014). Gender differences in suicide rates have been found to be smaller in Japan and South Korea than in the US and Australia, but in all these countries males had a higher prevalence of suicide than females (Hee Ahn et al. 2012). Hanging was the most common suicide method in these countries except for the US, where males were likely to use firearms and women were likely to use poison. For Japan, the use of hanging increased with age while poisoning decreased with age among both genders.

Why the suicide rate is so high in Japan is not entirely clear. Social tolerance towards the act should be considered. Historically, suicide was seen as 'the ultimate solution to an impossible situation' (Kadonaga and Fraser 2015) and 'a morally responsible action' (Ozawa-de Silva 2008). Factors that have been identified as possible reasons are social isolation, unemployment, financial problems, stressful life events, a personal or family history of suicide, and somatic illnesses (Hirokawa et al. 2012). A large study on risk factors for suicide using data from all 47 prefectures showed a number of gender differences (Ishii et al. 2013). Risk factors in 2007 that predicted suicide in 2008 among males were older age and unemployment, but marriage and annual savings via the Japan Post Bank protected against risk of suicide. For females, unemployment and colder weather (a lower annual mean temperature) were risk factors for suicide.

A strong association also exists between mental disorder and suicide. Hirokawa et al. (2012) conducted the first nationwide case-control study, matching 49 suicide cases to living community residents on similar characteristics. Approximately 65% of suicide cases had been suffering from a mental disorder. Mood disorders and major depressive disorder had the strongest associations with suicide—six to seven times the risk for suicide; disorders of anxiety, alcohol-related, and brief psychosis were also significantly related to suicide. The researchers further noted that more attention should be given to serious chronic physical conditions, as they were pertinent to the increased risk as well. Such conditions impair daily functioning, resulting in social isolation and withdrawal. Similarly, a comparison of adolescent mental health between Japanese, South Korean, and Chinese middle school students revealed feelings of Japanese youth that may put them at risk for depression and suicide (Houri et al. 2012). Compared to the others, Japanese adolescents reported greater feelings of powerlessness, unhappiness about themselves, and poorer interpersonal relationships. They were less likely to reveal family-related worries or vulnerabilities to others.

A couple of studies replicate the finding that social isolation, in particular a lack of familial relationships, for men increases the risk of suicide. Prospective data from the Miyagi prefecture of over 50,000 residents (aged 40–64 years) found that being widowed or divorced increases the risk of suicide among men, whereas these factors did not affect the risk of suicide among women (Fukuchi et al. 2013). Wives are usually seen as the centre of social support, so marriage offered the best protection against suicide risk for men because it offered social and community integration. In another study analysing suicide between 1957 and 2009, divorce was most pertinent as a risk factor for males, whereas for females, low fertility rates increased the risk of suicide (Andrés et al. 2011). In other words, men cannot live without wives, and women found it hard to live without children.

In contrast, the analysis of a number of data sources related to suicide rates between 1947 and 2010 showed that unemployment was the strongest predictor for suicide among men whereas, unexpectedly, a low fertility rate and a high divorce rate protected against suicide among women (Liu et al. 2013). This study addressed previous findings, explaining that male unemployment may lead to divorce and loss of social support while females may receive compensation after separation. Alternatively, factors influencing the suicide may change during different research periods.

A decrease in the risk of suicide for men and women between the ages of 40–69 years can be achieved through social support, as found in a large population study of over 50,000 people (Poudel-Tandukar et al. 2011). For both men and women, having four or more friends to meet once a week was protective against suicide risk, while having someone to support one's opinion and actions was protective for women only. Among young people, the factors may be different.

Using street-intercept techniques to survey Osaka youth (aged 15–24 years), factors associated with attempted suicide were found to be experiences of school bullying and a history of drug use. Specifically for males, low self-esteem and factors related to sexual experiences and sexuality were additional risks (Hidaka et al. 2008).

In some cases, certain individual traits may predispose someone to commit suicide. Tanji et al. (2014) conducted a natural experiment using the Eysenck Personality Questionnaire short form to examine the relationship between personality and suicide before and after the Asian Financial Crisis, which began in July 1997. The personality traits of neuroticism and psychoticism were related to an increased risk of suicide for the entire follow-up period from 1990 to 2008. After 1998, however, the risk of suicide increased for those who were high in neuroticism, while the risk decreased for those high in psychoticism. It was thought that those high in neuroticism were more susceptible to social stress which in turn led to developing depression; these findings were not explained by occupation or marital status. A 10-year follow-up of a representative sample of 70,213 individuals, aged 50–79 years, revealed that those who blamed themselves for or avoided their problems were more likely to commit suicide (Svensson et al. 2014). Those who attempted to solve their daily problems through planning, however, had a lower risk of committing suicide.

Motohashi (2011) summarises initiatives the Japanese government has implemented for suicide prevention: counselling and education programmes; publicity campaigns and commercials; dissemination of WHO guidelines for proper reporting of suicides; support for relatives of those who had committed suicide; controlling access to dangerous places and drugs; community-based programmes that emphasise civic participation and address poor mental health; commissioning of academic research and evaluation of suicide prevention measures; and increase in mental welfare volunteer activities. Evaluated initiatives have shown success in reducing suicide rates within towns. Plans to address mental disorder and suicide through better coordination between psychiatrists and medical doctors have been highlighted in the Plan to Accelerate Suicide Prevention Measures. Motohashi recommended that increased public knowledge would help in reducing stigma, and therefore encourage those who need psychiatric treatment to seek help. The most important conclusion was that a multidisciplinary and inter-professional approach was needed to create comprehensive suicide prevention.

Fujimoto and Park (1994) had questioned the 'safe society' reputation of Japan. Although interpersonal violence rates are low, the self-directed violence rate is very high—is Japan really a safe place if the risk of being stabbed by someone else is low, but the risk of stabbing yourself is high?

Hikikomori

Sociocultural changes in Japan are thought to contribute to *hikikomori*, which refers to complete social withdrawal for six months or more (Kato et al. 2012). Suwa and Suzuki (2013) believe that the phenomenon is attributed to a decline in conformity, face-to-face social interactions, and economic growth. The term first appeared in the mid-1980s, coined by Tomita Fujiya, the founder of *Friend Space*, a counselling centre for hikikomori (Horiguchi 2012). Fujiya understood hikikomori to be a psychological condition where one wants to have contact with others but finds that one cannot establish these social connections. The syndrome was first described in Japan and it was thought that it was culturally specific as well. A study using two case vignettes and questionnaires distributed to 239 clinicians in nine countries,[3] however, suggests that cases of hikikomori exist in urban areas in Asia, Australia, and the US (Kato et al. 2012).

A 'psycho-sociological phenomenon', hikikomori occurs among those under 30 years of age (Tajan 2015). Typically it affects adolescent males who avoid social contact by staying indoors. Onset is usually during adolescence or early adulthood, and cases first appear to clinicians, on average, four years after the start of the condition (Kato et al. 2016b).

---

[3]123 from Japan, 34 from South Korea, 22 from Australia, 19 from Taiwan, 10 each from Bangladesh, Iran, India, and the US, and 9 from Thailand.

The social withdrawal occurs when individuals have either graduated or dropped out from high school or university, and do not take up employment. Instead, they sever social contact and confine themselves to the family home (Suwa and Suzuki 2013). In some cases, they shut themselves away in their bedrooms and do not speak to family members.

Many hikikomori cases begin as school refusal, but in other cases, they may begin much later in life (Borovoy 2008). Hikikomori differs from school refusal in that it tends to affect adults and the withdrawal is unrelated to the school or its environment. A typical case of hikikomori is illustrated in this case study from Kato et al. (2016b):

> "Mr. T" is a 39-year-old unemployed man living with his parents. For the past 19 years, he has spent the vast majority of his time restricted to his room. He has never worked and describes his attitude toward life as "taking it easy". Video games and online shopping help him pass the time. At one point several years ago, his online shopping habits caused the equivalent of tens of thousands of dollars of debt. He views his parents' home as a complimentary hotel of sorts, with his parents tending to his basic needs. Mr. T's mother, a homemaker, prepares meals for him daily. Financially, he has supported his lifestyle with ongoing funds from his wealthy grandfather and, more recently, his father's retirement pension. When asked why he rarely leaves his home, his primary explanation is that he does not want to be seen by others, particularly in light of his lack of accomplishments... he lacked the motivation to obtain a job, and it was during this period that he began withdrawing into his room... At age 28, Mr. T's sister's health declined, and their mother began focusing her energies on her care, which led to Mr. T suddenly becoming physically aggressive toward his mother. (112)

The case of Mr. T highlights that violence may occur against family members from those with hikikomori. This is likely attributable to the kind of family dynamics and circumstances involved. In fact, a systematic review identified maladaptive parenting and family dysfunction as critical factors that lead to the development of hikikomori (Li and Wong 2015). In the case of Mr. T, the psychiatrists highlighted the overly dependent relationship between Mr. T and his mother, and the non-existent relationship he had with his absent father. The patient relied on his mother to provide him with food, shelter, and clothing, and that was why Mr. T had become jealous and angry when his sister received more care from their mother.

Related to hikikomori is a form of depression thought to be unique to Japanese youth, although it is not recognised officially (Kato et al. 2016a). Referred to as 'modern type depression' (MTD), it is described as comprising the following characteristics: (a) distress and reluctance to accept social norms; (b) avoidance of effort and rigorous work; and (c) the majority of sufferers are born after 1970, growing up during the era of Japan's high economic growth. The condition was denoted as MTD because psychiatrists in Japan had trouble in applying it to existing criteria in the ICD-10 and DSM-IV. Immature personalities are acknowledged to be an important factor for MTD. Whether this is an actual, distinct, and culturally bound condition is up for debate, but it relates to the manifestation of hikikomori.

Both conditions, MTD and hikikomori, are prevailing social problems among young people and are considered, to some extent, consequences of unhealthy family dynamics. These dynamics are prone to arise in Japan because of family relationships that stress interdependence, especially between the mother and child. Unlike in Western cultures where dependence is discouraged in children so that they become autonomous adults, dependence is encouraged in Japan so that children learn the life-long skill of fostering strong interpersonal relationships. Interdependent family relationships that have gone awry, as seen in cases of school refusal and hikikomori, may lead to filial violence.

Masataka (2002) observes that psychiatrists are unclear why exactly adolescents suffer from hikikomori, but they understand the context which produces it: pressure to be like everyone else. This pressure begins early in life. In a sample of 200 preschool children from 20 different classrooms in the Tokyo metropolitan area, the pressure to conform led to strong emotional control in the presence of interpersonal conflict (Masataka 2002). This may result in bottled up distress, which contributes to the hikikomori phenomenon. This may be why conduct disorder is less prevalent in Japan compared to countries like the US, because overt aggressive behaviour is strongly discouraged.

As a consequence, anger is suppressed. In a comparison of children in the US and Japan, Japanese children were less likely to externalise their blame as they were more inclined to experience shame and guilt (Bear et al. 2009). Japanese children were also more likely to experience anger. The result was attributed to the measure of anger: it was referred to experience and not to expression. The study considered that Japanese children were expected to self-regulate their emotions, and though they may experience anger, they were less prone to express it. This, however, has a negative side as the study discussed suicide, which was often linked to intense shame. Additionally worth noting is that suppressing the expression of anger may apply more to the public than to the private sphere.

Social withdrawal is thought to be indicative of other mental disorders such as depression or social anxiety disorder, but, because of its substantial prevalence, some researchers consider that social withdrawal is a separate mental disorder (Tajan 2015). Whether hikikomori is actually a mental disorder is controversial (Tajan 2015). What it is classed as, however, has implications for treatment. Support centres that often provide telephone consultation have been available since 2000 (Kato et al. 2016b). Psychiatrists use a variety of effective psychotherapeutic techniques such as group and family therapy, to treat hikikomori (Kato et al. 2012). Home visits have also proved effective in reducing violent behaviour. Some psychiatrists, however, believe that no psychiatric treatment is necessary and this view may be the result of the normalisation of hikikomori in Japanese society, as the syndrome has existed for a while. One promising proposal has been to use the game software, Pokémon Go, in an intervention, as it forces its players to go outside and communicate with other anonymous players (Tateno et al. 2016).

Challenges to Addressing Mental Disorder and Reoffending

Reoffending

The goal of the MTS Act, according to Nakatani (2012), is what distinguishes forensic mental health care in Japan from that of Western, industrialised countries. The MTS Act gives foremost priority to the reintegration into society of offenders with a mental disorder, whereas forensic mental health legislation in many European countries originated from the era of 'institutionalisation', which prioritised the notion of 'public protection from dangerous and unstable people' over the notion of 'providing treatment to people suffering from mental disorder'. Although the system of forensic mental health care introduced by the Act is a vast improvement, there are still issues to address.

One particular issue is reoffending, or recidivism. Because the Act focuses on rehabilitation, less attention has been given to the risk of reoffending. Indeed, according to Nakatani (2012), the guidelines for psychiatric evaluation do not specify the rates of reoffending as a condition of treatment. Its exclusion from the Act was the result of uncertainty over the predictive accuracy for reoffending. The government had originally suggested a hospital treatment order for anyone with a mental disorder who was at risk of committing a similar offence in the future. Now, however, it is unclear how successful these treatment orders are in reintegrating offenders with mental disorder into the community. In addition, no criteria exist under the MTS Act for admission based on recidivism risk. Risk assessments may be useful to evaluate whether treatment, as implemented by the MTS Act, is effective in reintegration and preventing recidivism. Assessments may also be useful for evaluating who is in need of more intensive treatment based on recidivism risk, monitoring progress, and as a way of identifying and targeting risk factors.

Data from a four-year survey, between 2005 and 2009, was used to identify risk factors for problematic behaviour, such as violence, substance abuse, and medical non-compliance, in 441 forensic outpatients (Ando et al. 2016). Risk factors included a positive diagnosis of substance misuse and having a history of being an inpatient. These types of nationwide studies will help to provide information for comprehensive and useful clinical guidelines in future revisions and updates of the MTS Act treatment system. One issue is that, although the MTS Act addresses forensic mental health needs, the number of psychiatrists who specialise in forensic mental health in Japan is low (Haraguchi et al. 2011). As a result, evaluations under the MTS Act may be conducted by general psychiatrists with little or no experience of forensic evaluations. Another problem is the exclusion of offenders with PDs. The omission of these offenders may be related to the low recidivism rate among offenders under the MTS Act (Fujii et al. 2014). Particular PDs such as ASPD and psychopathy are strongly related to criminal behaviour, and will need further investigation.

Stigma

The stigma associated with mental disorders may act as a barrier to treatment, especially for those who are suicidal (Desapriya and Iwase 2003). Even among the family, stigmatising attitudes were found to increase the risk of distress when caring for a family member with schizophrenia (Kageyama et al. 2016a). Comparisons to Western countries show that there is a higher prevalence of stigma towards people with mental disorders in Japan (Griffiths et al. 2006). A review of peer-reviewed studies since 2001 on stigmatisation towards mental disorder among the Japanese showed that most people thought that a weakness of personality caused mental disorder rather than biological factors, and that mental disorder could not be treated (Ando et al. 2013). Stigmatising attitudes among young Japanese (aged 15–18 years) towards people with mental disorder tend to be highest for schizophrenia and lowest for social phobia (Yoshioka et al. 2014). Males are more likely to have these attitudes than females, and mentally ill people were mainly perceived as weak and not sick, and as dangerous or unpredictable.

Attitudes may reflect stereotypes because of several murders by individuals who may have been diagnosed with schizophrenia in the late 1980s (Aoki et al. 2016). Part of the problem was believed to be the term used for schizophrenia. The old term, translated as 'Mind-Split Disease', was thought to lead to public misunderstanding and the unintentional association with criminality. The new term, introduced by the Japanese Society of Psychiatry and Neurology and translated as 'integration disorder', has been shown to be more associated with 'victim' than with 'criminal' (Takahashi et al. 2009). An investigation of news reports on schizophrenia and bipolar disorder before and after the name change found that, after the use of integration disorder, there was a significant decrease of reports on schizophrenia and danger, whereas an increase in reports associating bipolar disorder and danger was observed during the study period (Aoki et al. 2016). This could be the consequence of more awareness of mental disorder, which may lead to more prejudice towards certain types.

Borovoy (2008) uses the phenomenon of *hikikomori* as an example of Japan's views on mental disorder. The emphasis on mainstreaming and inclusion over individual rights, she argues, produces a kind of 'anti-psychology and psychiatry' societal attitude that views individual differences and distress as issues that are easily corrected by self-discipline and better coping and social skills. This is particularly prevalent in education and mental health care. Learning and development are considered to be shaped primarily by the environment, and little acknowledgement is given to innate abilities and predispositions. Measures that are perceived to marginalise, distinguish, or remove young people from mainstream society are avoided. A healthy and productive society is seen as one that promotes equality and shared social values. Borovoy observes that the stigma of mental disorder results in the refusal of doctors to diagnose individuals with any major disorder if possible, and mental health is viewed as the maintenance of positive attitudes. Psychiatrists tend to use terms that imply that conditions are caused externally, such as 'depressive state' instead of 'depression' or 'depressive illness'. Hikikomori could be seen as the consequence of individuals who are inadequately supported. Their psychological issues go unaddressed so they try their best to meet societal expectations but, ultimately, they retreat.

Conclusion

The recognition of crucial gaps in addressing forensic mental health has led to the implementation of the MTS Act. As part of the Act, forensic psychiatrists who work with offenders who are diagnosed with a mental disorder tend to be involved in assessing their criminal responsibility (Shiina et al. 2017). The likely diagnosis of these offenders tends to be schizophrenia. This could be why there is more of an association between offender and schizophrenia in Japan than with other mental disorders, and why the stigma of mental illness tends to be attributed to those with schizophrenia. From a public health viewpoint, other issues of mental health related to violence, particularly suicide and tôkôkyohi, should also be continually addressed.

References

American Psychiatric Association. 2013. *Diagnostic and Statistical Manual of Mental Disorders*. Washington, DC: Author.

Ando, Shuntaro, Sosei Yamaguchi, and Graham Thornicroft. 2013. "Review of Mental-Health-Related Stigma in Japan." *Psychiatry and Clinical Neuroscience* 67: 471–82.

Ando, Kumiko, Takahiro Soshi, Kanako Nakazawa, Takamasa Noda, and Takayuki Okada. 2016. "Risk Factors for Problematic Behaviors Among Forensic Outpatients Under the Medical Treatment and Supervision Act in Japan." *Frontiers in Psychiatry* 7 (144): 1–12.

Andrés, Antonio R., Ferda Halicioglu, and Eiji Yamamura. 2011. "Socio-Economic Determinants of Suicide in Japan." *Journal of Socio-Economics* 40 (6): 723–31.

Aoki, Ai, Yuta Aoki, Robert Goulden, Kiyoto Kasai, Graham Thornicroft, and Claire Henderson. 2016. "Change in Newspaper Coverage of Schizophrenia in Japan Over 20-Year Period." *Schizophrenia Research* 175 (1–3): 193–97.

Banner, Natalie F. 2013. "Mental Disorders Are Not Brain Disorders." *Journal of Evaluation in Clinical Practice* 19: 509–13.

Bear, George G., Ximena Uribe-Zarain, Maureen A. Manning, and Kunio Shiomi. 2009. "Shame, Guilt, Blaming, and Anger: Differences Between Children in Japan and the US." *Motivation and Emotion* 33 (3): 229–38.

Borovoy, Amy. 2008. "Japan's Hidden Youths: Mainstreaming the Emotionally Distressed in Japan." *Culture, Medicine, and Psychiatry* 32: 552–76.

Bruce, Matt, Deborah Cobb, Holly Clisby, David Ndegwa, and Sheilagh Hodgins. 2014. "Violence and Crime Among Male Inpatients with Severe Mental Illness: Attempting to Explain Ethnic Differences." *Social Psychiatry and Psychiatric Epidemiology* 49 (4): 549–58.

Chandler, Redonna K., Roger H. Peters, Gary Field, and Denise Juliano-Bult. 2004. "Challenges in Implementing Evidence-Based Treatment Practices for Co-occurring Disorders in the Criminal Justice System." *Behavioral Sciences and the Law* 22 (4): 431–48.

Desapriya, Ediriweera, and Nobutada Iwase. 2003. "New Trends in Suicide in Japan." *Injury Prevention* 9: 284–87.

Farrington, David P. 2004. "Conduct Disorder, Aggression and Delinquency." In *Handbook of Adolescent Psychology*, edited by Richard M. Lerner and Laurence Steinberg, 683–722. Chichester: Wiley.

Fazel, Seena, and John Danesh. 2002. "Serious Mental Disorder in 23000 Prisoners: A Systematic Review of 62 Surveys." *Lancet* 359 (9306): 545–50.

Fazel, Seena, and Rongqin Yu. 2011. "Psychotic Disorders and Repeat Offending: Systematic Review and Meta-Analysis." *Schizophrenia Bulletin* 37 (4): 800–810.

Fujii, Chiyo, Yusuke Fukuda, Kumiko Ando, Akiko Kikuchi, and Takayuki Okada. 2014. "Development of Forensic Mental Health Services in Japan: Working Towards the Reintegration of Offenders with Mental Disorders." *International Journal of Mental Health Systems* 8 (21): 1–11.

Fujimoto, Tetsuya, and Won-Kyu Park. 1994. "Is Japan Exceptional? Reconsidering Japanese Crime Rates." *Social Justice* 21 (2 (56)): 110–35.

Fukuchi, Naru, Masako Kakizaki, Yumi Sugawara, Fumiya Tanji, and Ikue Watanabe. 2013. "Association of Marital Status with the Incidence of Suicide: A Population-Based Cohort Study in Japan (Miyagi Cohort Study)." *Journal of Affective Disorders* 150 (3): 879–85.

Griffiths, Kathleen M., Yoshibumi Nakane, Helen Christensen, Kumiko Yoshioka, Anthony F. Jorm, and Hideyuki Nakane. 2006. "Stigma in Response to Mental Disorders: A Comparison of Australia and Japan." *BMC Psychiatry* 6 (21): 1–12.

Harada, Yuzuru, Yuri Satoh, and Ayako Sakuma. 2002. "Behavioral and Developmental Disorders Among Conduct Disorder." *Psychiatry and Clinical Neurosciences* 56: 621–25.

Harada, Yuzuru, Ayako Hayashida, Shouko Hikita, Junko Imai, Daimei Sasayama, Sari Masutani, Taku Tomita, Kazuhiko Saitoh, Shinsuke Washizuka, and Naoji Amano. 2009. "Impact of Behavioral/Developmental Disorders Comorbid with Conduct Disorder." *Psychiatry and Clinical Neurosciences* 63 (6): 762–68.

Haraguchi, Tadashi, Mihisa Fujisaki, Akihiro Shiina, Yoshito Igarashi, Naoe Okamura, Goro Fukami, Tetsuya Shiraishi, Michiko Nakazato, and Masaomi Iyo. 2011. "Attitudes of Japanese Psychiatrists Toward Forensic Mental Health as Revealed by a National Survey." *Psychiatry and Clinical Neurosciences* 65 (2): 150–57.

Hee Ahn, Myung, Subin Park, Kyooseob Ha, Soon Ho Choi, and Jin Pyo Hong. 2012. "Gender Ratio Comparisons of the Suicide Rates and Methods in Korea, Japan, Australia, and the United States." *Journal of Affective Disorders* 142 (1–3): 161–65.

Hidaka, Yasuharu, Don Operario, Mie Takenaka, Sachiko Omori, Seiichi Ichikawa, and Takuma Shirasaka. 2008. "Attempted Suicide and Associated Risk Factors Among Youth in Urban Japan." *Social Psychiatry and Psychiatric Epidemiology* 43 (9): 752–57.

Hirokawa, Seiko, Norito Kawakami, Toshihiko Matsumoto, and Akiko Inagaki. 2012. "Mental Disorders and Suicide in Japan: A Nation-Wide Psychological Autopsy Case—Control Study." *Journal of Affective Disorders* 140 (2): 168–75.

Horiguchi, Sachiko. 2012. "Hikikomori: How Private Isolation Caught the Public Eye." In *A Sociology of Japanese Youth: From Returnees to NEETs*, edited by Roger Goodman, Yuki Imoto, and Tuukka Toivonen, 122–38. New York: Routledge.

Houri, Daisuke, Eun Woo Nam, Eun Hee Choe, Liu Zhong Min, and Kenji Matsumoto. 2012. "The Mental Health of Adolescent School Children: A Comparison Among Japan, Korea, and China." *Global Health Promotion* 19 (3): 32–41.

Imai, Atsushi, Naoki Hayashi, Akihiro Shiina, Noriko Sakikawa, and Yoshito Igarashi. 2014. "Factors Associated with Violence Among Japanese Patients with Schizophrenia Prior to Psychiatric Emergency Hospitalization: A Case-Controlled Study." *Schizophrenia Research* 160 (1–3): 27–32.

Ishii, Nobuyoshi, Takeshi Terao, Yasuo Araki, Kentaro Kohno, Yoshinori Mizokami, Masano Arasaki, and Noboru Iwata. 2013. "Risk Factors for Suicide in Japan: A Model of Predicting Suicide in 2008 by Risk Factors of 2007." *Journal of Affective Disorders* 147 (1–3): 352–54.

Ishikawa, H., Norito Kawakami, and Ronald C. Keslser. 2016. "Lifetime and 12-Month Prevalence, Severity and Unmet Need for Treatment of Common Mental Disorders in Japan: Results from the Final Dataset of World Mental Health Japan Survey." *Epidemiology and Psychiatric Services* 25 (3): 217–29.

Johnson, David T. 2006. "The Vanishing Killer: Japan's Postwar Homicide Decline." *Social Science Japan Journal* 9 (1): 73–90.

Kadonaga, Tomoko, and Mark W. Fraser. 2015. "Child Maltreatment in Japan." *Journal of Social Work* 15 (3): 233–53.

Kageyama, Masako, Keiko Yokoyama, Satoko Nagata, Sachiko Kita, Yukako Nakamura, Sayaka Kobayashi, and Phyllis Solomon. 2015. "Rate of Family Violence Among Patients with Schizophrenia in Japan." *Asia-Pacific Journal of Public Health* 27: 652–60.

Kageyama, Masako, Phyllis Solomon, and Keiko Yokoyama. 2016a. "Archives of Psychiatric Nursing Psychological Distress and Violence Towards Parents of Patients with Schizophrenia." *Archives of Psychiatric Nursing* 30 (5): 614–19.

Kageyama, Masako, Phyllis Solomon, Sachiko Kita, Satoko Nagata, Keiko Yokoyama, Yukako Nakamura, Sayaka Kobayashi, and Chiyo Fujii. 2016b. "Factors Related to Physical Violence Experienced by Parents of Persons with Schizophrenia in Japan." *Psychiatry Research* 243: 439–45.

Kato, Takahiro A., Masaru Tateno, Naotaka Shinfuku, Daisuke Fujisawa, Alan R. Teo, and Norman Sartorius. 2012. "Does the 'Hikikomori' Syndrome of Social Withdrawal Exist Outside Japan? A Preliminary International Investigation." *Social Psychiatry and Psychiatric Epidemiology* 47: 1061–75.

Kato, Takahiro A., Ryota Hashimoto, and Kohei Hayakawa. 2016a. "Japan: A Proposal for a Different Diagnostic Approach to Depression Beyond the DSM-5." *Psychiatry and Clinical Neurosciences* 70: 7–23.

Kato, Takahiro A., Shigenobu Kanba, and Alan R. Teo. 2016b. "A 39-Year-Old 'Adolescent': Understanding Social Withdrawal in Japan." *American Journal of Psychiatry* 173 (2): 112–14.

Kumagami, Takashi, and Naomi Matsuura. 2009. "Prevalence of Pervasive Developmental Disorder in Juvenile Court Cases in Japan." *Journal of Forensic Psychiatry & Psychology* 20 (6): 974–87.

Li, Tim M. H., and Paul W. C. Wong. 2015. "Youth Social Withdrawal Behavior (Hikikomori): A Systematic Review of Qualitative and Quantitative Studies." *Australian and New Zealand Journal of Psychiatry* 49 (7): 595–609.

Liu, Yan, Ying Zhang, Y. T. Choc, Yoshihide Obayashia, Asuna Arai, and Hiko Tamashiroa. 2013. "Gender Differences of Suicide in Japan, 1947–2010." *Journal of Affective Disorders* 151 (1): 325–30.

Masataka, Nobuo. 2002. "Low Anger-Aggression and Anxiety-Withdrawal Characteristic to Preschoolers in Japanese Society Where 'Hikikomori' Is Becoming a Major Social Problem." *Early Education and Development* 13 (2): 187–200.

Matsuura, Naomi, Toshiaki Hashimoto, and Motomi Toichi. 2009. "Correlations Among Self-Esteem, Aggression, Adverse Childhood Experiences and Depression in Inmates of a Female Juvenile Correctional Facility in Japan." *Psychiatry and Clinical Neurosciences* 63 (4): 478–85.

Matsuura, Naomi, Toshiaki Hashimoto, and Motomi Toichi. 2013. "Associations Among Adverse Childhood Experiences, Aggression, Depression, and Self-Esteem in Serious Female Juvenile Offenders in Japan." *Journal of Forensic Psychiatry & Psychology* 24 (1): 111–27.

Ministry of Health and Welfare Japan. 2016. "Vital Statistics 2015." Tokyo: Author.

Monahan, John. 2002. "The MacArthur Studies of Violence Risk." *Criminal Behavior and Mental Health* 12: 67–72.

Motohashi, Yutaka. 2011. "Suicide in Japan." *The Lancet* 379 (9823): 1282–83.

Murray, Joseph, and David P. Farrington. 2010. "Risk Factors for Conduct Disorder and Delinquency: Key Findings from Longitudinal Studies." *The Canadian Journal of Psychiatry* 55 (10): 633–42.

Nagata, Takako, Atsuo Nakagawa, Satoko Matsumoto, Akihiro Shiina, Masaomi Iyo, Naotsugu Hirabayashi, and Yoshito Igarashi. 2016. "Characteristics of Female Mentally Disordered Offenders Culpable Under the New Legislation in Japan: A Gender Comparison Study." *Criminal Behaviour and Mental Health* 26 (1): 50–58.

Nakane, Yoshibumi, and Hideyuki Nakane. 2002. "Classification Systems for Psychiatric Diseases Currently Used in Japan." *Psychopathology* 35: 191–94.

Nakatani, Yoji. 2012. "Challenges in Interfacing Between Forensic and General Mental Health: A Japanese Perspective." *International Journal of Law and Psychiatry* 35 (5–6): 406–11.

Nakatani, Yoji, Miwa Kojimoto, Saburo Matsubara, and Isao Takayanagi. 2010. "New Legislation for Offenders with Mental Disorders in Japan." *International Journal of Law and Psychiatry* 33 (1): 7–12.

National Institute of Mental Health. 2015. "Autism Spectrum Disorder." Accessed 15 August 2017. https://www.nimh.nih.gov/health/topics/autism-spectrum-disorders-asd/index.shtml.

Ono, Yoshiro, and Andres J. Pumariega. 2008. "Violence in Youth." *International Review of Psychiatry* 20 (3): 305–16.

Ozawa-de Silva, Chikako. 2008. "Too Lonely to Die Alone: Internet Suicide Pacts and Existential Suffering in Japan." *Culture, Medicine, and Psychiatry* 32 (4): 516–51.

Poudel-Tandukar, Kalpana, Akiko Nanri, Tetsuya Mizoue, Yumi Matsushita, Yoshihiko Takahashi, Mitsuhiko Noda, Manami Inoue, and Shoichiro Tsugane. 2011. "Social Support and Suicide in Japanese Men and Women—The Japan Public Health Center (JPHC)-Based Prospective Study." *Journal of Psychiatric Research* 45 (12): 1545–50.

Shiina, Akihiro, Aika Tomoto, Soichiro Omiya, Aiko Sato, Masaomi Iyo, and Yoshito Igarashi. 2017. "Differences Between British and Japanese Perspectives on Forensic Mental Health Systems: A Preliminary Study." *World Journal of Psychiatry* 7 (1): 8–11.

Shin, Young, Eric Fombonne, Yun-Joo Koh, Soo-Jeong Kim, Keun-Ah Cheon, and Bennett L. Leventhal. 2014. "A Comparison of DSM-IV Pervasive Developmental Disorder and DSM-5 Autism Spectrum Disorder Prevalence in an Epidemiologic Sample." *Journal of the American Academy of Child and Adolescent Psychiatry* 53 (5): 500–508.

Stuart, Heather. 2003. "Violence and Mental Illness: An Overview." *World Psychiatry* 2 (2): 121–24.

Suwa, Mami, and Kunifumi Suzuki. 2013. "The Phenomenon of 'Hikikomori' (Social Withdrawal) and the Socio-Cultural Situation in Japan Today." *Journal of Psychopathology* 19 (3): 191–98.

Svensson, Thomas, Manami Inoue, Hadrien Charvat, Norie Sawada, Motoki Iwasaki, Shizuka Sasazuki, Taichi Shimazu, et al. 2014. "Coping Behaviors and Suicide in the Middle-Aged and Older Japanese General Population: The Japan Public Health Center-Based Prospective Study." *Annals of Epidemiology* 24: 199–205.

Tajan, Nicolas. 2015. "Social Withdrawal and Psychiatry: A Comprehensive Review of Hikikomori." *Neuropsychiatrie de L'enfance et de L'adolescence* 63: 324–31.

Takahashi, Hidehiko, Takashi Ideno, Shigetaka Okubo, Hiroshi Matsui, Kazuhisa Takemura, Masato Matsuura, Motoichiro Kato, and Yoshiro Okubo. 2009. "Impact of Changing the Japanese Term for 'Schizophrenia' for Reasons of Stereotypical Beliefs of Schizophrenia in Japanese Youth." *Schizophrenia Research* 112 (1–3): 149–52.

Tanji, Fumiya, Masako Kakizaki, Yumi Sugawara, Ikue Watanabe, Naoki Nakaya, Yuko Minami, Akira Fukao, and Ichiro Tsuji. 2014. "Personality and Suicide Risk: The Impact of Economic Crisis in Japan." *Psychological Medicine* 45 (3): 559–73.

Tateno, Masaru, Norbert Skokauskas, Takahiro A. Kato, Alan R. Teo, and Anthony P. S. Guerrero. 2016. "New Game Software (Pokémon Go) May Help Youth with Severe Social Withdrawal, Hikikomori." *Psychiatry Research* 246: 848–49.

Van Dorn, Richard, Jan Volavka, and Norman Johnson. 2012. "Mental Disorder and Violence: Is There a Relationship Beyond Substance Use?" *Social Psychiatry and Psychiatric Epidemiology* 47 (3): 487–503.

Watanabe, Norio. 2016. "Low Prevalence Rates of Common Mental Disorders in Japan: Does It Still Hold True?" *Epidemiology and Psychiatric Services* 25: 233–34.

Wibbelink, Carlijn J. M., Machteld Hoeve, Geert Jan J. M. Stams, and Frans J. Oort. 2017. "A Meta-Analysis of the Association Between Mental Disorders and Juvenile Recidivism." *Aggression and Violent Behavior* 33: 78–90.

World Health Organization. 1992. "The ICD-10 Classification of Mental and Behavioural Disorders Clinical Descriptions and Diagnostic Guidelines." Geneva: Author.

Xie, Liya. 2000. "Gender Difference in Mentally Ill Offenders: A Nationwide Japanese Study." *International Journal of Offender Therapy and Comparative Criminology* 44 (6): 714–24.

Yoshikawa, Kazuo, Pamela J. Taylor, Akira Yamagami, Takayuki Okada, Kumiko Ando, and Toshihiro Taruya. 2007. "Violent Recidivism Among Mentally Disordered Offenders in Japan." *Criminal Behaviour and Mental Health* 151: 137–51.

Yoshino, Aihide, Taihei Fukuhara, and Motoichiro Kato. 2000. "Premorbid Risk Factors for Alcohol Dependence in Antisocial Personality Disorder." *Alcoholism: Clinical and Experimental Research* 24 (I): 35–38.

Yoshioka, Kumiko, Nicola J. Reavley, Andrew J. Mackinnon, and Anthony F. Jorm. 2014. "Stigmatising Attitudes Towards People with Mental Disorders: Results from a Survey of Japanese High School Students." *Psychiatry Research* 215 (1): 229–36.

Yu, Rongqin, John R. Geddes, and Seena Fazel. 2012. "Personality Disorders, Violence, and Antisocial Behavior: A Systematic Review and Meta-Regression Analysis." *Journal of Personality Disorders* 26 (5): 775–92.

8

Biosocial Interactions

The notion of the 'born criminal' makes many criminologists wary. The assumption was that there were genetically inferior and superior groups of people; those born with 'bad' genes, a circumstance beyond their control, were fated to live a life harming others and society. The solution was that these people should be eradicated. This was exactly the logic of Nazi Germany, which advanced eugenic measures against Jews and anyone thought inferior to the Aryan race—ideas based on dubious history and evidence. Japan during the Second World War, as an ally of Germany, also involved itself in the eugenics movement by enacting the National Eugenics Law (Yokoyama 2013).

This legacy has left a substantial 'stink' on the study of biological explanations for crime. Early biological findings also had major short-comings: they were unscientific, unicausal, and simplistic (Fishbein 1990). Biological theorists were no better as they failed to present a rational explanation for criminal behaviour.

The big misconception is that biology is destiny. Raine (2002b) believes that it is possible to change biological predispositions that influence violence. Many of these changes are nonthreatening because they focus on health and nutrition, so success in crime prevention can be considerably enhanced if biological factors are included. Biological

© The Author(s) 2019
L. Bui and D. P. Farrington, *Crime in Japan*, Palgrave Advances in Criminology and Criminal Justice in Asia, https://doi.org/10.1007/978-3-030-14097-7_8

factors have been identified in twin and adoption studies and they include genes, psychophysiology, brain impairments, birth complications, nutrition, and neurochemistry (Raine 2002b).

In recent decades, research on biological factors has gained sophistication and more consideration of the social context. Specific genetic polymorphisms can be isolated and patterns of brain functioning can be observed (Rocque et al. 2014). Findings indicate that biology alone does not influence behaviour, but they do so in interaction with the environment. For a while now, science has known a number of things about the environment and, specifically, genes (Hannay 2015): children can inherit both from their parents; genes can motivate people to change their environments; and, in particular, the environment can alter the effects of our genes. Genes themselves do not produce behaviour but are responsible for constructing the brain that produces our behaviour. To add to this, our brains are malleable. They adapt and respond to everyday experiences that can cause biological changes within them. No longer is the debate between nature and nurture in criminology: it is now about nurture versus biosocial interactions.

The idea of a biosocial approach is nothing new. Sir Leon Radzinowicz (1999), a pioneer of British criminology, had advocated this approach almost twenty years ago: 'There is still the need for mental readjustment on the part of researchers in sorting out the often deep schism between those attaching a greater weight to individual disposition and those emphasising environmental conditioning. These two influences are in fact interconnected, constantly interacting: a complex relationship varying not only between broad categories of offences, but even within particular offences' (p. 450). It seems baffling that the nature versus nurture debate was able to exist for such a long time as a neat dichotomy and a point of contention among scholars, but Radzinowicz (1999) believed that the controversy exasperated issues on how best to approach social and educational policy that it hindered the two sides from working together. But there now seems to be some progress.

A basic tenet of psychology is that the interaction between the individual and the environment produces behaviour (Farrington and Jolliffe

2015). Likewise, the biosocial approach to crime assumes that human behaviour is the result of a complex interaction between biological and environmental factors. According to Pinker (2015), gene-environment interactions do not mean that the environment is required for genes to function. Rather it refers to the observation that genes will affect someone's behaviour in one way in one environment and in another way in a different environment.

These interactions can be divided into five areas (Barnes and Boutwell 2015): (1) Evolutionary criminology; (2) Bio/physiological criminology; (3) Molecular genetics; (4) Behaviourial genetics; and (5) Neurocriminology. The fifth area, neurocriminology, is meant to bring the four other areas together in explaining how environmental, biological, and genetic factors influence behaviour via their impact on brain functioning. An obstacle in the study of antisocial behaviour, especially in criminology, is the lack of integration of findings among disciplines. Raine (2005) argues that interdisciplinary rivalries between genetic, biological, psychological, and social perspectives have hindered progress in the study of antisocial and aggressive behaviour. The reluctance of criminologists to accept biological explanations is unusual when few psychologists or psychiatrists would deny their relevance in understanding crime (Raine 2002b). Biological approaches, however, are now making more inroads into criminology, as evidenced by the new Division of Biopsychosocial Criminology of the American Society of Criminology.

To date, two main conclusions may be drawn from patterns of biosocial interactions (Raine 2005): first, when biological and social risk factors influence antisocial behaviour, the presence of both factors increases the likelihood of antisocial behaviour more than if only one type of factor was present. Second, when biological functioning is the outcome, social factors will moderate the relationship between antisocial behaviour and biology, so that this relationship will be strongest in harmless social environments. We will now look at this in more detail.

Biological factors are likely be most important in explaining antisocial behaviour for children who lack social risks, whereas biological factors will be less prominent in explaining antisocial behaviour if a child has been exposed to an adverse early home environment. The example Raine (2002a) gives is that any biological risk will be more noticeable in children who live in a benign home environment, whereas social risks will be more obvious in children who live in an unfavourable home environment such as being raised in poverty or who have a parent who has been imprisoned. This is known as the social push hypothesis: no social factors are present to *push* an individual towards antisocial behaviour from benign home backgrounds, and that is why biology tends to better explain antisocial behaviour for these individuals. For example, low resting heart rate may be a stronger characteristic of antisocial individuals from privileged middle-class backgrounds with intact families.

There is little research on the biosocial approach in Japan, and this is probably because most Japanese criminologists were trained as sociologists. While there seem to be no studies explicitly identified as biosocial criminology, research from the disciplines of psychiatry and psychology in Japan support similar findings from other countries.

Neuropsychological/Cognitive Deficits

One of the strongest factors for later offending is childhood neuropsychological deficits (Rocque et al. 2014). Individuals with these deficits have difficulty in conforming to social expectations and delaying gratification because they have poor executive functioning—poor skills in organisation, selective attention, and inhibitory control. Low intelligence is usually an observable measure of general cognitive deficits and impairment. Some of these deficits may have initially been the result of genetic or environmental factors.

Some of the studies on offenders and cognitive deficits in Japan deal with mental disorder as well. They all present evidence that poor executive functioning is related to offending, albeit differently depending on the type of mental disorder. Among 221 young male first-time offenders with conduct disorder, recidivism was related to younger age, changes in parent or guardian, and poor executive functioning (Miura and Fuchigami 2017). At intake, the first-time offenders were 16 and they were followed until age 19, before they reached adulthood. Miura (2009) compared 317 non-violent and violent adolescent male delinquents, both groups diagnosed with conduct disorder, who were admitted to a

Juvenile Classification Home (JCH) for the first time in Nagoya. Violent adolescents had lower executive functioning compared to non-violent adolescents. Miura examined whether familial environmental factors were also related to violence, but there were no significant findings.

Although violent offending is not a general characteristic of schizophrenia, a considerable number of repeat violent behaviours tend to be committed by those with this mental disorder (Kuroki et al. 2017). The association between schizophrenia and violence may be cognitively mediated. Kashiwagi et al. (2015) compared neurocognitive characteristics of male patients with schizophrenia who were either hospitalised as part of the MTS Act for committing a serious violent offence ($n = 30$) or hospitalised with no history of violence ($n = 24$). All those who were hospitalised under the Act were thought to have committed the violent offence because of delusions or hallucinations, though most had offended impulsively. The patients who had been violent had better working memory and executive functioning than the patients with no history of violence. These results suggested that the violent group had better functioning in the dorsolateral prefrontal cortex (DLPFC), the front of the brain, which is related to control, planning, and goal attainment. This enabled them to plan and commit their offences, despite committing some acts that were carried out impulsively.

Kuroki and colleagues (2017) recently compared gray matter volume in the brains of two groups with schizophrenia and similar demographics as those found in Kashiwagi et al. (2015). The violent group was split into two sub-groups, one where violence was premeditated and another where it was not. Their results identified structural differences in several brain regions between violent and non-violent males. Those who had been violent, whether premeditated or not, had smaller regional volumes in some areas of the brain. Some of these abnormal regions, the temporal pole and insula, have been identified in individuals with psychopathy or antisocial behavioural problems (see Kuroki et al. 2017), suggesting that being violent may depend on the same areas in the brain. The temporal pole helps in social and emotional processing while the insula helps to imagine, observe, and execute an experience. Both studies on violent individuals with schizophrenia suggest that multiple brain areas, whether functioning or not, may be related to violence.

Sexual Offending

Sex offences are considered 'hidden offences' and may make up a substantial portion of Japan's dark figure of crime. Suzuki (2016) describes several forms of sexual violence towards women that exist in Japan: rape, indecent assault, and, the most common, frotteurism. Frotteurism is widely known as *chikan*, and it usually refers to middle-aged men who fondle or rub themselves against victims—typically young female school and university students—in crowded trains. In some cases, the perpetrators may wait in empty lots and grope unsuspecting victims or expose themselves in public places.

Chikan is a common form of sex offence (Suzuki 2016), probably because perpetrators rely on the belief that victims often will not make a big deal over it. Compared to other sex offences, it is thought that it may be physically harmless, often committed by strangers, and unlikely to cause a sense of shame in victims, but some have argued that it leads to increased fear of crime (Horii and Burgess 2012). Perpetrators of chikan are dubbed *oyaji*, referring to salarymen who were once the face of Japan's male-dominated economic success until the bubble burst. Now oyaji is associated with sexual molestation. Although those under the age of 20 are considered children, unwanted sexual contact with those under 18 years of age is not considered a sex crime when coercion cannot be proven in court (Sudo et al. 2006), and the age of consent in Japan is 13 years (Katsuta and Hazama 2016).

For a little more than a decade, measures have been taken by the Ministry of Justice to prevent sex crimes, such as sharing the addresses of sexual offenders with the National Police Agency and providing systematic treatment for all sexual offenders in prison (Sudo et al. 2006). As primary prevention, police list incidents involving individuals who seem likely to sexually offend against women and children in online reports (Kikuchi 2015). Examples include children who were told they would be given candy if they went along with the suspicious individual, or women who were stalked. Based on these reports, generic email warnings are sent to the general public. What makes these individuals 'suspicious' is left to the discretion of the police. The assumption is that such incidents increase the risk for the occurrence of a serious sex crime. Kikuchi

(2015) found that this prevention strategy was accurate in predicting later sex crimes, as their likelihood of occurring was higher in areas close to where the initial incident had happened and decreased the further away it was in distance and time. This finding, however, seemed most applicable to incidents involving middle-school aged children or older.

Early prevention that focuses on the individual, however, is limited. Understanding why someone commits a sex offence is only attempted once that person has become a sex offender, and attention is then focused on the sexual reoffending. Prevention then becomes the responsibility of the criminal justice system. Miller (2014) reviewed the international literature on rape. Impairment in the brain has been shown to be linked to sex offences, because of difficulties in tasks that are sensitive to verbal skills, attention, and behavioural inhibition, but there is no 'rape centre' in the brain. Not only may perpetrators have brain impairment, but so can victims. Trauma can impair attention due to neuro-alterations in brain functioning and damage to the brain. Ogasawara (2011) noted that the initial responses of medical personnel are crucial to the emotional recovery of victims. Assuring them that their victimisation was not their fault, for example, is important. In terms of social factors, studies have shown that a substantial number of different types of sex offenders have experienced childhood abuse and poor parental attachment and these do differentiate them from other types of offenders (Miller 2014).

Prison cognitive-behavioural therapy (CBT) programmes in Japan were developed and implemented for sex offenders either on probation or parole, based on similar programmes used by the Canadian correctional service (Yamamoto and Mori 2016). They followed the Risk-Needs-Responsivity principles (RNR), which are guidelines for effective correctional treatment (Matsushima 2016). According to Matsushima (2016), the CBT programme was the first to use evidence-based practice in Japanese corrections. Its use of risk assessment set an example for other criminal justice rehabilitation programmes, because it enabled officers to gauge the risk level and provided a systematic way of administering treatment and rehabilitation.

Yamamoto and Mori (2016) describe the programme: adult sex offenders are placed in either low, moderate, or high intensity groups, depending on the results of a risk assessment. The high intensity group is required to attend the core programme, comprising five sessions of group work. In the first session, offenders reflect on their offence process and the factors that led to their offending as the basis for a self-prevention plan. Second, cognitive distortions, such as rationalising the offending behaviour or minimising responsibility for offending, are addressed. Third, officers provide training to offenders on problem-solving skills in interpersonal relationships. Fourth, emotional management skills training is provided, and in the fifth session offenders learn to increase empathy. Afterwards, depending on their sentence, offenders may attend follow-up sessions which could include family support (Katsuta and Hazama 2016).

In a comparative analysis of cognitive distortions among male sex offenders, child molesters scored significantly higher in rationalising their criminal behaviour than did non-offenders, and scored significantly higher in minimising their responsibility for offending than did non-offenders or sex offenders who were not child molesters (Katsuta and Hazama 2016). One explanation for the difference in scores between child molesters and other sex offenders on minimisation was that child molesters found difficulty in justifying their behaviour, as it involved children, so they used more excuses to try to alleviate their contradictory state of mind. The findings suggest that reasoning abilities are there, but the researchers did not explore impairment in cognition.

Whether the CBT programme is effective is debatable. A comparison of those who attended 90% or more of the programme with those who did not showed mixed support for the programme's ability to reduce reoffending (Yamamoto and Mori 2016). These individuals were subsequently released and followed for three years between 2007 and 2011. Of those who had good programme attendance, 21.9% reoffended, while of those who did not attend the programme or had poor attendance, 29.6% reoffended. Although the programme seemed to reduce reoffending generally, suggesting that it was effective in combating antisocial tendencies, the reduction in sexual reoffending was not significant. It could reflect pre-existing differences between the groups.

Recently, young offenders in Japan have been treated with CBT as well, and the programme concentrates on modifying cognitive distortions by improving executive functioning (Miyaguchi et al. 2012). It does this by helping young people to enhance positive, prosocial behaviour and thoughts, as well as interpersonal skills. A challenge to treatment is that the effectiveness varies in diverse groups. Juvenile sex offenders with low IQ, for example, show lower executive functioning than non-sex offenders with low IQ (Miyaguchi and Shirataki 2014). Between the two groups, however, no difference was found for visual cognitive functioning and reasoning abilities. It should be noted that these differences were not identified between sex offenders and non-sex offenders when those with high IQ were included. Low IQ sex offenders, therefore, may have undetected developmental issues that might affect their treatment progress.

Psychopathy

Psychopathy is a personality disorder marked by low interpersonal affect and antisocial characteristics (Gao et al. 2010). Examples of the former are manipulativeness and lack of emotion, and of the latter, aggression and impulsivity. These characteristics describe someone who has reduced ability for remorse and has poor behavioural controls (Blair 2000). Unlike British forensic psychiatrists who believe that psychopathy is a mental disorder, Japanese practitioners are not so sure that it is (Shiina et al. 2017).

Psychopathy is mistakenly thought to be synonymous with criminality. This is not true, but those who are evaluated as having high psychopathy commit more crimes than the average offender and have higher rates of violent recidivism, institutional misconduct, and conditional release failure (Burt et al. 2016). Growing evidence supports the notion that neurological dysfunction may influence the emergence of psychopathic traits.

The amygdala is considered to be one of the core neural systems that influences psychopathy (Blair 2000). Its impairment hinders effective socialisation in distinguishing between what is morally right or wrong. As children, we are socialised through aversive conditioning and instrumental learning. To learn that a behaviour is bad, it has to be associated with adverse consequences or empathising with the victim; this is similar to the idea of the 'conscience' proposed by Hans Eysenck. An impaired amygdala causes difficulty in processing others' emotions and in moral judgement (Glenn and Raine 2014). Studies from Japan have made advances in this area of research, but the findings are drawn from samples of university students and focus on psychopathy in the general population.

In Western studies, the gold-standard measure for psychopathy is the Psychopathy Checklist-Revised (PCL-R) (Wallinius et al. 2012), developed by Robert Hare (1991) in Canada. None of the studies in English in Japan use the PCL-R. Part of the reason may be that forensic psychiatrists, because of their duty to judge criminal responsibility through the MTS Act, deal more with schizophrenic offenders, so they concentrate less on personality disorders like psychopathy (Shiina et al. 2017). The Primary and Secondary Psychopathy Scales (PSPS), Levenson's Self-report Psychopathy Scale (LSPS), and the Psychopathic Personality Inventory-Revised (PPI-R) are translated and used in Japan, because they are more sensitive to subclinical samples. Whether these instruments are directly applicable to Japan are uncertain. In some cases, they may need to be modified. Yokota (2012) examined the validity of the PPI-R in a group of Hokkaido University students ($n = 160$), with a focus on cultural influences, as some psychopathic traits may be expressed differently or be less relevant in Japan. Although the factors were similar, the items that composed each factor were different from those found in US studies, suggesting that psychopathy characteristics are influenced by the social context.

Psychopathy, too, is often confused with antisocial personality disorder (ASPD), but a simplistic way to distinguish the two is that psychopathy emphasises emotional impairment. Most of the antisocial behaviour that is exhibited by psychopaths is instrumental, whereby the behaviour is goal-directed, as an attempt to achieve something. Impulsivity, although it seems contradictory, must be seen within the context of the attempt to achieve: psychopaths plan for what they want but do not consider the long-term consequences.

Poor behavioural controls in psychopaths were reported in a group of 40 Japanese university students (mean age = 19 years) (Masui and

Nomura 2011). They were assessed for psychopathy using the LSPS and asked to participate in a task that measured inhibitory ability (in other words, self-control) using the stop-signal paradigm. When there were high levels of rewards and punishments, the stop-signal response times of those with high psychopathy scores varied little from their response times when there were no rewards or punishments. The authors suggested that those with clinical and non-clinical psychopathy may suffer from a deficit in response inhibitory capabilities, as they were unable to distinguish between conditions.

Another study of 50 university students investigated the relationship between non-clinical psychopathy and altruistic punishment, and contributed knowledge on egocentricity in this area (Masui et al. 2011). Students played a game where they could choose to give their own points to another player or not. Altruistic punishment refers to the condition where students can choose to apply penalty points to punish another player, but in some cases, it would cost them as well. Those rated as high in psychopathy received high levels of emotional gratification when they engaged in altruistic punishment. From the findings it seems that those who have high scores seem to engage in masochistic punishment to gratify themselves.

Several recent studies have studied attention in those rated high on psychopathy. Psychopathy impacts affect, and it is thought that attention may be related to low empathy and anxiety in individuals. Among those with low attention, Sugiura and Sugiura (2012) found that high psychopathy was associated with difficulty in gauging increasing threats and danger, and this could be why psychopathic individuals partake in more risk taking. This, too, suggests that decreased executive functioning may be an issue. High risk taking by psychopathic individuals indicates that they prefer rewards regardless of uncertainty and they do not take losses under such conditions seriously (Takahashi et al. 2014).

Tamura et al. (2014) found that individuals with high psychopathy also had low empathy and anxiety, and it was thought that this was because their attention was directed elsewhere, to irrelevant cues. Tamura and colleagues (2016) confirmed these previous findings, demonstrating that reduced attention moderated the relationship between psychopathy and empathy. In other words, people who score higher in psychopathy tend to be less empathetic because their attention is directed towards attaining a goal. Their tunnel vision results in their missing other pertinent information in their surrounding environment.

Psychopaths may live among the general population and have no criminal history. These individuals are considered to be 'successful psychopaths', because they share similar traits to convicted 'unsuccessful psychopaths', such as egocentricity and superficial charm. They are, however, considered high-functioning, often working as businessmen, physicians, or scientists (Gao and Raine 2010).

Based on the idea of the 'successful and unsuccessful psychopath', studies in Japan have investigated altruistic punishment. Osumi and Ohira (2010) found that, among a group of 28 university students, those rated high on psychopathy were more likely to accept unfair offers than those rated low on psychopathy. Electrodermal responses to fair and unfair offers, and photos of faces supposedly making those offers, were assessed for each participant using skin conductance. Low psychopathy students often exhibited an electrodermal response when unfair offers appeared and, in some cases, their response suggested an irrational rejection of an offer, stemming from negative emotions such as anger. In contrast, high psychopathy students showed no difference in response between types of offers and the faces associated with them. These results have implications for the success of psychopaths in the general population. Their reduced emotional connection with others may enable them to make more rational decisions in social exchanges.

Osumi and colleagues (2012) scanned the brains of 20 male students using functional magnetic resonance imaging (fMRI) to examine the neural pathways for frustration-induced aggression among psychopaths in the general population. Everyone was tasked with choosing to inflict punishment on others who proposed unfair offers for distributing money between themselves and the participants. Results from the fMRI showed that those with high psychopathy were less likely to inflict punishment on those who made unfair offers and, during this decision, there was less activity in the amygdala. The authors concluded that it is amygdala dysfunction that is related to the affective deficits of psychopathy. In spite of this, successful psychopaths are able to quell impulses for reactive aggression.

Gao and Raine (2010) explain, in their review of successful and unsuccessful psychopaths, that both types exhibit similar cognitive and emotional deficits, but these seem less severe in successful types. Successful types are able to evade conviction for criminal acts and this could be because they rely more on relational than on physical aggression—they plan when to strike rather than strike on impulse. The studies they reviewed included international studies as well and many used samples of university students. The authors highlight that this latter fact, of course, affects the number of those considered successful psychopaths and what characteristics are thought to identify them. University students are better educated than the general population and it is unclear whether they have been detected by law enforcement. Another limitation is that, though psychopathic individuals are identified among university students, it is unclear whether they go on to be 'occupationally' successful.

Risks in Nutrients and Childbirth

Poor nutrition and problems related to childbirth are considered to be within the realm of biology, but could arguably belong more to social influences. For example, some researchers consider nutrition deficiency to be a social factor more than a biological one, because accessibility to good nutrition is dependent on socioeconomic status and the type of neighbourhood in which one resides. The same could be said about obstetric issues. Maternal smoking and birth complications happen externally, not internally to the individual child. In turn, they affect the child's biological development. Because these factors, as mechanisms, are so close to biological changes, compared to undisputed social factors such as low socioeconomic status, they are often included in the literature on biological explanations for crime. Nevertheless, these factors provide evidence for the existence of biosocial interactions in criminology.

Omega-3

The causes of violence are thought to start even before infancy, beginning when the child is in the womb. Poor nutrition during pregnancy has been found to influence gene expression and to predispose an individual to a host of behavioural and mental problems (Raine et al. 2015). A deficiency in omega-3 essential fatty acids, mainly obtained by eating less fish, has been of particular interest in the link between nutrition and violence. Virkkunen et al. (1987) were the first to report low levels of omega-3 among violent and impulsive offenders compared to healthy controls and offenders who were not (Hibbeln et al. 2006).

A large body of literature supports the effects of omega-3 on mental health and violence (Hibbeln et al. 2006). It is thought that a deficiency in long-chain essential fatty acids during critical phases of neurodevelopment—the prenatal phase and childhood—leads to cognitive impairments, which in turn leads to aggression and violence. A nutritional deficiency in early life may result in neurotransmitter changes, causing susceptibility to poor mental health and behaviour in otherwise healthy individuals. Gajos and Beaver (2016) found support for the relationship between omega-3 consumption and aggression in their meta-analysis, but it was unclear whether omega-3 supplementation could be used to reduce or prevent aggressive behaviour. In other words, is lack of omega-3 supplementation a cause for aggressive behaviour? In a recent study, however, it was found that omega-3 supplementation in children, in Mauritius, could lead to improvements in child externalising behaviour scores and long-term reductions in intimate partner violence between the child's parents, specifically in psychological aggression (Portnoy et al. 2018).

A significant study conducted by Hibbeln (2001) showed a strong correlation between levels of fish consumption and homicide rates among 26 countries using data from the World Health Organization (Pearson's $r = -0.63$). Countries that had the lower amount of seafood consumption had higher rates of homicide. For example, Bulgaria ate the least seafood and had the most deaths by murder, whereas Japan ate the most seafood and had the least number of deaths by murder.[1] Hibbeln concluded that consuming fish may have 'biological psychotropic effects' of reducing impulsivity and violence. Although the analyses were simplistic as they did not control for other factors, these results contribute to the growing evidence of the influence of omega-3 on violence.

The effects of omega-3 on aggression were investigated for three months in schoolchildren, ages 9–12 in Japan (Itomura et al. 2005). Previously fish oil was found to prevent an increase in aggression during stressful moments (exam periods) in a group of 41 Japanese university students (Hamazaki et al. 1996). A group of children ($n = 83$) were given omega-3 in their food while another group of children ($n = 83$) were given placebo supplements. Aggression significantly increased in the control group whereas no changes were reported in the fish oil group. By gender, the scientists treated both boys and girls equally but it seemed that fish oil affected girls more. The change in physical aggression was found only in girls, and impulsivity was reduced in girls among the fish oil group.

Omega-3 deficiency has been shown to increase the risk for suicide. Previous studies in other countries had shown a link between high omega-3 intake and reduced suicide risk, but this was not found in Japan using the Japan Public Health Center-based (JPHC) Prospective Study (Poudel-Tandukar et al. 2011). Dietary patterns and food frequency were examined in 89,037 participants, ages 40–69, in the JPHC (Nanri et al. 2013). A diet characterised by potatoes, seaweed, vegetables, fruits, soy products, mushrooms, and fish was associated with a decreased suicide risk, but a traditional Japanese diet, comprising a high intake of fish and seafood, had no association with suicide risk. The authors explained that perhaps there was a threshold where additional fish intake offered no additional benefits in countries like Japan that already had high fish consumption.

---

[1]The US was excluded because its homicide rate was too high (10-fold above the mean) and its inclusion would have skewed the results. In other words, because of the wide availability of firearms in the US, these would have been a stronger influence in homicide than fish consumption.

Obstetric Influences

Biosocial interactions receive most support from studies on influences from childbirth. Obstetric influences fall into three domains: birth complications, prenatal nicotine exposure, and minor physical anomalies (Raine 2005). Babies who suffer from birth complications are at increased risk of developing conduct disorder, or adult antisocial behaviour and criminality, but only when psychosocial factors are also present (Raine 2013). Essentially, adult violence arises from the interaction between obstetric factors and psychosocial risk factors.

No studies have directly investigated obstetric factors on later adult antisocial and offending behaviour in Japan. Research on obstetric factors, however, shows associations with poor health and behavioural prospects for children. Considering the many similar findings between Japan and other countries, and the plethora of evidence supporting the effects of early life risks on later antisocial behaviour in other countries, it seems likely that the obstetric influences-antisocial behaviour relationship will be found in Japan as well.

Anti-smoking campaigns and policies in Japan have been successful, as they have significantly decreased smoking in the general population. Regardless of this success, contemporary young Japanese women smoke at higher rates than young women in past generations (Fujioka et al. 2012). Levels of smoking while pregnant in Japan is considered to be high. It has been attributed to lower taxation of cigarettes compared to Western countries, so Japanese women can afford to smoke more (Shiozaki et al. 2011). Maternal smoking has been shown to be related to the incidence of six types of birth complications: threatened premature delivery before 37 completed weeks of pregnancy; cervical insufficiency; pregnancy-induced hypertension; placental abruption; preterm, premature rupture of the membrane before 37 completed weeks of pregnancy; and chorioamnionitis[2] (Hayashi et al. 2011). Birth complications as the result of smoking while pregnant were confirmed in a study of risk factors for birth complications. Findings showed that risk

---

[2]Inflammation of the foetal membranes due to a bacterial infection that occurs before or during labour.

factors were generally similar in Japan and Western countries, except for in vitro fertilisation and embryo transfer (IVF-ET), which were risks for placenta previa.[3] The relations between smoking during pregnancy and chorioamnionitis and pregnancy-induced hypertension[4] were significant among Japanese women (Shiozaki et al. 2011). The consequences of prenatal nicotine exposure include low-weight babies, earlier deliveries, and of course, birth complications.

Low birth weight is related to an increased risk of behavioural problems as well as educational and intellectual difficulties among children. In Nagasaki, babies who weighed under 1500 grams were assessed as having lower interaction ability, motor, and state control skills than babies who were of normal birth weight (Ohgi et al. 2003). In addition, low birth weight babies had deficiencies in their neonatal behaviour, which are related to later behavioural problems such as conduct problems and hyperactivity. The weight of babies have social implications as it may be influenced by the environment (Fujiwara et al. 2013). Increases in income inequality at the prefectural level were associated with low birth weight, where children of fathers with less than a university education were most likely to be impacted. The researchers of this study proposed that less educated fathers may have been more negatively affected by the greater income discrepancy, experiencing more financial or emotional stress, and this may increase the likelihood of domestic violence or low emotional support. In fact, the best replicated biosocial interaction for future antisocial behaviour seems to be between birth complications and adverse home environments (Raine 2005).

After the baby is born, other issues that have been shown to be directly related to brain impairment arise. The leading cause of death for children who are abused is being shaken or suffering head trauma, and in Japan, 2015, the cause of death for 38% of abused children under the age of three was abusive head trauma (Isumi and Fujiwara 2016).

---

[3] The placenta is located unusually low in the uterus and partially or completely covers the cervix; this causes bleeding from the mother.

[4] High blood pressure during pregnancy and can lead to a serious condition called pre-eclampsia; it prevents the placenta from receiving enough blood, meaning that the baby receives inadequate food and oxygen.

In some cases children survive the abuse and head trauma, but may suffer from cognitive difficulties, resulting in another pathway towards later offending. Miura and colleagues (2005) reported research that found a higher prevalence of prior head or face trauma in young offenders. They investigated this in a sample of 1136 male and females in the Nagoya JCH who were separated into two groups: one with a history of epilepsy/severe head injury and one with no such history. Of those with a history, over 80% showed neurodevelopmental problems, revealed by an electroencephalograph (EEG), and they were likely to have a history of psychiatric treatment and a family history of drug abuse compared to those with no history of head trauma or epilepsy. Neither group, however, was more likely to commit violence. The study indicates that neuro-deficits because of environmental circumstances reveal a host of other issues that may, too, have contributed.

How do other issues contribute to this unfortunate set of circumstances of abuse, head trauma, neuro-deficits, and offending? It is believed that an intergenerational transmission of abuse gives rise to child abusive head trauma. Isumi and Fujiwara (2016) found partial evidence for this, although parents' adverse childhood experiences such as maltreatment were not found to be associated with infant smothering or shaking in a sample of 7652 caregivers in Chiba prefecture. Rather, it was caregivers who had witnessed violence between their parents as children who were more likely to shake their infant. Isumi and Fujiwara (2016) believed that maternal depression may mediate this relationship and, indeed, they confirmed this finding, although these results were not presented in their study.

Maternal depression has been shown to be related to many poor behavioural and developmental outcomes for children. Sugawara et al. (1999) found that maternal postnatal depression was linked to the infant's daily rhythms and this was reciprocal in Kawasaki. The baby's everyday demands, if irregular, disrupted the mother's daily activities, which increased the risk of maternal depression. In turn, this depression obstructed the mother from caring for her baby, which then affected the baby's daily rhythms. The results suggest that these infants are more vulnerable to stress from early infancy, and in late infancy they are likely to develop a fear of strangers and strange situations.

Biological Prevention

Calls have been made to move beyond merely identifying risk factors and to advance knowledge on a 'social neurocriminology' perspective (Choy et al. 2015), which would make progress towards more accurate prediction of violence and antisocial behaviour. This perspective is concerned with social influences on biology and the brain that, in turn, influence offending.

Most modern approaches to crime prevention that include biological factors recognise that biosocial interactions are commonplace, and that the best way to tackle such risks is to alter the environment (Rocque et al. 2012). How this prevention would look is similar to the targeted programmes advocated by developmental crime prevention: the enhancement of cognitive skills, parent training, prenatal and maternal care, and nutritional enrichment. The idea is to intervene early, especially during critical developmental stages, and to prevent the manifestation of biological risk factors. The debate against child institutionalisation in Japan contains arguments rooted in its detrimental effects on child development because of the lack of familial and parental attachment (Goldfarb 2015). Scholars and activists who criticise the Japanese child welfare system cite an increased risk of attachment disorders, neural atrophy, developmental delay, disability, and persisting psychological damage.

A challenge to prevention is to clarify how much of the risk is environmental, in cases where it is impossible to intervene very early in life—if prevention is focused on children or adolescents, is that too late to intervene? CBT, for example, has been recommended as an effective treatment for sex offenders and juvenile offenders. This is assuming, however, that many of these cognitive deficits are the result of the environment and not genes or brain impairment. Miyaguchi et al. (2012) evaluated CBT for improving IQ in Japanese juvenile offenders. Their results suggested that external factors from a negative environment contributed to the low IQ of the juvenile offenders, because CBT was effective in boosting cognitive functioning and intelligence. Many of the juveniles in their sample had come from deprived homes and had exhibited early childhood antisocial behaviour. As they aged, social institutions failed to detect and provide them with special educational services because the juveniles had other issues such as maltreatment and bullying. In other cases, the deficits are genetic, and the environment only aggravates behavioural problems.

Psychopathy was thought to develop independently of adverse parental influences, but this is clearly not true (see Farrington and Bergstrøm 2018). In a community sample from Mauritius, Gao et al. (2010) found that disrupted parental bonding, in which low maternal care and poor paternal bonding were important relevant factors, was related to increased levels of adult psychopathic personality. Compared to childhood abuse, parental bonding seemed more relevant to the development of psychopathy. They concluded that the early psychosocial environment may be critical to brain development. Likewise, the interaction between low family support and high psychopathy in relation to antisocial behaviour was identified in a group of 48 Japanese university students (Masui et al. 2012).

It is thought that the social environment contributes to the relationship between psychopathy and aggression. Masui et al. (2013) found that the reason psychopaths developed aggressive humour styles was because they felt socially excluded. These researchers acknowledged that cultural differences may have played a role in their findings, as previous studies from other countries showed that psychopathy was related to a self-defeating sense of humour. In Japan, perhaps the aggressive style for socially excluded psychopaths may be more relevant, a style that comprises mocking, criticising, and offending others because of lack of respect.

Another matter to consider is that of cultural differences. In each country, certain values and beliefs are prioritised more than others and this may produce cross-national differences. Findings of biosocial research in Japan suggest that there are similarities with findings in other countries, but there is much terrain to explore. For example, Japan has been considered a shame culture and the US a guilt culture (Benedict 1946). Guilt occurs because of one's conscience or concerns with others' judgement, whereas shame, or embarrassment, is a public emotion that arises because of concern about what others—real or imagined—might think of one as result of the perceived faux pas. Guilt is pertinent to the violation of moral conventions, while embarrassment is pertinent to the violation of social conventions.

Both forms of emotion seem to operate differently in the brain, as examined in a small group ($n = 19$) of Japanese adults recruited from the community (Takahashi et al. 2004). Both emotions can be considered to be self-conscious types, because they both have similar activation patterns in the medial prefrontal cortex (MPFC), left posterior superior temporal sulcus (STS), and visual cortex, although embarrassment seemed to be a more complex process than guilt, involving more brain regions. The findings indicate that cultural influences, as social factors, may have different impacts on the brain, and in turn, this may have implications for the cross-cultural study of biosocial interactions for antisocial behaviour. In understanding why children from Japan, Korea, and China exhibited higher levels of self-control compared to Western children, however, Lewis et al. (2009) highlighted the difficulty of identifying specific cultural mechanisms that may be responsible.

Conclusion

Research on biological factors for violence and offending has been expanding in Western countries, emphasising an interaction with social factors to predispose someone to criminality. Research directly related to biological factors in criminology appears to be non-existent in Japan, possibly because of the past involvement with eugenics and because the study of biology and crime has only recently been revived in the West. Some scholarly ventures in the fields of psychology and psychiatry in Japan, however, show similar findings to that of the Western biosocial literature, although they mainly serve as implications for the development of antisocial behaviour.

From findings in the West, it seems that crime prevention may be improved if biological factors are included. Studies on omega-3 deficiency and maternal smoking in Japan show later developmental complications for children, and these have been found in studies from other countries to be linked to later antisocial behaviour. Investigations into biological factors for crime and their interaction with the environment may be promising for crime prevention in Japan. Already the country, overall, consumes a large amount of seafood, and this has been associated with lower homicide rates. Perhaps establishing a public health initiative to ensure that all people have access to adequate levels of omega-3, and good nutrition generally, will be a less drastic and more effective long-term crime prevention strategy.

References

Barnes, J. C., and Brian B. Boutwell. 2015. "Biosocial Criminology: The Emergence of a New and Diverse Perspective." *Criminal Justice Studies* 28 (1): 1–5.

Benedict, Ruth. 1946. *The Chrysanthemum and the Sword*. Boston: Houghton Mifflin.

Blair, James R. 2000. "Neurobiological Basis of Psychopathy." *British Journal of Psychiatry* 182: 5–7.

Burt, Grant N., Mark E. Olver, and Stephen C. P. Wong. 2016. "Investigating Characteristics of the Nonrecidivating Psychopathic Offender." *Criminal Justice and Behavior* 43 (12): 1741–60.

Choy, Olivia, Adrian Raine, Jill Portnoy, Anna Rudo-Hutt, Yu Gao, and Liana Soyfer. 2015. "The Mediating Role of Heart Rate on the Social Adversity-Antisocial Behavior Relationship: A Social Neurocriminology Perspective." *Journal of Research in Crime and Delinquency* 52 (3): 303–41.

Farrington, David P., and Darrick Jolliffe. 2015. "Personality and Crime." In *International Encyclopedia of the Social and Behavioral Sciences*, edited by James D. Wright, Vol. 17, 774–79. Oxford: Elsevier.

Farrington, David P., and Henriette Bergstrøm. 2018. "Family Background and Psychopathy." In *Handbook of Psychopathy*, edited by Christopher J. Patrick, 354–79. London: Guildford Press.

Fishbein, Diana. 1990. "Biological Perspectives in Criminology." *Criminology* 28 (1): 27–72.

Fujioka, Nami, Toshio Kobayashi, and Sue Turale. 2012. "Short-Term Behavioral Changes in Pregnant Women After a Quit-Smoking Program via E-Learning: A Descriptive Study from Japan." *Nursing and Health Science* 14: 304–11.

Fujiwara, Takeo, Jun Ito, and Ichiro Kawachi. 2013. "Income Inequality, Parental Socioeconomic Status, and Birth Outcomes in Japan." *American Journal of Epidemiology* 177 (10): 1042–52.

Gajos, Jamie M., and Kevin M. Beaver. 2016. "The Effect of Omega-3 Fatty Acids on Aggression: A Meta-Analysis." *Neuroscience and Biobehavioral Reviews* 69: 147–158.

Gao, Yu, and Adrian Raine. 2010. "Successful and Unsuccessful Psychopaths: A Neurobiological Model." *Behavioral Sciences and the Law* 210: 194–210.

Gao, Yu, Adrian Raine, Frances Chan, Peter H. Venables, and Sarnoff A. Mednick. 2010. "Early Maternal and Paternal Bonding, Childhood Physical Abuse and Adult Psychopathic Personality." *Psychological Medicine* 40: 1007–16.

Glenn, Andrea L., and Adrian Raine. 2014. *Psychopathy: An Introduction to Biological Findings and Their Implications*. New York: New York University Press.

Goldfarb, Kathryn E. 2015. "Social Science & Medicine Developmental Logics: Brain Science, Child Welfare, and the Ethics of Engagement in Japan." *Social Science & Medicine* 143: 271–78.

Hamazaki, Tomohito, Shigeki Sawazaki, Miho Itomura, Etsuko Asaoka, Yoko Nagao, Nozomi Nishimura, Kazunaga Yazawa, Toyomi Kuwamori, and Masashi Kobayashi. 1996. "The Effect of Docosahexaenoic Acid on Aggression in Young Adults." *Journal of Clinical Investigation* 97 (4): 1129–33.

Hannay, Timo. 2015. "Nature Versus Nurture." In *This Idea Must Die*, edited by John Brockman, 179–81. New York: HarperCollins.

Hare, Robert D. 1991. *The Psychopathy Checklist—Revised (PCL–R)*. Toronto: Multi-Health Systems.

Hayashi, Kunihiko, Yoshio Matsuda, Yayoi Kawamichi, Arihiro Shiozaki, and Shigeru Saito. 2011. "Smoking During Pregnancy Increases Risks of Various Obstetric Complications: A Case-Cohort Study of the Japan Perinatal Registry Network Database." *Journal of Epidemiology* 21 (1): 61–66.

Hibbeln, Joseph R. 2001. "Seafood Consumption and Homicide Mortality: A Cross-National Ecological Analysis." *World Review of Nutritional Dietetics* 88: 41–46.

Hibbeln, Joseph R., Teresa A. Ferguson, Tanya L. Blasbalg. 2006. "International Review of Psychiatry Omega-3 Fatty Acid Deficiencies in Neurodevelopment, Aggression and Autonomic Dysregulation: Opportunities for Intervention." *International Review of Psychiatry* 18 (2): 107–18.

Horii, Mitsutoshi, and Adam Burgess. 2012. "Constructing Sexual Risk: 'Chikan', Collapsing Male Authority and the Emergence of Women-Only Train Carriages in Japan." *Health, Risk and Society* 14 (1): 41–55.

Isumi, Aya, and Takeo Fujiwara. 2016. "Association of Adverse Childhood Experiences with Shaking and Smothering Behaviors Among Japanese Caregivers." *Child Abuse & Neglect* 57: 12–20.

Itomura, Miho, Kei Hamazaki, Shigeki Sawazaki, and Makoto Kobayashi. 2005. "The Effect of Fish Oil on Physical Aggression in Schoolchildren—A Randomized, Double-Blind, Placebo-Controlled Trial." *Journal of Nutritional Biochemistry* 16: 163–71.

Kashiwagi, Hiroko, Noriomi Kuroki, Satoru Ikezawa, Masateru Matsushita, Masanori Ishikawa, Kazuyuki Nakagome, Naotsugu Hirabayashi, and Manabu Ikeda. 2015. "Neurocognitive Features in Male Patients with Schizophrenia Exhibiting Serious Violence: A Case Control Study." *Annals of General Psychiatry* 21 (2): 307–17.

Katsuta, Satoshi, and Kyoko Hazama. 2016. "Cognitive Distortions of Child Molesters on Probation or Parole in Japan." *Japanese Psychological Research* 58 (2): 163–74.

Kikuchi, George. 2015. "Precursor Events of Sex Crimes in Japan: A Spatio-Temporal Analysis of Reports of Contacts with Suspicious Persons by Target Age Groups." *International Journal of Criminal Justice Sciences* 10 (2): 122–38.

Kuroki, Noriomi, Hiroko Kashiwagi, Miho Ota, Masanori Ishikawa, Hiroshi Kunugi, Noriko Sato, Naotsugu Hirabayashi, and Toshio Ota. 2017. "Brain Structure Differences Among Male Schizophrenic Patients with History of Serious Violent Acts: An MRI Voxel-Based Morphometric Study." *BMC Psychiatry* 17 (1): 105.

Lewis, Charlie, Masuo Koyasu, Seungmi Oh, Ayako Ogawa, Benjamin Short, and Zhao Huang. 2009. "Culture, Executive Function, and Social Understanding." *New Directions in Child and Adolescent Development*, 123: 69–85.

Masui, Keita, and Michio Nomura. 2011. "The Effects of Reward and Punishment on Response Inhibition in Non-clinical Psychopathy." *Personality and Individual Differences* 50 (1): 69–73.

Masui, Keita, Shouichi Iriguchi, Michio Nomura, and Mitsuhiro Ura. 2011. "Amount of Altruistic Punishment Accounts for Subsequent Emotional Gratification in Participants with Primary Psychopathy." *Personality and Individual Differences* 51 (7): 823–28.

Masui, Keita, Shouichi Iriguchi, Miki Terada, Michio Nomura, and Mitsuhiro Ura. 2012. "Lack of Family Support and Psychopathy Facilitates Antisocial Punishment Behavior in College Students." *Psychology* 3 (3): 284–88.

Masui, Keita, Hiroshi Fujiwara, and Mitsuhiro Ura. 2013. "Social Exclusion Mediates the Relationship Between Psychopathy and Aggressive Humor Style in Noninstitutionalized Young Adults." *Personality and Individual Differences* 55 (2): 180–84.

Matsushima, Yuko. 2016. "The Inter-Rater Reliability of the Psychopathy Checklist-Revised in Practical Field Settings." Masters thesis, Southern Illinois University, Carbondale.

Miller, Laurence. 2014. "Rape: Sex Crime, Act of Violence, or Naturalistic Adaptation?" *Aggression and Violent Behavior* 19 (1): 67–81.

Miura, Hideki. 2009. "Differences in Frontal Lobe Function Between Violent and Nonviolent Conduct Disorder in Male Adolescents." *Psychiatry and Clinical Neurosciences* 63: 161–66.

Miura, Hideki, and Yasuyuki Fuchigami. 2017. "Impaired Executive Function in 14- to 16-Year-Old Boys with Conduct Disorder Is Related to Recidivism: A Prospective Longitudinal Study." *Criminal Behaviour and Mental Health* 27 (2): 136–45.

Miura, Hideki, Masumi Fujiki, Arihiro Shibata, and Kenji Ishikawa. 2005. "Influence of History of Head Trauma and Epilepsy on Delinquents in a Juvenile Classification Home." *Psychiatry and Clinical Neurosciences* 59 (6): 661–65.

Miyaguchi, Koji, and Sadaaki Shirataki. 2014. "Executive Functioning Problems of Juvenile Sex Offenders with Low Levels of Measured Intelligence." *Journal of Intellectual & Developmental Disability* 39 (3): 253–60.

Miyaguchi, Koji, Naomi Matsuura, Sadaaki Shirataki, and Kiyoshi Maeda. 2012. "Cognitive Training for Delinquents Within a Residential Service in Japan." *Children and Youth Services Review* 34 (9): 1762–68.

Nanri, Akiko, Tetsuya Mizoue, Kalpana Poudel-tandukar, Mitsuhiko Noda, and Masayuki Kato. 2013. "Dietary Patterns and Suicide in Japanese Adults: The Japan Public Health Center-Based Prospective Study." *British Journal of Psychiatry* 203: 422–27.

Ogasawara, Kazumi. 2011. "Current Status of Sex Crimes and Measures for the Victims in Japan." *Journal of Medical Association Journal* 139 (3): 164–67.

Ohgi, Shohei, Tatsuya Takahashi, J. Kevin Nugent, and Kokichi Arisawa. 2003. "Neonatal Behavioral Characteristics and Later Behavioral Problems." *Clinical Pediatrics* 42 (8): 679–86.

Osumi, Takahiro, and Hideki Ohira. 2010. "The Positive Side of Psychopathy: Emotional Detachment in Psychopathy and Rational Decision-Making in the Ultimatum Game." *Personality and Individual Differences* 49 (5): 451–56.

Osumi, Takahiro, Takashi Nakao, Yukinori Kasuya, and Jun Shinoda. 2012. "Amygdala Dysfunction Attenuates Frustration-Induced Aggression in Psychopathic Individuals in a Non-criminal Population." *Journal of Affective Disorders* 142 (1–3): 331–38.

Pinker, Steven. 2015. "Behavior = Genes + Environment." In *This Idea Must Die*, edited by John Brockman, 188–91. New York: HarperCollins.

Portnoy, Jill, Adrian Raine, Jianghong Liu, and Joseph R. Hibbeln. 2018. "Reductions of Intimate Partner Violence Resulting from Supplementing Children with Omega-3 Fatty Acids: A Randomised, Double-Blind, Placebo-Controlled, Stratified, Parallel-Group Trial." *Aggressive Behavior.* https://doi.org/10.1002/ab.21769.

Poudel-Tandukar, Kalpana, Akiko Nanri, Motoki Iwasaki, Tetsuya Mizoue, Yumi Matsushita, Yoshihiko Takahashi, Mitsuhiko Noda, Manami Inoue, and Shoichiro Tsugane. 2011. "Long Chain N-3 Fatty Acids Intake, Fish Consumption and Suicide in a Cohort of Japanese Men and Women—The Japan Public Health Center-Based (JPHC) Prospective Study." *Journal of Affective Disorders* 129 (1–3): 282–88.

Radzinowicz, Leon. 1999. *Adventures in Criminology.* London: Routledge.

Raine, Adrian. 2002a. "Biosocial Studies of Antisocial and Violent Behavior in Children and Adults: A Review." *Journal of Abnormal Child Psychology* 30 (4): 311–26.

———. 2002b. "The Basis Biological of Crime." In *Crime: Public Policies for Crime Control,* edited by James Q. Wilson and Joan Petersilia, 43–74. Oakland: ICS Press.

———. 2005. "The Interaction of Biological and Social Measures in the Explanation of Antisocial and Violent Behavior." In *Developmental Psychobiology of Aggression,* edited by David M. Stoff and Elizabeth J. Susman, 13–42. Cambridge: Cambridge University Press.

———. 2013. *The Anatomy of Violence: The Biological Roots of Crime.* New York: Vintage Books.

Raine, Adrian, Jill Portnoy, Jianghong Liu, Tashneem Mahoomed, and Joseph R. Hibbeln. 2015. "Reduction in Behavior Problems with Omega-3 Supplementation in Children Aged 8–16 Years: A Randomized, Double-Blind, Placebo-Controlled, Stratified, Parallel-Group Trial." *Journal of Child Psychology and Psychiatry and Allied Disciplines* 56 (5): 509–20.

Rocque, Michael, Brandon C. Welsh, and Adrian Raine. 2012. "Biosocial Criminology and Modern Crime Prevention." *Journal of Criminal Justice* 40 (4): 306–12.

———. 2014. "Policy Implications of Biosocial Criminology: Crime Prevention and Offender Rehabilitation." In *The Nurture vs. Biosocial Debate in Criminology: On the Origins of Criminal Behavior and Criminality,* edited by Kevin M. Beaver, J. C. Barnes, Brian B. Boutwell, 431–45. New York: Sage.

Shiina, Akihiro, Aika Tomoto, Soichiro Omiya, Aiko Sato, Masaomi Iyo, and Yoshito Igarashi. 2017. "Differences Between British and Japanese Perspectives on Forensic Mental Health Systems: A Preliminary Study." *World Journal of Psychiatry* 7 (1): 8–11.

Shiozaki, Arihiro, Yoshio Matsuda, Kunihiko Hayashi, Shoji Satoh, and Shigeru Saito. 2011. "Comparison of Risk Factors for Major Obstetric Complications Between Western Countries and Japan: A Case—Cohort Study." *Journal of Obstetrics and Gynaecology Research* 37 (10): 1447–54.

Sudo, Junya, Makoto Sato, Shugo Obata, and Akira Yamagami. 2006. "Exploring the Possibility of Risk Assessment of Japanese Sexual Offenders Using Static-99." *Criminal Behaviour and Mental Health* 16: 146–54.

Sugawara, Masumi, Toshinori Kitamura, Mari Aoki Toda, and Satoru Shima. 1999. "Longitudinal Relationship Between Maternal Depression and Infant Temperament in a Japanese Population." *Journal of Clinical Psychology* 55 (7): 869–80.

Sugiura, Yoshinori, and Tomoko Sugiura. 2012. "Psychopathy and Looming Cognitive Style: Moderation by Attentional Control." *Personality and Individual Differences* 52 (3): 317–22.

Suzuki, Yumi E. 2016. "Sexual Violence in Japan: Implications of the Lay Judge System on Victims of Sexual Violence." *Journal of Law and Criminal Justice* 4 (1): 75–81.

Takahashi, Hidehiko, Noriaki Yahata, Michihiko Koeda, Tetsuya Matsuda, Kunihiko Asai, and Yoshiro Okubo. 2004. "Brain Activation Associated with Evaluative Processes of Guilt and Embarrassment: An fMRI Study." *NeuroImage* 23 (3): 967–74.

Takahashi, Taiki, Haruto Takagishi, Hirofumi Nishinaka, Takaki Makino, and Hiroki Fukui. 2014. "Neuroeconomics of Psychopathy: Risk Taking in Probability Discounting of Gain and Loss Predicts Psychopathy." *Neuroendocrinology Letters* 35 (6): 510–17.

Tamura, Ayame, Yoshinori Sugiura, Tomoko Sugiura, and Jun Moriya. 2016. "Attention Moderates the Relationship Between Primary Psychopathy and Affective Empathy in Undergraduate Students." *Psychological Reports* 119 (3): 608–29.

Tamura, Ayame, Keiji Takata, Yoshinori Sugiura, Jun Moriya, Yoshitake Takebayashi, and Keisuke Tanaka. 2014. "Moderation of the Relationship Between Psychopathy and Empathy by Attention." *Personality and Individual Differences* 60 (April): S62.

Virkkunen, Matti. E., David F. Horrobin, Douglas K. Jenkins, and Mehar S. Manku. 1987. "Plasma Phospholipids, Essential Fatty Acids and

Prostaglandins in Alcoholic, Habitually Violent and Impulsive Offenders." *Biological Psychiatry* 22 (9): 1087–96.

Wallinius, Märta, Thomas Nilsson, Björn Hofvander, Henrik Anckarsäter, and Gunilla Stålenheim. 2012. "Facets of Psychopathy Among Mentally Disordered Offenders: Clinical Comorbidity Patterns and Prediction of Violent and Criminal Behavior." *Psychiatry Research* 198 (2): 279–84.

Yamamoto, Mana, and Takemi Mori. 2016. "Assessing the Effectiveness of the Correctional Sex Offender Treatment Program." *Online Journal of Japanese Clinical Psychology* 3: 1–13.

Yokota, Kunihiro. 2012. "The Validity of a Three-Factor Model in PPI-R and Social Dominance Orientation in Japanese Sample." *Personality and Individual Differences* 53 (7): 907–11.

Yokoyama, Minoru. 2013. "Development of Criminology in Japan from a Sociological Perspective." In *Handbook of Asian Criminology*, edited by Jianhong Liu, Bill Hebenton, and Susyan Jou, 223–30. New York: Springer.

9

Conclusions

This case study of Japan has highlighted its particular crime issues from a psychological perspective, and how that relates to psychology and crime in other countries. The psychological perspective on crime is founded on values that include respect for human diversity and the complexity of human behaviour (Bonta and Andrews 2017). Traditionally, criminology was seen as a gathering of diverse disciplinary perspectives that shared an interest in investigating crime and its related phenomena. These different perspectives, however, seldom worked together, preferring to contribute knowledge on crime that was derived solely from their own discipline. Linking sociological explanations to those that are psychological is one way of understanding the full impact of criminological phenomena.

The difficulty, though, is that different explanations sometimes seem to be at odds with each other. Some reasons are historical, because sociological explanations dominated because of conditions after the World Wars. Other reasons are concerned with differences in emphasis, where the sociological perspective focuses more on crime originating from the macro-level while the psychological perspective focuses more on crime stemming from the micro-level; psychologists focus more on individual

© The Author(s) 2019
L. Bui and D. P. Farrington, *Crime in Japan*, Palgrave Advances in Criminology and Criminal Justice in Asia, https://doi.org/10.1007/978-3-030-14097-7_9

and biological factors, whereas sociologists focus more on national, cultural, community, and neighbourhood factors. Both, however, are interested in family, peer, and school factors. These differences in emphasis have implications for crime prevention and reduction. For example, the psychological perspective is likely to view crime as behaviour, which suggests that it is to some extent malleable. The sociological opinion is that psychology is the bandage over the wound—it doesn't bother looking at why the wound occurred in the first place in order to properly treat it. Hence, sociologists would recommend changes in society.

The conflict between the two disciplines can be summarised by an incident experienced by the penologist Nigel Walker (2003):

> English sociologists were taking their cues from America, and spent a great deal of energy in trying to discredit psychology, perhaps because as Philip Burgess once put it, one of the jobs of psychologists is to follow the cavalry of sociology with the shovel of empirical research. I had not realised how much antagonism there was between the two disciplines, and early in my time at Oxford made the mistake of inviting the Halseys to meet the Argyles for dinner in our home. Halsey, an LSE sociologist, attacked Michael Argyle the social psychologist with a venom I have seldom seen equalled, even on television, and never at a dinner-table. (98)

If disciplinary differences are set aside, it makes sense to connect these two perspectives to illuminate our understanding of criminological phenomena, and to establish how the macro exactly affects the micro and vice versa. After all, it is people who are the focus of both perspectives. For those who believe that only the environment—immediate or broader—matters more than what goes on in an individual in 'shaping' behaviour, Pinker (2015) points out that, for the environment to affect an individual, it would need to be processed by that individual and only some of that information is absorbed, in complex ways: 'which information is taken in, how it's transformed, and how it affects the organism all depend on the organism's innate organization' (p. 189). Another way of putting this is that psychology cannot be ignored when understanding how social institutions and structures affect an individual's behaviour.

We presented seven explanations for crime in Japan that could be illuminated by psychological research. Based on our reviews, high-quality research is needed to replicate results that previous studies, in and outside of Japan, have produced, and to evaluate the effectiveness of interventions. As the purposes are to replicate and evaluate, a scientific approach would be useful to gain more certainty about the following: what findings are most relevant to Japanese crime and criminal justice; how these findings are connected to the broader social and global context; and what forms of crime prevention are needed and are most effective. Exactly what type of high-quality research is needed are now discussed for each chapter.

In Chapter 2, the cultural explanation is one that foreign scholars are often attracted to because it enables unfamiliar territory to become accessible by comparing relevant behaviours and their underlying beliefs and values. The assumption is that the culture reflects cherished notions and held views of the world that manifest in the operations and prioritisation of institutions and the behaviours of individual members of society. To understand a culture is to, in some sense, understand the core of that society or the group's main concerns. The primary issue, however, is that this explanation risks essentialism. From a sociological stance, culture is seen as a macro-phenomenon because it is formed by groups of people, including societies, to provide them with a set of values and beliefs that are not only entrenched in the social system but also in individual minds (Karstedt 2012). To what extent culture affects individual behaviour—especially criminal and deviant behaviour—is less clear. There is evidence that it does have some impact, as individual members must adhere to the informal social control of their in-groups in order to enjoy social benefits, but culture is a dynamic force, changing with time, though this change can be slow. Recall that, often, Japan is assumed to be a collectivist, rather than an individualist, culture, but this seems to have not been rigorously and empirically tested with a large, representative sample in recent years.[1] It is important to test theories, and to

---

[1] An exception is the Asian Barometer Survey (Center for East Asian Democratic Studies 2012), which collected data from Japan in 2016. There is a measure of traditionalism, but the survey is focused more on political values and governance.

assess the extent to which they are falsifiable. Theory and data should go together, and the relationship should be mutualistic, characterised by informing and enriching each other (see Bottoms 2008).

The life course was introduced in Chapter 3, as well as some interesting longitudinal research that either had been conducted or was being conducted by government researchers. Although juvenile and adult criminal records have been recently connected in Japan, more knowledge about the development of offending can be gained with prospective longitudinal studies using community samples (Farrington 2012). Measuring and comparing self-reported and official offending over the life course is vital to evaluate the effectiveness of the police and courts, as well as to evaluate interventions that usually only use official measures of recidivism to determine success.

The family, in Chapter 4, is often highlighted as a significant reason why crime goes up. It is even considered the cause of quite a few societal ills. In addition, the social structure has consequences for the prevalence and reporting of family violence. Witnessing and experiencing such violence has been shown to be associated with and even predictive of later violent offending. The intergenerational transmission of crime has yet to be investigated in Japan, and this would, too, be best examined using a prospective longitudinal study. It would require information about offending as well as, ideally, developmental and situational information on at least two generations of families, specifically on parents and their children. A question that could also be addressed by this research is: 'to what extent do family factors predict offending after controlling for genetic influences?' (Farrington 2012).

The underlying causes of youth crime and violence in Chapters 5 and 6, whether out in the streets, in the home, or at school, seem to involve the breakdown of social relationships and bonds, particularly in the family. It seems that the family bears a heavy responsibility for upholding morality and order in society. Whether the family is deserving of a large proportion of the blame for societal ills, including crime in Japan, is hard to say. It seems to be an easy target as it is the family which is the initial and long-term institution of socialisation. The discourse on the family in Japan, however, could be the result of this ingrained idea that the family is a vital pillar of society.

Targeting families, however, is not unique to Japan. It has been the strategy of criminal justice and social agencies in the UK as well. Some sociological critics argue that this strategy is misguided and distracts from real injustices that might encourage crime, namely social and economic inequality. It is, however, more realistic and feasible to support and develop strategies at the familial level rather than at the societal level. To establish with any certainty whether prevention strategies focused on the family are effective in reducing offending, it is important to evaluate the impact of family interventions, and randomised trials may be the best option. Numerous measures should be used to gauge the influence of interventions during a number of years, and it is preferable if intended outcomes are measured before and after the intervention. As discussed in Chapter 5, it seems that these interventions should be outside the justice system. Interventions should not only focus on offending, but on other associated life outcomes. In Japan, it seems that improving the quality of social relationships, rather than reducing offending among young people, should be a major focus.

Areas that are in need of more consideration in Japan are mental disorders, discussed in Chapter 7, and biosocial interactions, discussed in Chapter 8, and there are promising research developments on these topics. The implementation of the Medical Treatment and Supervision Act for offenders suffering from mental disorder may result in advances in our understanding of the relationship between mental disorders and crime in Japan. Evaluations of what types of rehabilitative programmes are effective in preventing and treating offending should measure outcomes other than recidivism to assess how these interventions impact different aspects of an individual's life, such as mental and physical health, employment, and social relationships. This can further advance knowledge about desistance. In addition, research on the effectiveness of rehabilitative programmes can be enhanced by conducting a large-scale study using interview data, and, ideally, using a mixed-methods approach.

There has not been much investigation of biosocial interactions, but there has been research in Japan on some biological factors such as omega-3 consumption and obstetric influences, although the latter research has not directly studied effects on offending and violence. Criminological research in this area is needed and can begin by collaborating with those already studying biological factors in related fields.

Developing an Inclusive Criminology

Cross-national studies are important but they are not carried out enough because they are not easy tasks. According to Farrington (2015), for such a study to succeed in advancing knowledge, collaboration between at least one knowledgeable researcher from each country may be the most helpful in overcoming language barriers and possible misinterpretations. Using this collaborative method, a long-term and meaningful collaboration among international researchers can emerge. At least two large-scale international comparative studies, based on this method, exist: the International Crime Victims Survey (ICVS) has collected victimisation information six times between 1989 and 2010, and has been conducted in over 80 countries (van Kesteren et al. 2014); and the International Self-Report Delinquency Survey (ISRD) has collected information, thrice, on delinquency, substance use, and victimisation among young people, approximately ages 12–14 years, in a number of countries. Their third data collection is currently on-going with 35 participating countries including Japan (Northeastern University 2014).

One big question is whether it is possible to develop a universal knowledge base in criminology. Developing criminology, according to Liu (2007), requires validating or extending assumed universal findings, and it appears that, in the field, there has been an increase in seeking a more general theoretical understanding. Proponents of this approach echo similar sentiments, believing that universal results can be established as well as culture-specific occurrences (Farrington 2015).

So, what would such a knowledge base for crime look like exactly?

The study of crime is problematic because crime itself is a hazy concept. Its definition fluctuates and is dictated by the law and those who make the law, although the majority of offences are similar in most countries. Psychologists have focused on either broad forms of antisocial behaviour and aggression, or on more serious forms such as violence. All of these are manifestations of deviance but are not reliant on legal definitions to label which behaviours are criminal. This method is also able to capture the 'true extent' of 'criminal behaviour' that otherwise may have gone undetected by formal criminal justice agencies. When creating a universal knowledge base, the many challenges of comparative work arise, particularly what definitions to use and what types of crime should be included and compared.

Another issue to consider is how universals are created: who gets to say what are the universals, and whose rubric should be used to measure this knowledge against. Already comparative criminologists have privileged the English language, and this case study on Japan is no exception. The practical matter of including scholars who are not versed in English and their studies needs attention as it has consequences for whose viewpoints are included.

Last, and related to the previous point, to create a universal knowledge base also involves a question of how disciplinary work should be approached. It is assumed that universals would be established by including different disciplinary perspectives, and interdisciplinary work would be preferable. Recently some higher education institutions and funding bodies are even encouraging such an approach to conducting research. An interdisciplinary approach seems ideal but caution should be taken as this line of thinking has been followed before. Radzinowicz (1962) had warned about this over fifty years ago:

> A closer liaison, leading to a more productive exchange of views concerning methods and objectives, is needed. There can be no doubt that a particular project of research undertaken by a penologist, for instance, could gain in richness and depth if some parts of it could be reviewed by a social psychologist. But I cannot help thinking that, except in very rare instances indeed, an inquiry embracing several disciplines from the start, and depending on the coordination of their individual methods and distinctive terminologies, would carry the seeds of its own failure and would inevitably fall apart into as many undertakings. This interdisciplinary fusion breeds centrifugal confusion. Yet at the conceptional and consultative stage it undoubtedly contains great advantages. (177)

What gets included in this universal knowledge base in terms of disciplinary approaches needs more thought. It could result in a smaller version of what contemporary criminology already is—a subject of many disparate perspectives. This is not inherently a bad thing, but there is an overwhelming amount of information from different disciplines, and knowledge would be advanced if these are brought together in order to decipher meaningful connections and comparisons.

This case study has made connections on two main levels: first, how crime in Japan and our understanding of it links to crime in other countries and the larger criminological literature. Second, how a psychological perspective connects with the larger criminological literature where the sociological perspective is often dominant. Our purpose was to highlight Japan and the psychological research that may contribute more insights into issues of crime and antisocial behaviour there, and also globally. Therefore, the main thing that this case study has offered, as the art critic John Berger would have it, is 'ways of seeing'.

References

Bonta, James, and Donald A. Andrews. 2017. *The Psychology of Criminal Conduct*. New York: Routledge.

Bottoms, Anthony. 2008. "The Relationship Between Theory and Empirical Observations in Criminology." In *Doing Research on Crime and Justice*, edited by Roy D. King and Emma Wincup, 75–116. Oxford: Oxford University Press.

Center for East Asia Democratic Studies, National Taiwan University. 2012. "The Asian Barometer Survey" [online]. Available at http://asianbarometer. org/. Accessed 10 December 2018.

Farrington, David P. 2012. "Foreword: Looking Back and Forward." In *The Future of Criminology*, edited by Rolf Loeber and Brandon Welsh, xxii–xxiv. Oxford: Oxford University Press.

Farrington, David P. 2015. "Cross-National Comparative Research on Criminal Careers, Risk Factors, Crime and Punishment." *European Journal of Criminology* 12 (4): 386–99.

Karstedt, Susanne. 2012. "Comparing Justice and Crime Across Cultures." In *The Sage Handbook of Criminological Research Methods*, edited by David Gadd, Susanne Karstedt, and Steven F. Messner, 373–90. London: Sage.

Liu, Jianhong. 2007. "Developing Comparative Criminology and the Case of China: An Introduction." *International Journal of Offender Therapy and Comparative Criminology* 51 (1): 3–8.

Northeastern University. 2014. "The International Self-Report Delinquency Study" [online]. Available at https://web.northeastern.edu/isrd/. Accessed 10 December 2018.

Pinker, Steven. 2015. "Behavior = Genes + Environment." In *This Idea Must Die*, edited by John Brockman, 188–91. New York: HarperCollins.

Radzinowicz, Leon. 1962. *In Search of Criminology*. Cambridge: Harvard University Press.

van Kesteren, John, Jan van Dijk, and Pat Mayhew. 2014. "The International Crime Victims Surveys: A Retrospective." *International Review of Victimization* 20 (1): 49–69.

Walker, Nigel. (2003). *A Man Without Loyalties: A Penologist's Afterthoughts*. Chichester: Barry Rose Law Publishers.

References

Adler, Freda. 1983. *Nations Not Obsessed with Crime*. Littleton: Fred B. Rothman and Co.

Agozino, Biko. 2004. "Imperialism, Crime and Criminology: Towards the Decolonisation of Criminology." *Crime, Law and Social Change* 41 (4): 343–58.

Ainsworth, Mary S., and John Bowlby. 1991. "An Ethological Approach to Personality Development." *American Psychologist* 46 (4): 333–41.

Aldous, Christopher, and Frank Leishman. 2000. *Enigma Variations: Reassessing the Kôban*. Oxford: Nissan Institute of Japanese Studies.

Ambaras, David R. 2006. *Bad Youth: Juvenile Delinquency and the Politics of Everyday Life in Modern Japan*. Berkeley: University of California Press.

Amemiya, Airi, and Takeo Fujiwara. 2016. "Association Between Maternal Intimate Partner Violence Victimization During Pregnancy and Maternal Abusive Behavior Towards Infants at 4 Months of Age in Japan." *Child Abuse & Neglect* 55: 32–39.

American Psychiatric Association. 2013. *Diagnostic and Statistical Manual of Mental Disorders*. Washington, DC: Author.

Ando, Kumiko. 2004. "Current Adolescent Forensic Psychiatry in Japan." *Current Opinion in Psychiatry* 17 (5): 417–22.

Ando, Kumiko, Takahiro Soshi, Kanako Nakazawa, Takamasa Noda, and Takayuki Okada. 2016. "Risk Factors for Problematic Behaviors Among Forensic Outpatients Under the Medical Treatment and Supervision Act in Japan." *Frontiers in Psychiatry* 7 (144): 1–12.

© The Editor(s) (if applicable) and The Author(s) 2019
L. Bui and D. P. Farrington, *Crime in Japan*, Palgrave Advances in Criminology and Criminal Justice in Asia, https://doi.org/10.1007/978-3-030-14097-7

Ando, Shuntaro, Sosei Yamaguchi, and Graham Thornicroft. 2013. "Review of Mental-Health-Related Stigma in Japan." *Psychiatry and Clinical Neuroscience* 67: 471–82.

Andrés, Antonio R., Ferda Halicioglu, and Eiji Yamamura. 2011. "Socio-Economic Determinants of Suicide in Japan." *Journal of Socio-Economics* 40 (6): 723–31.

Andrews, Donald A., and James Bonta. 2010. "Rehabilitating Criminal Justice Policy and Practice." *Psychology, Public Policy, and Law* 16 (1): 39–55.

Anme, Tokie. 2004. "A Study of Elder Abuse and Risk Factors in Japanese Families: Focused on the Social Affiliation Model." *Geriatrics and Gerontology International* 4 (s1): S262–63.

Anme, Tokie, Mary McCall, and Toshio Tatara. 2005. "An Exploratory Study of Abuse Among Frail Elders Using Services in a Small Village in Japan." *Journal of Elder Abuse and Neglect* 17 (2): 1–20.

Aoki, Ai, Yuta Aoki, Robert Goulden, Kiyoto Kasai, Graham Thornicroft, and Claire Henderson. 2016. "Change in Newspaper Coverage of Schizophrenia in Japan Over 20-Year Period." *Schizophrenia Research* 175 (1–3): 193–97.

Ariga, Michio, Toru Uehara, Kazuo Takeuchi, Yoko Ishige, Reiko Nakano, and Masahiko Mikuni. 2008. "Trauma Exposure and Posttraumatic Stress Disorder in Delinquent Female Adolescents." *Journal of Child Psychology and Psychiatry* 49 (1): 79–87.

Aspinall, Robert W. 2016. "Children's Rights in a Risk Society: The Case of Schooling in Japan." *Japan Forum* 28 (2): 135–54.

Baba, Sachiko, Aya Goto, and Michael R. Reich. 2014. "Recent Pregnancy Trends Among Early Adolescent Girls in Japan." *Journal of Obstetrics and Gynaecology Research* 40 (1): 125–32.

Babinski, Leslie M., Carolyn S. Hartsough, and Nadine M. Lambert. 2001. "A Comparison of Self-Report of Criminal Involvement and Official Arrest Records." *Aggressive Behavior* 27: 44–54.

Baglivio, Michael T., Katherine Jackowski, Mark A. Greenwald, and James C. Howell. 2014. "Serious, Violent, and Chronic Juvenile Offenders: A Statewide Analysis of Prevalence and Prediction of Subsequent Recidivism Using Risk and Protective Factors." *Criminology and Public Policy* 13 (1): 1–34.

Bandura, Albert. 1977. *Social Learning Theory.* Oxford: Prentice-Hall.

Banner, Natalie F. 2013. "Mental Disorders Are Not Brain Disorders." *Journal of Evaluation in Clinical Practice* 19: 509–13.

Barry, Monica. 2017. "Young Offenders' Views of Desistance in Japan: A Comparison with Scotland." In *Comparative Criminology in Asia*, edited by Jianhong Liu, Max Travers, Max Chang, 119–29. New York: Springer.

Barnes, J. C., and Brian B. Boutwell. 2015. "Biosocial Criminology: The Emergence of a New and Diverse Perspective." *Criminal Justice Studies* 28 (1): 1–5.

Bayley, David H. 1976. *Forces of Order: Policing Modern Japan.* Berkeley: University of California Press.

Bear, George G., Ximena Uribe-Zarain, Maureen A. Manning, and Kunio Shiomi. 2009. "Shame, Guilt, Blaming, and Anger: Differences Between Children in Japan and the US." *Motivation and Emotion* 33 (3): 229–38.

Becker, Carl B. 1988. "Report from Japan: Causes and Controls of Crime in Japan." *Journal of Criminal Justice* 16 (5): 425–35.

Benedict, Ruth. 1946. *The Chrysanthemum and the Sword.* Boston: Houghton Mifflin.

Besemer, Sytske. 2012. *Intergenerational Transmission of Criminal and Violent Behaviour.* Leiden: Sidestone Press.

Besemer, Sytske, Victor van der Geest, Joseph Murray, Catrien Bijleveld, and David P. Farrington. 2011. "The Relationship Between Parental Imprisonment and Offspring in England and the Netherlands." *British Journal of Criminology* 51: 413–37.

Blair, James R. 2000. "Neurobiological Basis of Psychopathy." *British Journal of Psychiatry* 182: 5–7.

Blumstein, Alfred, Jacqueline Cohen, Jeffrey A. Roth, and Christy A. Visher. 1986. "Criminal Careers and 'Career Criminals'." Panel on Research on Career Criminals, Committee on Research on Law Enforcement and the Administration of Justice, Commission on Behaviorial and Social Sciences and Education, National Research Council. Washington, DC: National Academy Press.

Blumstein, Alfred, Jacqueline Cohen, David P. Farrington. 1988. "Criminal Career Research: Its Value for Criminology." *Criminology* 26: 1–35.

Bonta, James, and Donald A. Andrews. 2017. *The Psychology of Criminal Conduct.* New York: Routledge.

Borovoy, Amy. 2008. "Japan's Hidden Youths: Mainstreaming the Emotionally Distressed in Japan." *Culture, Medicine, and Psychiatry* 32: 552–76.

Bottoms, Anthony. 2008. "The Relationship Between Theory and Empirical Observations in Criminology." In *Doing Research on Crime and Justice*, edited by Roy D. King and Emma Wincup, 75–116. Oxford: Oxford University Press.

Bouffard, Jeff A., Jessica M. Craig, and Alex R. Piquero. 2015. "Comparing Attitudinal and Situational Measures of Self-Control Among Felony Offenders." *Criminal Behavior and Mental Health* 25: 112–25.

Bowlby, John. 1944. "Forty-Four Juvenile Thieves: Their Characters and Home-Life." *The International Journal of Psycho-Analysis* 25 (107): 19–52.

Braithwaite, John. 1989. *Crime, Shame and Reintegration.* Cambridge: Cambridge University Press.

Bruce, Matt, Deborah Cobb, Holly Clisby, David Ndegwa, and Sheilagh Hodgins. 2014. "Violence and Crime Among Male Inpatients with Severe Mental Illness: Attempting to Explain Ethnic Differences." *Social Psychiatry and Psychiatric Epidemiology* 49 (4): 549–58.

Bui, Laura. 2012. "Youth Offending in Japan: Context, Applicability and Risk Factors." Doctoral dissertation, University of Cambridge.

———. 2014. "Examining the Relationship Between Parenting, Risk-Taking, and Delinquency in Japan: Context and Empirical Applicability." *Asian Journal of Criminology* 9 (3): 171–87.

———. 2018. "Examining the Academic Achievement–Delinquency Relationship Among Southeast Asian Americans." *International Journal of Offender Therapy and Comparative Criminology* 62 (6): 1556–72.

Bui, Laura, David P. Farrington, Mitsuaki Ueda, and Karl G. Hill. 2014. "Prevalence and Risk Factors for Self-Reported Violence of Osaka and Seattle Male Youths." *International Journal of Offender Therapy and Comparative Criminology* 58 (12): 1540–57.

Bui, Laura, David P. Farrington, and Mitsuaki Ueda. 2016. "Potential Risk and Promotive Factors for Serious Delinquency in Japanese Female Youth." *International Journal of Comparative and Applied Criminal Justice* 40 (3): 209–24.

———. 2018. "Risk and Protective Factors for Serious Delinquency in the Japanese Context: Findings from Osaka Male Youths." In *Crime and Justice in Contemporary Japan*, edited by Jianghong Liu and Setsuo Miyazawa, 119–35. New York: Springer.

Burt, Grant N., Mark E. Olver, and Stephen C. P. Wong. 2016. "Investigating Characteristics of the Nonrecidivating Psychopathic Offender." *Criminal Justice and Behavior* 43 (12): 1741–60.

Cao, Liqun, and Steven Stack. 2005. "Confidence in the Police Between America and Japan." *Policing: An International Journal of Police Strategies & Management* 28 (1): 139–51.

Cao, Liqun, Steven Stack, and Yi Sun. 1998. "Public Attitudes Toward the Police: A Comparative Study Between Japan and America." *Journal of Criminal Justice* 26 (4): 279–89.

Castellini, Alessandro. 2014. "Silent Voices: Mothers Who Kill Their Children and the Women's Liberation Movement in 1970s Japan." *Feminist Review* 106 (1): 9–26.

Center for East Asia Democratic Studies, National Taiwan University. 2012. "The Asian Barometer Survey." Available at http://asianbarometer.org/. Accessed 10 December 2018.

Chan, Darius K. S., Michele J. Gelfand, Harry C. Triandis, and Oliver Tzeng. 1996. "Tightness-Looseness Revisited: Some Preliminary Analyses in Japan and the United States." *International Journal of Psychology* 31 (1): 1–12.

Chandler, Redonna K., Roger H. Peters, Gary Field, and Denise Juliano-Bult. 2004. "Challenges in Implementing Evidence-Based Treatment Practices for Co-occurring Disorders in the Criminal Justice System." *Behavioral Sciences and the Law* 22 (4): 431–48.

Chesney-Lind, Meda, and Randall G. Sheldon. 2014. *Girls, Delinquency, and Juvenile Justice*. West Sussex: Wiley.

Chol, Hyung, Gilbert C. Gee, and David Takeuchi. 2009. "Discrimination and Health Among Asian American Immigrants: Disentangling Racial from Language Discrimination." *Social Science & Medicine* 68 (4): 726–32.

Choy, Olivia, Adrian Raine, Jill Portnoy, Anna Rudo-Hutt, Yu Gao, and Liana Soyfer. 2015. "The Mediating Role of Heart Rate on the Social Adversity-Antisocial Behavior Relationship: A Social Neurocriminology Perspective." *Journal of Research in Crime and Delinquency* 52 (3): 303–41.

Chu, Rebekah, Craig Rivera, and Colin Loftin. 2000. "Herding and Homicide: An Examination of the Nisbett-Reaves Hypothesis." *Social Forces* 78 (3): 971–87.

Crystal, David S., Gerrod W. Parrott, Yukiko Okazaki, and Hirozumi Watanabe. 2001. "Examining Relations Between Shame and Personality Among University Students in the United States and Japan: A Developmental Perspective." *International Journal of Behavioral Development* 25 (2): 113–23.

Deater-Deckard, Kirby, Kenneth A. Dodge, John E. Bates, and Gregory S. Pettit. 1996. "Physical Discipline Among African American and European American Mothers: Links to Children's Externalizing Behaviors." *Developmental Psychology* 32 (6): 1065–72.

DeLisi, Matt, and Alex R. Piquero. 2011. "New Frontiers in Criminal Careers Research, 2000–2011: A State-of-the-Art Review." *Journal of Criminal Justice* 39 (4): 289–301.

de Ruiter, Corine, and Leena K. Augimeri. 2012. "Making Delinquency Prevention Work with Children and Adolescents: From Risk Assessment to Effective Interventions." In *Managing Clinical Risk*, edited by C. Logan and L. Johnstone, 199–223. London: Routledge.

Derzon, James H. 2010. "The Correspondence of Family Features with Problem, Aggressive, Criminal, and Violent Behavior: A Meta-Analysis." *Journal of Experimental Criminology* 6 (3): 263–92.

Desapriya, Ediriweera, and Nobutada Iwase. 2003. "New Trends in Suicide in Japan." *Injury Prevention* 9: 284–87.

Doi, Takeo. 1973. *The Anatomy of Dependence*. Tokyo: Kodansha.

Durkheim, Emile. 1924. *Sociology and Philosophy*. New York: Free Press.

———. 1951. *Suicide: A Study in Sociology*. Glencoe: Free Press.

Dussich, John P. J., and Chie Maekoya. 2007. "Physical Child Harm and Bullying-Related Behaviors in Japan, South Africa, and the United States." *International Journal of Offender Therapy and Comparative Criminology* 51 (5): 495–509.

Elliott, Amy, Brian Francis, Keith Soothill, and Arjan Blokland. 2017. "Changing Crime Mix Patterns of Offending Over the Life Course: A Comparative Study in England and Wales and the Netherlands." In *The Routledge International Handbook of Life-Course Criminology*, edited by Arjan Blokland and Victor van der Geest, 89–111. New York: Routledge.

Ellis, Tom, and Akira Kyo. 2017. "Youth Justice in Japan." In *Oxford Handbook of Crime and Criminal Justice*, edited by Michael Tonry. Oxford: Oxford University Press.

Enoki, Hiroaki and Kiyohiko Katahira. 2014. "Statistical Relationship Between Elderly Crime and the Social Welfare System in Japan: Preventative Welfare Approach for the Deterrence of Elderly Crime." *Niigata Journal of Health and Welfare* 14 (1): 48–57.

Erbe, Annette. 2003. "Youth in Crisis: Public Perceptions and Discourse on Deviance and Juvenile Problem Behavior in Japan." In *Juvenile Delinquency in Japan: Reconsidering the "Crisis,"* edited by Gesine Foljanty-Jost, 51–74. Leiden: Brill.

Eysenck, Hans J. 1977. *Crime and Personality*. London: Routledge.

Farrington, David P. 1973. "Self-Reports of Deviant Behavior: Predictive and Stable?" *Journal of Criminal Law and Criminology* 64 (1): 99–110.

————. 1977. "The Effects of Public Labeling." *British Journal of Criminology* 17: 112–25.

————. 1986. "Age and Crime." In *Crime and Justice, Vol. 7*, edited by Michael Tonry and Norval Morris, 189–250. Chicago: University of Chicago Press.

————. 1988. "Studying Change Within Individuals: The Causes of Offending." *Studies of Psychosocial Risk: The Power of Longitudinal Data*, edited by Michael Rutter, 158–83. Cambridge: Cambridge University Press.

————. 1993. "Understanding and Preventing Bullying." In *Crime and Justice, Vol. 17*, edited by Michael Tonry, 381–458. Chicago: University of Chicago Press.

————. 1997. "Evaluating a Community Crime Prevention Program." *Evaluation* 3 (2): 157–173.

————. 2000. "Explaining and Preventing the Globalization of Knowledge— The American Society of Criminology 1999 Presidential Address." *Criminology* 38 (1): 1–25.

————. 2001. "Key Results from the First Forty Years of the Cambridge Study in Delinquent Development." In *Taking Stock of Delinquency: An Overview of Findings from Contemporary Longitudinal Studies*, edited by Terence P. Thornberry and Marvin D. Krohn, 137–83. New York: Kluwer/Plenum.

————. 2003. "Developmental and Life-Course Criminology: Key Theoretical and Empirical Issues—The 2002 Sutherland Award Address." *Criminology* 41 (2): 221–55.

————. 2004. "Conduct Disorder, Aggression and Delinquency." In *Handbook of Adolescent Psychology*, edited by Richard M. Lerner and Laurence Steinberg, 683–722. Chichester: Wiley.

————. 2005a. *Integrated Developmental and Life-Course Theories of Offending*. New Brunswick: Transaction.

————. 2005b. "Childhood Origins of Antisocial Behavior." *Clinical Psychology and Psychotherapy* 12 (3): 177–90.

————. 2007. "Childhood Risk Factors and Risk-Focussed Prevention." In *The Oxford Handbook of Criminology*, edited by Mike Maguire, Rodney Morgan, and Robert Reiner, 4th ed., 602–40. Oxford: Oxford University Press.

————. 2011. "Families and Crime." In *Crime and Public Policy*, edited by James Q. Wilson and Joan Petersilia, 130–57. Oxford: Oxford University Press.

————. 2012. "Foreword: Looking Back and Forward." In *The Future of Criminology*, edited by Rolf Loeber and Brandon Welsh, xxii–xxiv. Oxford: Oxford University Press.

————. 2013. "Longitudinal and Experimental Research in Criminology." *Crime and Justice* 42 (1): 453–527.

————. 2015a. "Cross-National Comparative Research on Criminal Careers, Risk Factors, Crime and Punishment." *European Journal of Criminology* 12 (4): 386–99.

————. 2015b. "The Developmental Evidence Base: Prevention." In *Forensic Psychology*, edited by David A. Crighton and Graham J. Towl, 141–59. West Sussex: Wiley.

————. 2017. "Developmental Criminology." In *The Routledge Companion to Criminological Theory and Concepts*, edited by Avi Brisman, Eamonn Carrabine, and Nigel South, 60–64. London: Routledge.

Farrington, David P., and Brandon C. Welsh. 2007. *Saving Children from a Life of Crime*. New York: Oxford University Press.

Farrington, David P., and Darrick Jolliffe. 2015. "Personality and Crime." In *International Encyclopedia of the Social and Behavioral Sciences*, edited by James D. Wright, vol. 17, 774–79. Oxford: Elsevier.

Farrington, David P., and Henriette Bergstrøm. 2018. "Family Background and Psychopathy." In *Handbook of Psychopathy*, edited by Christopher J. Patrick, 354–79. London: Guildford Press.

Farrington, David P., and Maria M. Ttofi. 2011. "Protective and Promotive Factors in the Development of Offending." In *Antisocial Behavior and Crime: Contributions of Developmental and Evaluation Research to Prevention and Intervention*, edited by Thomas Bliesener, Andreas Beelmann, and Mark Stemmler, 71–88. Cambridge: Hogrefe.

Farrington, David P., and Rolf Loeber. 2000. "Epidemiology of Juvenile Violence." *Child and Adolescent Psychiatric Clinics of North America* 9 (4): 733–48.

Farrington, David P., Darrick Jolliffe, Rolf Loeber, Magda Stouthamer-Loeber, and Larry M. Kalb. 2001. "The Concentration of Offenders in Families, and Family Criminality in the Prediction of Boys' Delinquency." *Journal of Adolescence* 24 (5): 579–96.

Farrington, David P., Rolf Loeber, Yanming Yin, and Stewart J. Anderson. 2002. "Are Within-Individual Causes of Delinquency the Same as Between-Individual Causes?" *Criminal Behavior and Mental Health* 12 (1): 53–68.

Farrington, David P., Darrick Jolliffe, J. David Hawkins, Richard F. Catalano, Karl G. Hill, and Rick Kosterman. 2003a. "Comparing Delinquency Careers in Court Records and Self-Reports." *Criminology* 41 (3): 933–58.

Farrington, David P., Rolf Loeber, and Magda Stouthamer-Loeber. 2003b. "How Can the Relationship Between Race and Violence Be Explained?" In *Violent Crime: Assessing Race and Ethnic Differences*, edited by Darnell F. Hawkins, 213–37. Cambridge: Cambridge University Press.

Farrington, David P., Yutaka Harada, Hiroyuki Shinkai, and Tetsuki Moriya. 2015. "Longitudinal and Criminal Career Research in Japan." *Asian Journal of Criminology* 10 (4): 255–76.

Farrington David P., Maria M. Ttofi, and Rebecca V. Crago. 2017a. "Intergenerational Transmission of Convictions for Different Types of Offenses." *Victims & Offenders* 12 (1): 1–20.

Farrington, David P., Hannah Gaffney, Friedrich Lösel, and Maria M. Ttofi. 2017b. "Systematic Reviews of the Effectiveness of Development Prevention Programs in Reducing Delinquency, Aggression, and Bullying." *Aggression and Violent Behavior* 33: 91–106.

Fazel, Seena, and John Danesh. 2002. "Serious Mental Disorder in 23000 Prisoners: A Systematic Review of 62 Surveys." *Lancet* 359 (9306): 545–50.

Fazel, Seena, and Rongqin Yu. 2011. "Psychotic Disorders and Repeat Offending: Systematic Review and Meta-Analysis." *Schizophrenia Bulletin* 37 (4): 800–10.

Fenwick, Mark. 2013. "'Penal Populism' and Penological Change in Contemporary Japan." *Theoretical Criminology* 17 (2): 215–31.

Finch, Andrew. 2000. "Criminal Statistics in Japan: The White Paper on Crime, Hanzai Hakusho and Hanzai Tokeisho." *Social Science Japan Journal* 3 (2): 237–49.

Fishbein, Diana. 1990. "Biological Perspectives in Criminology." *Criminology* 28 (1): 27–72.

Folijanty-Jost, Gesine, and Manuel Metzler. 2003a. "Juvenile Delinquency in Japan: A Self-Preventing Prophecy." *Social Science Japan* 25: 39–43.

———. 2003b. "Juvenile Delinquency in Japan: Reconsidering the Crisis." In *Juvenile Delinquency in Japan: Reconsidering the "Crisis"*, edited by Gesine Foljanty-Jost, 1–17. Leiden: Brill.

Francis, Brian, Keith Soothill, and Rachel Fligelstone. 2004. "Identifying Patterns and Pathways of Offending Behaviour a New Approach to Typologies of Crime." *European Journal of Criminology* 1 (1): 47–87.

Fujii, Chiyo, Yusuke Fukuda, Kumiko Ando, Akiko Kikuchi, and Takayuki Okada. 2014. "Development of Forensic Mental Health Services in Japan: Working Towards the Reintegration of Offenders with Mental Disorders." *International Journal of Mental Health Systems* 8 (21): 1–11.

Fujimoto, Tetsuya, and Won-Kyu Park. 1994. "Is Japan Exceptional? Reconsidering Japanese Crime Rates." *Social Justice* 21 (2 (56)): 110–35.

Fujioka, Nami, Toshio Kobayashi, and Sue Turale. 2012. "Short-Term Behavioral Changes in Pregnant Women After a Quit-Smoking Program Via E-Learning: A Descriptive Study from Japan." *Nursing and Health Science* 14: 304–11.

Fujiwara, Takeo, Makiko Okuyama, and Mayuko Izumi. 2012a. "The Impact of Childhood Abuse History, Domestic Violence and Mental Health Symptoms on Parenting Behaviour Among Mothers in Japan." *Child: Care, Health and Development* 38 (4): 530–37.

———. 2012b. "Factors That Contribute to the Improvement in Maternal Parenting After Separation from a Violent Husband or Partner." *Journal of Interpersonal Violence* 27 (2): 380–95.

Fujiwara, Takeo, Keiko Natsume, Makiko Okuyama, Takuyo Sato, and Ichiro Kawachi. 2012c. "Do Home-Visit Programs for Mothers with Infants Reduce Parenting Stress and Increase Social Capital in Japan?" *Journal of Epidemiology and Community Health* 66 (12): 1167–76.

Fujiwara, Takeo, Jun Ito, and Ichiro Kawachi. 2013. "Income Inequality, Parental Socioeconomic Status, and Birth Outcomes in Japan." *American Journal of Epidemiology* 177 (10): 1042–52.

Fukayama, Francis. 1998. "Asian Values and Civilization." In *ICAS Fall Symposium, Asia's Challenges Ahead*. University of Pennsylvania.

Fukuchi, Naru, Masako Kakizaki, Yumi Sugawara, Fumiya Tanji, and Ikue Watanabe. 2013. "Association of Marital Status with the Incidence of Suicide: A Population-Based Cohort Study in Japan (Miyagi Cohort Study)." *Journal of Affective Disorders* 150 (3): 879–85.

Fukushima, Miyuki, Susan F. Sharp, and Emiko Kobayashi. 2009. "Bond to Society, Collectivism, and Conformity: A Comparative Study of Japanese and American College Students." *Deviant Behavior* 30 (5): 434–66.

Fukuzawa, Rebecca Erwin. 1994. "The Path to Adulthood According to Japanese Middle Schools." *Journal of Japanese Studies* 20 (1): 61–86.

Gajos, Jamie M., and Kevin M. Beaver. 2016. "The Effect of Omega-3 Fatty Acids on Aggression: A Meta-Analysis." *Neuroscience and Biobehavioral Reviews* 69: 147–58.

Gao, Yu, and Adrian Raine. 2010. "Successful and Unsuccessful Psychopaths: A Neurobiological Model." *Behavioral Sciences and the Law* 210: 194–210.

Gao, Yu, Adrian Raine, Frances Chan, Peter H. Venables, and Sarnoff A. Mednick. 2010. "Early Maternal and Paternal Bonding, Childhood Physical Abuse and Adult Psychopathic Personality." *Psychological Medicine* 40: 1007–16.

Gelfand, Michele J. 2012. "Culture's Constraints International Differences in the Strength of Social Norms." *Current Directions in Psychological Science* 21 (6): 420–24.

Gelfand, Michele J., Lisa H. Nishii, and Jana L. Raver. 2006. "On the Nature and Importance of Cultural Tightness-Looseness." *The Journal of Applied Psychology* 91 (6): 1225–44.

Gelfand, Michele J., Jana L. Raver, Lisa Nishii, Lisa M. Leslie, Janetta Lun, Beng Chong Lim, Lili Duan, et al. 2011. "Differences Between Tight and Loose Cultures: A 33-Nation Study." *Science* 332 (6033): 1100–104.

Glenn, Andrea L., and Adrian Raine. 2014. *Psychopathy: An Introduction to Biological Findings and Their Implications*. New York: New York University Press.

Goldfarb, Kathryn E. 2015. "Social Science & Medicine Developmental Logics: Brain Science, Child Welfare, and the Ethics of Engagement in Japan." *Social Science & Medicine* 143: 271–78.

Goold, Benjamin. 2004. "Idealizing the Other? Western Images of the Japanese Criminal Justice System." *Criminal Justice Ethics* 23 (2): 14–25.

Gottfredson, Michael R., and Travis Hirschi. 1990. *A General Theory of Crime*. Stanford: Stanford University Press.

Griffiths, Kathleen M., Yoshibumi Nakane, Helen Christensen, Kumiko Yoshioka, Anthony F. Jorm, and Hideyuki Nakane. 2006. "Stigma in Response to Mental Disorders: A Comparison of Australia and Japan." *BMC Psychiatry* 6 (21): 1–12.

Haas, Henriette, David P. Farrington, Martin Killias, and Ghazala Sattar. 2004. "The Impact of Different Family Configurations on Delinquency." *British Journal of Criminology* 44 (4): 520–32.

Hamada, Shoko, Hitoshi Kaneko, Masayoshi Ogura, Aya Yamawaki, Andre Sourander, Shuji Honjo, Junko Maezono, and Lauri Sillanm. 2018. "Association Between Bullying Behavior, Perceived School Safety, and Self-Cutting: A Japanese Population-Based School Survey." *Child and Adolescent Mental Health* 23 (3): 141–47.

Hamai, Koichi. 2011. "Review of Dag Leonardsen Crime in Japan: Paradise Lost?" *Social Science Japan Journal* (September): 4–6.

Hamai, Koichi, and Thomas Ellis. 2006. "Crime and Criminal Justice in Modern Japan: From Re-integrative Shaming to Popular Punitivism." *International Journal of the Sociology of Law* 34 (3): 157–78.

———. 2008. "Japanese Criminal Justice: Was Reintegrative Shaming a Chimera?" *Punishment & Society* 10 (1): 25–46.

Hamamura, Takeshi. 2012. "Are Cultures Becoming Individualistic? A Cross-Temporal Comparison of Individualism-Collectivism in the United States and Japan." *Personality and Social Psychology Review* 16 (1): 3–24.

Hamazaki, Tomohito, Shigeki Sawazaki, Miho Itomura, Etsuko Asaoka, Yoko Nagao, Nozomi Nishimura, Kazunaga Yazawa, Toyomi Kuwamori, and Masashi Kobayashi. 1996. "The Effect of Docosahexaenoic Acid on Aggression in Young Adults." *Journal of Clinical Investigation* 97 (4): 1129–33.

Hannay, Timo. 2015. "Nature Versus Nurture." In *This Idea Must Die*, edited by John Brockman, 179–81. New York: HarperCollins.

Hanson, Karl R., and Andrew J. R. Harris. 2000. "Where Should We Intervene?: Dynamic Predictors of Sexual Offense Recidivism." *Criminal Justice and Behavior* 27 (1): 6–35.

Hara, Hideki. 2002. "Justifications for Bullying Among Japanese Schoolchildren." *Asian Journal of Social Psychology* 5: 197–204.

Harada, Yutaka. 1992. "A Retrospective Study on the Relationship of Delinquent History in Junior High School to Later School and Employment Careers." *Reports of the National Research Institute of Police Science* 33: 1–13.

———. 1995. "Adjustment to School, Life Course Transitions, and Changes in Delinquent Behavior in Japan." In *Current Perspectives on Aging and the Life Cycle: Delinquency and Disrepute in the Life Course, Vol. 4*, edited by Zena Smith Blau and John Hagan, vol. 33, 35–60. Greenwich: JAI Press.

Harada, Yuzuru, Yuri Satoh, and Ayako Sakuma. 2002. "Behavioral and Developmental Disorders Among Conduct Disorder." *Psychiatry and Clinical Neurosciences* 56: 621–25.

Harada, Yuzuru, Ayako Hayashida, Shouko Hikita, Junko Imai, Daimei Sasayama, Sari Masutani, Taku Tomita, Kazuhiko Saitoh, Shinsuke Washizuka, and Naoji Amano. 2009. "Impact of Behavioral/Developmental Disorders Comorbid with Conduct Disorder." *Psychiatry and Clinical Neurosciences* 63 (6): 762–68.

Haraguchi, Tadashi, Mihisa Fujisaki, Akihiro Shiina, Yoshito Igarashi, Naoe Okamura, Goro Fukami, Tetsuya Shiraishi, Michiko Nakazato, and Masaomi Iyo. 2011. "Attitudes of Japanese Psychiatrists Toward Forensic Mental Health as Revealed by a National Survey." *Psychiatry and Clinical Neurosciences* 65 (2): 150–57.

Hare, Robert D. 1991. *The Psychopathy Checklist—Revised (PCL–R)*. Toronto: Multi-Health Systems.

Harzing, Anne-Wil. 2006. "Response Styles in Cross-National Survey Research: A 26-Country Study." *International Journal of Cross Cultural Management* 6 (2): 243–66.

Hashimoto, Akiko, and John W. Traphagan. 2008. "Changing Japanese Families." In *Imagined Families, Lived Families: Culture and Kinship in Contemporary Japan*, edited by Akiko Hashimoto and John W. Traphagan, 1–12. New York: SUNY Press.

Hashimoto, Hirofumi, Yang Li, and Toshio Yamagishi. 2011. "Beliefs and Preferences in Cultural Agents and Cultural Game Players." *Asian Journal of Social Psychology* 14 (2): 140–47.

Hawkins, David J., Richard F. Catalano, and Janet Y. Miller. 1992. "Risk and Protective Factors for Alcohol and Other Drug Problems in Adolescence and Early Adulthood: Implications for Substance Abuse Prevention." *Psychological Bulletin* 112 (1): 64–105.

Hawkins, David J., Todd I. Herrenkohl, David P. Farrington, Devon Brewer, Richard F. Catalano, and Tracy W. Harachi. 2000. *Predictors of Youth Violence.* Washington, DC: Office of Juvenile Justice and Delinquency Prevention.

Hayashi, Kunihiko, Yoshio Matsuda, Yayoi Kawamichi, Arihiro Shiozaki, and Shigeru Saito. 2011. "Smoking During Pregnancy Increases Risks of Various Obstetric Complications: A Case-Cohort Study of the Japan Perinatal Registry Network Database." *Journal of Epidemiology* 21 (1): 61–66.

Hayashi, Yoko. 2016. "Elder Abuse and Family Transformation." In *Family Violence in Japan: A Life Course Perspective*, edited by Fumie Kumagai and Masako Ishii-Kuntz, 123–51. New York: Springer.

Hechter, Michael, and Satoshi Kanazawa. 1993. "Group Solidarity and Social Order in Japan." *Journal of Theoretical Politics* 5 (4): 455–93.

Hee Ahn, Myung, Subin Park, Kyooseob Ha, Soon Ho Choi, and Jin Pyo Hong. 2012. "Gender Ratio Comparisons of the Suicide Rates and Methods in Korea, Japan, Australia, and the United States." *Journal of Affective Disorders* 142 (1–3): 161–65.

Hibbeln, Joseph R. 2001. "Seafood Consumption and Homicide Mortality: A Cross-National Ecological Analysis." *World Review of Nutritional Dietetics* 88: 41–46.

Hibbeln, Joseph R., Teresa A. Ferguson, Tanya L. Blasbalg. 2006. "International Review of Psychiatry Omega-3 Fatty Acid Deficiencies in Neurodevelopment, Aggression and Autonomic Dysregulation: Opportunities for Intervention." *International Review of Psychiatry* 18 (2): 107–18.

Hidaka, Yasuharu, Don Operario, Mie Takenaka, Sachiko Omori, Seiichi Ichikawa, and Takuma Shirasaka. 2008. "Attempted Suicide and Associated Risk Factors Among Youth in Urban Japan." *Social Psychiatry and Psychiatric Epidemiology* 43 (9): 752–57.

Hilton, Jeanne. M., Linda Anngela-Cole, and Juri Wakita. 2010. "A Cross-Cultural Comparison of Factors Associated with School Bullying in Japan and the United States." *The Family Journal* 18 (4): 413–22.

Hino, Kimihiro, Masaya Uesugi, and Yasushi Asami. 2018. "Official Crime Rates and Residents' Sense of Security Across Neighborhoods in Tokyo, Japan." *Urban Affairs Review* 54 (1): 165–89.

Hiraiwa-Hasegawa, Mariko. 2005. "Homicide by Men in Japan, and Its Relationship to Age, Resources and Risk Taking." *Evolution and Human Behavior* 26 (4): 332–43.

Hiramura, Hidetoshi, Masayo Uji, Noriko Shikai, Zi Chen, Nao Matsuoka, and Toshinori Kitamura. 2010. "Understanding Externalizing Behavior from Children's Personality and Parenting Characteristics." *Psychiatry Research* 175 (1–2): 142–47.

Hirokawa, Seiko, Norito Kawakami, Toshihiko Matsumoto, and Akiko Inagaki. 2012. "Mental Disorders and Suicide in Japan: A Nation-Wide Psychological Autopsy Case—Control Study." *Journal of Affective Disorders* 140 (2): 168–75.

Hiroyuki, Kuzuno. 2005. "Juvenile Diversion and the Get-Tough Movement in Japan." *Ryukoku Law Review* 22: 1–21.

Hirschi, Travis. 1969. *Causes of Delinquency*. Berkeley: University of California Press.

———. 2004. "Self-Control and Crime." In *Handbook of Self-Regulation*, edited by Roy Baumeister and Kathleen Vohs, 537–52. New York: Guilford Press.

Hoeve, Machteld, Judith Semon Dubas, Veroni I. Eichelsheim, Peter H. van der Laan, Wilma Smeenk, and Jan R. M. Gerris. 2009. "The Relationship Between Parenting and Delinquency: A Meta-Analysis." *Journal of Abnormal Child Psychology* 37 (6): 749–75.

Hoeve, MacHteld, Geert Jan J. M. Stams, Claudia E. Van Der Put, Judith Semon Dubas, Peter H. Van Der Laan, and Jan R. M. Gerris. 2012. "A Meta-Analysis of Attachment to Parents and Delinquency." *Journal of Abnormal Child Psychology* 40 (5): 771–85.

Hofstede, Geert. 1983. "National Cultures in Four Dimensions: A Research-Based Theory of Cultural Differences Among Nations." *International Studies of Management and Organization* Xlll (1): 46–74.

Hollin, Clive R. 2002. "Criminological Psychology." In *The Oxford Handbook in Criminology and Criminal Justice*, edited by Mike Maguire, Rod Morgan, and Robert Reiner, 144–74. Oxford: Oxford University Press.

———. 2013. *Psychology and Crime: An Introduction to Criminological Psychology*. London: Routledge.

Holloway, Susan D. 2010. *Women and Family in Contemporary Japan*. Cambridge: Cambridge University Press.

Horiguchi, Sachiko. 2012. "Hikikomori: How Private Isolation Caught the Public Eye." In *A Sociology of Japanese Youth: From Returnees to NEETs*, edited by Roger Goodman, Yuki Imoto, and Tuukka Toivonen, 122–38. New York: Routledge.

Horii, Mitsutoshi, and Adam Burgess. 2012. "Constructing Sexual Risk: 'Chikan', Collapsing Male Authority and the Emergence of Women-Only Train Carriages in Japan." *Health, Risk and Society* 14 (1): 41–55.

Houri, Daisuke, Eun Woo Nam, Eun Hee Choe, Liu Zhong Min, and Kenji Matsumoto. 2012. "The Mental Health of Adolescent School Children: A Comparison Among Japan, Korea, and China." *Global Health Promotion* 19 (3): 32–41.

Howard, Gregory J., Graeme Newman, and William Alex Pridemore. 2000. "Theory, Method, and Data in Comparative Criminology." *Criminal Justice* 4: 139–211.

Hughes, Christopher W. 1998. "Japan's Aum Shinrikyo, the Changing Nature of Terrorism, and the Post-Cold War Security Agenda." *Pacifica Review: Peace, Security & Global Change* 10 (1): 39–60.

Imada, Hiroshi, and Junko Tanaka-Matsumi. 2016. "Psychology in Japan." *International Journal of Psychology* 51 (3): 220–31.

Imada, Toshie. 2012. "Cultural Narratives of Individualism and Collectivism: A Content Analysis of Textbook Stories in the United States and Japan." *Journal of Cross-Cultural Psychology* 43 (4): 576–91.

Imai, Atsushi, Naoki Hayashi, Akihiro Shiina, Noriko Sakikawa, and Yoshito Igarashi. 2014. "Factors Associated with Violence Among Japanese Patients with Schizophrenia Prior to Psychiatric Emergency Hospitalization: A Case-Controlled Study." *Schizophrenia Research* 160 (1–3): 27–32.

Ireland, Timothy O., and Carolyn A. Smith. 2009. "Living in Partner-Violent Families: Developmental Links to Antisocial Behavior and Relationship Violence." *Journal of Youth and Adolescence* 38 (3): 323–39.

Ishida, Hiroshi, and Satoshi Miwa. 2012. "School Discipline and Academic Achievement in Japan." In *Improving Learning Environments: School Discipline and Student Achievement in Comparative Perspective*, edited by Richard Arum and Melissa Velez. Stanford: Stanford University Press.

Ishii-Kuntz, Masako. 1994. "Paternal Involvement and Perception Towards Fathers' Roles: A Comparison Between Japan and the United States." *Journal of Family Issues* 15 (1): 30–48.

———. 2016. "Child Abuse: History and Current State in Japanese Context." In *Family Violence in Japan: A Life Course Perspective*, edited by Fumie Kumagai and Masako Ishii-Kuntz, 49–78. New York: Springer.

Ishii, Nobuyoshi, Takeshi Terao, Yasuo Araki, Kentaro Kohno, Yoshinori Mizokami, Masano Arasaki, and Noboru Iwata. 2013. "Risk Factors for Suicide in Japan: A Model of Predicting Suicide in 2008 by Risk Factors of 2007." *Journal of Affective Disorders* 147 (1–3): 352–54.

Ishikawa, H., Norito Kawakami, and Ronald C. Keslser. 2016. "Lifetime and 12-Month Prevalence, Severity and Unmet Need for Treatment of Common Mental Disorders in Japan: Results from the Final Dataset of World Mental Health Japan Survey." *Epidemiology and Psychiatric Services* 25 (3): 217–29.

Isumi, Aya, and Takeo Fujiwara. 2016. "Association of Adverse Childhood Experiences with Shaking and Smothering Behaviors Among Japanese Caregivers." *Child Abuse & Neglect* 57: 12–20.

Itomura, Miho, Kei Hamazaki, Shigeki Sawazaki, and Makoto Kobayashi. 2005. "The Effect of Fish Oil on Physical Aggression in Schoolchildren—A Randomized, Double-Blind, Placebo-Controlled Trial." *Journal of Nutritional Biochemistry* 16: 163–71.

Jensen-Campbell, Lauri A., Jennifer M. Knack, Amy M. Waldrip, and Shaun D. Campbell. 2007. "Do Big Five Personality Traits Associated with Self-Control in Influence the Regulation of Anger and Aggression ?" *Journal of Research in Personality* 41 (2): 403–24.

Johnson, David T. 2003. "Above the Law? Police Integrity in Japan." *Social Science Japan Journal* 6 (1): 19–37.

———. 2006. "The Vanishing Killer: Japan's Postwar Homicide Decline." *Social Science Japan Journal* 9 (1): 73–90.

———. 2007. "Book Review: Park, W.-K. (2006). Trends in Crime Rates in Postwar Japan: A Structural Perspective. The Law and Political Science Series of the University of Kitakyushu, 20. Morioka City, Iwate Prefecture, Japan: Shinzansha Co., Pp. Xii, 255." *International Criminal Justice Review* 17 (2): 153–55.

———. 2008. "The Homicide Drop in Postwar Japan." *Homicide Studies* 12 (1): 146–60.

Jolliffe, Darrick, and David P. Farrington. 2009. "A Systematic Review of the Relationship Between Childhood Impulsiveness and Later Violence." In *Personality, Personality Disorder and Violence*, edited by Mary McMurran and Richard C. Howard, 38–61. Chichester: Wiley.

Jolliffe, Darrick, David P. Farrington, David J. Hawkins, Richard F. Catalano, Karl G. Hill, and Rick Kosterman. 2003. "Predictive, Concurrent, Prospective and Retrospective Validity of Self-Reported Delinquency." *Criminal Behaviour and Mental Health* 13: 179–97.

Jolliffe, Darrick, David P. Farrington, Rolf Loeber, and Dustin Pardini. 2016. "Protective Factors for Violence: Results from the Pittsburgh Youth Study." *Journal of Criminal Justice* 45: 32–40.

Jones, David W. 2008. *Understanding Criminal Behaviour: Psychosocial Approaches to Criminality.* Cullompton: Willan.

Jones, Shayne E., Joshua D. Miller, and Donald R. Lynam. 2011. "Personality, Antisocial Behavior, and Aggression: A Meta-Analytic Review." *Journal of Criminal Justice* 39 (4): 329–37.

Juby, Heather, and David P. Farrington. 2001. "Disentangling the Link Between Disrupted Families and Delinquency." *British Journal of Criminology* 41 (1): 22–40.

Kadonaga, Tomoko, and Mark W. Fraser. 2015. "Child Maltreatment in Japan." *Journal of Social Work* 15 (3): 233–53.

Kadowaki, Atsushi. 2003. "Changes in Values and Life Orientation Among Japanese Youth." In *Juvenile Delinquency in Japan: Reconsidering the "Crisis"*, edited by Gesine Foljanty-Jost, 75–90. Leiden: Brill.

Kageyama, Masako, Keiko Yokoyama, Satoko Nagata, Sachiko Kita, Yukako Nakamura, Sayaka Kobayashi, and Phyllis Solomon. 2015. "Rate of Family Violence Among Patients with Schizophrenia in Japan." *Asia-Pacific Journal of Public Health* 27: 652–60.

Kageyama, Masako, Phyllis Solomon, and Keiko Yokoyama. 2016a. "Archives of Psychiatric Nursing Psychological Distress and Violence Towards Parents of Patients with Schizophrenia." *Archives of Psychiatric Nursing* 30 (5): 614–19.

Kageyama, Masako, Phyllis Solomon, Sachiko Kita, Satoko Nagata, Keiko Yokoyama, Yukako Nakamura, Sayaka Kobayashi, and Chiyo Fujii. 2016b. "Factors Related to Physical Violence Experienced by Parents of Persons with Schizophrenia in Japan." *Psychiatry Research* 243: 439–45.

Kameguchi, Kenji, and Stephen Murphy-Shigematsu. 2001. "Family Psychology and Family Therapy in Japan." *The American Psychologist* 56 (1): 65–70.

Kanetsuna, Tomoyuki, Peter K. Smith, and Yohji Morita. 2006. "Coping with Bullying at School: Children's Recommended Strategies and Attitudes to School-Based Interventions in England and Japan." *Aggressive Behaviour* 32 (3): 570–80.

Karstedt, Susanne. 2001. "Comparing Cultures, Comparing Crime: Challenges, Prospects and Problems for a Global Criminology." *Crime, Law and Social Change* 36 (3): 285–308.

———. 2006. "Democracy, Values, and Violence: Paradoxes, Tensions, and Comparative Advantages of Liberal Inclusion." *The Annals of the American Academy of Political and Social Science* 605 (1): 50–81.

———. 2012. "Comparing Justice and Crime Across Cultures." In *The Sage Handbook of Criminological Research Methods*, edited by David Gadd, Susanne Karstedt, and Steven F. Messner, 373–90. London: Sage.

Kashiwagi, Hiroko, Noriomi Kuroki, Satoru Ikezawa, Masateru Matsushita, Masanori Ishikawa, Kazuyuki Nakagome, Naotsugu Hirabayashi, and Manabu Ikeda. 2015. "Neurocognitive Features in Male Patients with Schizophrenia Exhibiting Serious Violence: A Case Control Study." *Annals of General Psychiatry* 21 (2): 307–17.

Kashiwagi, Hiroko, Akiko Kikuchi, Koyama Mayuko, Dalsuke Salto, and Naotsugu Hirabayashi. 2018. "Strength Based Assessment for Future Violence Risk: A Retrospective Validation Study of the Structured Assessment of PROtective Factors for Violence Risk (SAPROF) Japanese Version in Forensic Psychiatric Inpatients." *Annals of General Psychiatry* 17 (5): 1–8.

Kataoka, Yaeko, Yukari Yaju, Hiromi Eto, and Shigeko Horiuchi. 2010. "Self-Administered Questionnaire Versus Interview as a Screening Method for Intimate Partner Violence in the Prenatal Setting in Japan: A Randomised Controlled Trial." *BMC Pregnancy and Childbirth* 10: 84.

Kato, Takahiro A., Masaru Tateno, Naotaka Shinfuku, Daisuke Fujisawa, Alan R. Teo, and Norman Sartorius. 2012. "Does the 'Hikikomori' Syndrome of Social Withdrawal Exist Outside Japan ? A Preliminary International Investigation." *Social Psychiatry and Psychiatric Epidemiology* 47: 1061–75.

Kato, Takahiro A., Shigenobu Kanba, and Alan R. Teo. 2016a. "A 39-Year-Old 'Adolescent': Understanding Social Withdrawal in Japan." *American Journal of Psychiatry* 173 (2): 112–14.

Kato, Takahiro A., Ryota Hashimoto, and Kohei Hayakawa. 2016b. "Japan: A Proposal for a Different Diagnostic Approach to Depression Beyond the DSM-5." *Psychiatry and Clinical Neurosciences* 70: 7–23.

Katsuta, Satoshi, and Kyoko Hazama. 2016. "Cognitive Distortions of Child Molesters on Probation or Parole in Japan." *Japanese Psychological Research* 58 (2): 163–74.

Kawabata, Naoto. 2001. "Adolescent Trauma in Japanese Schools: Two Case Studies of Ijime (Bullying) and School Refusal." *The Journal of the American Academy of Psychoanalysis* 29 (1): 85–103.

Kawabata, Yoshito, Nicki R. Crick, and Yoshikazu Hamaguchi. 2010. "The Role of Culture in Relational Aggression: Associations with Social-Psychological Adjustment Problems in Japanese and US School-Aged Children." *International Journal of Behavioral Development* 34 (4): 354–62.

Kazemian, Lila, David P. Farrington, and Marc Le Blanc. 2009. "Can We Make Accurate Long-Term Predictions About Patterns of de-escalation in Offending Behavior?" *Journal of Youth and Adolescence* 38 (3): 384–400.

Kikuchi, George. 2015. "Precursor Events of Sex Crimes in Japan: A Spatio-Temporal Analysis of Reports of Contacts with Suspicious Persons by Target Age Groups." *International Journal of Criminal Justice Sciences* 10 (2): 122–38.

Kita, Sachiko, Kataoka Yaeko, and Sarah E. Porter. 2014. "Prevalence and Risk Factors of Intimate Partner Violence Among Pregnant Women in Japan." *Health Care for Women International* 35 (4): 442–57.

Kitagawa, Yuko, Shinji Shimodera, Yuji Okazaki, and Atsushi Nishida. 2014. "Suicidal Feelings Interferes with Help-Seeking in Bullied Adolescents." *PLoS One* 9 (9): 1–7.

Kitamura, Toshinori, Nobuhiko Kijima, Noboru Iwata, Yukiko Senda, Koji Takahashi, and Ikue Hayashi. 1999. "Frequencies of Child Abuse in Japan: Hidden but Prevalent Crime." *International Journal of Offender Therapy and Comparative Criminology* 43 (1): 21–33.

Kitayama, Shinobu, and Hyekyung Park. 2007. "Cultural Shaping of Self, Emotion, and Well-Being: How Does It Work?" *Social and Personality Psychology Compass* 1 (1): 202–22.

Klomek, Anat Brunstein, Andre Sourander, and Henrik Elonheimo. 2015. "Bullying by Peers in Childhood and Effects on Psychopathology, Suicidality, and Criminality in Adulthood." *Lancet Psychiatry* 2: 930–41.

Kluckhohn, Clyde. 1954. "Culture and Behavior." In *Handbook of Social Psychology*, edited by Gardner Lindzey, 921–76. Cambridge: Addison-Wesley.

Kobayashi, Emiko, Harold R. Kerbo, and Susan F. Sharp. 2009. "Differences in Individualistic and Collectivistic Tendencies Among College Students in Japan and the United States." *International Journal of Comparative Sociology* 51 (1–2): 59–84.

Kobayashi, Emiko, Alexander T. Vazsonyi, Pan Chen, and Susan F. Sharp. 2010. "A Culturally Nuanced Test of Gottfredson and Hirschi's 'General Theory': Dimensionality and Generalizability in Japan and the United States." *International Criminal Justice Review* 20 (2): 112–31.

Kobayashi, Emiko, David P. Farrington, and Molly Buchanan. 2018. "Peer Reactions, Peer Behavior, Student Attitudes, and Student Deviance: A Comparison of College Students in Japan and the USA." *Asian Journal of Criminology*. https://doi.org/10.1007/s11417-018-9276-y.

Komiya, Nobuo. 1999. "A Cultural Study of the Low Crime Rate in Japan." *British Journal of Criminology* 39 (3): 369–90.

Konishi, Takako. 2000. "Cultural Aspects of Violence Against Women in Japan." *Lancet* 355 (9217): 1810.

Konishi, Tokikazu. 2013. "Diversity Within an Asian Country: Japanese Criminal Justice and Criminology." In *Handbook of Asian Criminology*, edited by Jianhong Liu, Bill Hebenton, and Susyan Jou, 213–22. New York: Springer.

———. 2014. "Strengthening the Child Guidance Functions in the Child Welfare System: Toward Early Solutions for Child Maltreatment and Delinquency Cases." *Waseda Bulletin of Comparative Law* 32: 1–10.

Kouno, Akihisa, and Charles F. Johnson. 1995. "Child Abuse and Neglect in Japan: Coin-Operated-Locker Babies." *Child Abuse and Neglect* 19 (1): 25–31.

Koyama, Asuka, Yuko Miyake, Norito Kawakami, Masao Tsuchiya, Hisateru Tachimori, and Tadashi Takeshima. 2010. "Lifetime Prevalence, Psychiatric Comorbidity and Demographic Correlates of 'Hikikomori' in a Community Population in Japan." *Psychiatry Research* 176 (1): 69–74.

Kozu, Junko. 1999. "Domestic Violence in Japan." *American Psychologist* 54 (1): 50–54.

Kraemer, Helena C., Alan E. Kazdin, David R. Offord, Ronald C. Kessler, Peter S. Jensen and David J. Kupfer. 1997. "Coming to Terms with the Terms of Risk." *Archives of General Psychiatry* 54 (4): 337–43.

Kuklinski, Margaret R., Abigail A. Fagan, David J. Hawkins, John S. Briney, and Richard F. Catalano. 2015. "Benefit-Cost Analysis of a Randomized Evaluation of Communities That Care: Monetizing Intervention Effects on the Initiation of Delinquency and Substance Use Through Grade 12." *Jounral of Experimental Criminology* 11: 165–92.

Kumagai, Fumie. 1983. "Filial Violence: A Peculiar Parent-Child Relationship in the Japanese Family Today." *Journal of Comparative Family Studies* 12 (3): 337–49.

———. 2016a. "Conclusion: Prevention and Intervention of Violence in Japan." In *Family Violence in Japan: A Life Course Perspective*, edited by Fumie Kumagai and Masako Ishii-Kuntz, 153–64. New York: Springer.

———. 2016b. "Introduction: Toward a Better Understanding of Family Violence in Japan." In *Family Violence in Japan: A Life Course Perspective*, edited by Fumie Kumagai and Masako Ishii-Kuntz, 1–48. Singapore: Springer.

———. 2016c. "Preface." In *Family Violence in Japan: A Life Course Perspective*, edited by Fumie Kumagai and Masako Ishii-Kuntz, v–vii. New York: Springer.

Kumagami, Takashi, and Naomi Matsuura. 2009. "Prevalence of Pervasive Developmental Disorder in Juvenile Court Cases in Japan." *Journal of Forensic Psychiatry & Psychology* 20 (6): 974–87.

Kuroki, Noriomi, Hiroko Kashiwagi, Miho Ota, Masanori Ishikawa, Hiroshi Kunugi, Noriko Sato, Naotsugu Hirabayashi, and Toshio Ota. 2017. "Brain Structure Differences Among Male Schizophrenic Patients with History of Serious Violent Acts: An MRI Voxel-Based Morphometric Study." *BMC Psychiatry* 17 (1): 105.

Laser, Julie, Tom Luster, and Toko Oshio. 2007. "Promotive and Risk Factors Related to Deviant Behavior in Japanese Youth." *Criminal Justice and Behavior* 34 (11): 1463–80.

Lebra, Takie Sugiyama. 1976. *Japanese Patterns of Behavior*. Honolulu: University Press of Hawaii.

Lee, Maggy, and Karen Joe Laider. 2013. "Doing Criminology from the Periphery: Crime and Punishment in Asia." *Theoretical Criminology* 17 (2): 141–57.

Leonardsen, Dag. 2002. "The Impossible Case of Japan." *Australian and New Zealand Journal of Criminology* 35 (2): 203–29.

―――. 2003. "Crime in Japan–A Lesson for Criminological Theory? The Cultural Dimension in Crime–What Can the Japanese Experience Tell Us?" Accessed 10 June 2011. http://www.britsoccrim.org/volume6/008.pdf.

Lewis, Chris, Graham Brooks, Thomas Ellis, and Koichi Hamai. 2009a. "Comparing Japanese and English Juvenile Justice: Reflections on Change in the Twenty-First Century." *Crime Prevention and Community Safety* 11 (2): 75–89.

Lewis, Charlie, Masuo Koyasu, Seungmi Oh, Ayako Ogawa, Benjamin Short, and Zhao Huang. 2009b. "Culture, Executive Function, and Social Understanding." *New Directions in Child and Adolescent Development* 123: 69–85.

Li, Tim M. H., and Paul W. C. Wong. 2015. "Youth Social Withdrawal Behavior (Hikikomori): A Systematic Review of Qualitative and Quantitative Studies." *Australian and New Zealand Journal of Psychiatry* 49 (7): 595–609.

Lie, John. 2001. "Ruth Benedict's Legacy of Shame: Orientalism and Occidentalism in the Study of Japan." *Asian Journal of Social Science* 29 (2): 249–61.

Lipsey, Mark W., and James H. Derzon. 1998. "Predictors of Violent or Serious Delinquency in Adolescence and Early Adulthood: A Synthesis of Longitudinal Research." In *Serious and Violent Juvenile Offenders: Risk Factors and Successful Interventions*, edited by Rolf Loeber and David P. Farrington, 86–106. Thousand Oaks: Sage.

Liu, Jianhong. 2007. "Developing Comparative Criminology and the Case of China: An Introduction." *International Journal of Offender Therapy and Comparative Criminology* 51 (1): 3–8.

―――. 2009. "Asian Criminology—Challenges, Opportunities, and Directions." *Asian Journal of Criminology* 4 (1): 1–9.

Liu, Jianhong, and Setsuo Miyazawa. 2018. *Crime and Justice in Contemporary Japan*. Cham: Springer.

Liu, Yan, Ying Zhang, Y. T. Choc, Yoshihide Obayashia, Asuna Arai, and Hiko Tamashiroa. 2013. "Gender Differences of Suicide in Japan, 1947–2010." *Journal of Affective Disorders* 151 (1): 325–30.

Loeber, Rolf, and David P. Farrington. 1998. *Serious and Violent Juvenile Offenders: Risk Factors and Successful Interventions*. Thousand Oaks: Sage.

Loeber, Rolf, and Magda Stouthamer-Loeber. 1986. "Family Factors as Correlates and Predictors of Juvenile Conduct Problems and Delinquency."

In *Crime and Justice*, edited by Michael Tonry and Norval Morris, 29–149. Chicago: University of Chicago Press.

Loeber, Rolf, and Marc Le Blanc. 1990. "Toward a Developmental Criminology." In *Crime and Justice*, edited by Michael Tonry and Norval Morris, 375–473. Chicago: University of Chicago Press.

Loeber, Rolf, David P. Farrington, Magda Stouthamer-Loeber, and Helene Raskin White. 2008. *Violence and Serious Theft: Development and Prediction from Childhood to Adulthood*. New York: Routledge.

Lösel, Friedrich, and David P. Farrington. 2012. "Direct Protective and Buffering Protective Factors in the Development of Youth Violence." *American Journal of Preventive Medicine* 43 (2S1): S8–23.

Lussier, Patrick, David P. Farrington, and Terrie E. Moffitt. 2009. "Is the Antisocial Child Father of the Abusive Man? A 40-Year Prospective Longitudinal Study on the Developmental Antecedents of Intimate Partner Violence." *Criminology* 47 (3): 741–80.

Maguin, Eugene, and Rolf Loeber. 1996. "Academic Performance and Delinquency." *Crime and Justice* 20: 145–264.

Mair, George. 1995. "Evaluating the Impact of Community Penalties." *The University of Chicago Law School Roundtable* 2 (2): Article 6.

Marshall, Ineke Haen. 2001. "The Criminological Enterprise in Europe and the United States: A Contextual Exploration." *European Journal on Criminal Policy and Research* 9 (3): 235–58.

Martinez, Dolores P. 2007. *Modern Japan Culture and Society*. London: Routledge.

Martinson, Robert M. 1974. "What Works?—Questions and Answers About Prison Reform." *The Public Interest* 35: 22–54.

Maruna, Shadd. 2001. *Making Good: How Ex-convicts Reform and Rebuild Their Lives*. Washington, DC: American Psychological Association.

Maruyama, Mika, and Frank R. Ascione. 2008. "Animal Abuse: An Evolving Issue in Japanese Society." In *The International Handbook of Animal Abuse and Cruelty: Theory, Research, and Practice*, edited by Frank R. Ascione, 269–304. West Lafayette: Purdue University Press.

Masataka, Nobuo. 2002. "Low Anger-Aggression and Anxiety-Withdrawal Characteristic to Preschoolers in Japanese Society Where 'Hikikomori' Is Becoming a Major Social Problem." *Early Education and Development* 13 (2): 187–200.

Masui, Keita, and Michio Nomura. 2011. "The Effects of Reward and Punishment on Response Inhibition in Non-clinical Psychopathy." *Personality and Individual Differences* 50 (1): 69–73.

Masui, Keita, Shouichi Iriguchi, Michio Nomura, and Mitsuhiro Ura. 2011. "Amount of Altruistic Punishment Accounts for Subsequent Emotional Gratification in Participants with Primary Psychopathy." *Personality and Individual Differences* 51 (7): 823–28.

Masui, Keita, Shouichi Iriguchi, Miki Terada, Michio Nomura, and Mitsuhiro Ura. 2012. "Lack of Family Support and Psychopathy Facilitates Antisocial Punishment Behavior in College Students." *Psychology* 3 (3): 284–88.

Masui, Keita, Hiroshi Fujiwara, and Mitsuhiro Ura. 2013. "Social Exclusion Mediates the Relationship Between Psychopathy and Aggressive Humor Style in Noninstitutionalized Young Adults." *Personality and Individual Differences* 55 (2): 180–84.

Matsumoto, David, and Linda Juang. 2013. *Culture and Psychology*. Belmont: Wadsworth/Thompson Learning.

Matsushima, Yuko. 2016. "The Inter-Rater Reliability of the Psychopathy Checklist-Revised in Practical Field Settings." Masters thesis, Southern Illinois University Carbondale.

Matsuura, Naomi, Toshiaki Hashimoto, and Motomi Toichi. 2009. "Correlations Among Self-Esteem, Aggression, Adverse Childhood Experiences and Depression in Inmates of a Female Juvenile Correctional Facility in Japan." *Psychiatry and Clinical Neurosciences* 63 (4): 478–85.

———. 2013. "Associations Among Adverse Childhood Experiences, Aggression, Depression, and Self-Esteem in Serious Female Juvenile Offenders in Japan." *Journal of Forensic Psychiatry & Psychology* 24 (1): 111–27.

McAra, Lesley, and Susan McVie. 2017. "Developmental and Life-Course Criminology: Innovations, Impacts, and Applications." In *The Oxford Handbook of Criminology*, edited by Alison Liebling, Shadd Maruna, and Lesley McAra, 607–33. Oxford: Oxford University Press.

Messner, Steven F. 2014. "Social Institutions, Theory Development, and the Promise of Comparative Criminological Research." *Asian Journal of Criminology* 9 (1): 49–63.

Messner, Steven F. 2015. "When West Meets East: Generalizing Theory and Expanding the Conceptual Toolkit of Criminology." *Asian Journal of Criminology* 10 (2): 117–29.

Metzler, Manuel, and Gesine Folijanty-Jost. 2003. "Problem Behavior and Social Control in Japan's Junior High Schools." In *Juvenile Delinquency in*

Japan: Reconsidering the "Crisis", edited by Gesine Folijanty-Jost, 253–66. Leiden: Brill.

Mieko, Yoshihama. 1999. "Domestic Violence: Japan's 'Hidden Crime.'" *Japan Quarterly* 46 (3): 76–82.

Miller, Alan, and Satoshi Kanazawa. 2000. *Order by Accident: The Origins and Consequences of Conformity in Contemporary Japan.* Boulder: Westview.

Miller, Laurence. 2014. "Rape: Sex Crime, Act of Violence, or Naturalistic Adaptation ?" *Aggression and Violent Behavior* 19 (1): 67–81.

Ministry of Health and Welfare Japan. 2016. "Vital Statistics 2015." Tokyo: Author.

Ministry of Justice Japan. 2009. "White Paper on Crime 2008—The Circumstances and Attributes of Elderly Offenders and Their Treatment." Tokyo: Author.

Ministry of Justice Japan. 2015. "White Paper on Crime, 2014." Tokyo: Author.

Ministry of Justice Japan. 2016. "White Paper on Crime, 2015." Tokyo: Author.

Ministry of Justice Japan. 2018. "White Paper on Crime, 2017." Tokyo: Author.

Mino, Tamaki. 2006. "Ijime (Bullying) in Japanese Schools: A Product of Japanese Education Based on Group Conformity." In *Rhizomes: Re-visioning Boundaries*, 24–25. http://espace.library.uq.edu.au/view/UQ:7721.

Misumi, Jyuji. 1989. "Introduction: Applied Psychology in Japan." *Applied Psychology* 38 (4): 309–20.

Miura, Hideki. 2009. "Differences in Frontal Lobe Function Between Violent and Nonviolent Conduct Disorder in Male Adolescents." *Psychiatry and Clinical Neurosciences* 63: 161–66.

Miura, Hideki, and Yasuyuki Fuchigami. 2017. "Impaired Executive Function in 14- to 16-Year-Old Boys with Conduct Disorder Is Related to Recidivism: A Prospective Longitudinal Study." *Criminal Behaviour and Mental Health* 27 (2): 136–45.

Miura, Hideki, Masumi Fujiki, Arihiro Shibata, and Kenji Ishikawa. 2005. "Influence of History of Head Trauma and Epilepsy on Delinquents in a Juvenile Classification Home." *Psychiatry and Clinical Neurosciences* 59 (6): 661–65.

Miyaguchi, Koji, and Sadaaki Shirataki. 2014. "Executive Functioning Problems of Juvenile Sex Offenders with Low Levels of Measured Intelligence." *Journal of Intellectual & Developmental Disability* 39 (3): 253–60.

Miyaguchi, Koji, Naomi Matsuura, Sadaaki Shirataki, and Kiyoshi Maeda. 2012. "Cognitive Training for Delinquents Within a Residential Service in Japan." *Children and Youth Services Review* 34 (9): 1762–68.

Miyazawa, Setsuo. 2012. "The Enigma of Japan as a Testing Ground for Cross-Cultural Criminological Studies." *International Annals of Criminology* 50 (1/2): 153–75.

Moffitt, Terrie E. 1993. "Adolescence-Limited and Life-Course-Persistent Antisocial Behavior: A Developmental Taxonomy." *Psychological Review* 100 (4): 674–701.

Moffitt, Terrie E., Louise Arseneault, Daniel Belsky, Nigel Dickson, Robert J. Hancox, and Honalee Harrington. 2011. "A Gradient of Childhood Self-Control Predicts Health, Wealth, and Public Safety." *Proceedings of the National Academy of Sciences of the United States of America* 108 (7): 2693–98.

Monahan, John. 2002. "The MacArthur Studies of Violence Risk." *Criminal Behavior and Mental Health* 12: 67–72.

Moore, Robin. 2015. "*A Compendium of Research and Analysis on the Offender Assessment System (Oasys) 2009–2013.*" London: National Offender Management Service.

Mori, Takemi, Masura Takahashi, and Daryl G. Kroner. 2017. "Can Unstructured Clinical Risk Judgment Have Incremental Validity in the Prediction of Recidivism in a Non-Western Juvenile Context?" *Psychological Services* 14 (1): 77–86.

Morita, Yohji. 1996. "Bullying as a Contemporary Behaviour Problem in the Context of Increasing 'Societal Privatization' in Japan." *Prospects* 26 (2): 311–29.

Motohashi, Yutaka. 2011. "Suicide in Japan." *The Lancet* 379 (9823): 1282–83.

Muncie, John. 2015. *Youth and Crime.* London: Sage.

Murai, Toshikuni. 1988. "Current Problems of Juvenile Delinquency in Japan." *Hitotsubashi Journal of Law and Politics* 16: 1–10.

Muramatsu, Naoko, and Hiroko Akiyama. 2011. "Japan: Super-Aging Society Preparing for the Future." *The Gerontologist* 51 (4): 425–32.

Murray, Joseph, and David P. Farrington. 2010. "Risk Factors for Conduct Disorder and Delinquency: Key Findings from Longitudinal Studies." *The Canadian Journal of Psychiatry* 55 (10): 633–42.

Murray, Joseph, David P. Farrington, and Manuel P. Eisner. 2009. "Drawing Conclusions About Causes from Systematic Reviews of Risk Factors: The Cambridge Quality Checklists." *Journal of Experimental Criminology* 5 (1): 1–23.

Nagae, Miyoko, and Barbara L. Dancy. 2010. "Japanese Women's Perceptions of Intimate Partner Violence (IPV)." *Journal of Interpersonal Violence* 25 (4): 753–66.

Nagai, Susumu. 2017. "Status of Victims of Spousal Violence and the Future Tasks: The Case of Japan." In *Domestic Violence in International Context,* edited by Diana Schaff Peterson and Julie A. Schroeder, 136–46. Oxon: Routledge.

Nagata, Takako, Atsuo Nakagawa, Satoko Matsumoto, Akihiro Shiina, Masaomi Iyo, Naotsugu Hirabayashi, and Yoshito Igarashi. 2016. "Characteristics of Female Mentally Disordered Offenders Culpable Under the New Legislation in Japan: A Gender Comparison Study." *Criminal Behaviour and Mental Health* 26 (1): 50–58.

Nagin, Daniel, and Richard E. Tremblay. 1999. "Trajectories of Boys' Physical Aggression, Opposition, and Hyperactivity on the Path to Physically Violent and Non-violent Juvenile Delinquency." *Child Development* 70 (5): 1181–96.

Naito, Takashi, and Uwe P. Gielen. 2005. "Bullying and Ijime in Japanese Schools." In *Violence in Schools: Cross-National and Cross-Cultural Perspectives*, edited by Florence L. Denmark, Herbert H. Krauss, Robert W. Wesner, Elizabeth Midlarsky, and Uwe P. Gielen, 169–90. Boston: Springer.

Nakadaira, Hiroto, Masaharu Yamamoto, and Toh Matsubara. 2006. "Mental and Physical Effects of Tanshin Funin, Posting Without Family, on Married Male Workers in Japan." *Journal of Occupational Health* 48 (2): 113–23.

Nakane, Chie. 1970. *Japanese Society*. Tokyo: Tuttle.

Nakane, Yoshibumi, and Hideyuki Nakane. 2002. "Classification Systems for Psychiatric Diseases Currently Used in Japan." *Psychopathology* 35: 191–94.

Nakanishi, Miharu, Yumiko Hoshishiba, Nobuyuki Iwama, Tomoko Okada, Etsuko Kato, and Hiroshi Takahashi. 2009. "Impact of the Elder Abuse Prevention and Caregiver Support Law on System Development Among Municipal Governments in Japan." *Health Policy* 90 (2–3): 254–61.

Nakatani, Yoji. 2012. "Challenges in Interfacing Between Forensic and General Mental Health: A Japanese Perspective." *International Journal of Law and Psychiatry* 35 (5–6): 406–11.

Nakatani, Yoji, Miwa Kojimoto, Saburo Matsubara, and Isao Takayanagi. 2010. "New Legislation for Offenders with Mental Disorders in Japan." *International Journal of Law and Psychiatry* 33 (1): 7–12.

Nanri, Akiko, Tetsuya Mizoue, Kalpana Poudel-Tandukar, Mitsuhiko Noda, and Masayuki Kato. 2013. "Dietary Patterns and Suicide in Japanese Adults: The Japan Public Health Center-Based Prospective Study." *British Journal of Psychiatry* 203: 422–27.

National Institute of Mental Health. 2015. "Autism Spectrum Disorder." Accessed 15 August 2017. https://www.nimh.nih.gov/health/topics/autism-spectrum-disorders-asd/index.shtml.

Nawa, Shinpei. 2006. "Postwar Fourth Wave of Juvenile Delinquency and Tasks of Juvenile Police." In *Current Juvenile Police Policy in Japan*, edited by Police Policy Research Center, National Police Academy of Japan, 1–19. Tokyo: Research Foundation for Safe Society.

Nelken, David. 2009. "Comparative Criminal Justice: Beyond Ethnocentrism and Relativism." *European Journal of Criminology* 6 (4): 291–311.

Nesdale, Drew, and Mikako Naito. 2005. "Individualism-Collectivism and the Attitudes to School Bullying of Japanese and Australian Students." *Journal of Cross-Cultural Psychology* 36 (5): 537–56.

Ng, Jennifer C., Sharon S. Lee, and Yoon K. Pak. 2007. "Contesting the Model Minority and Perpetual Foreigner Stereotypes: A Critical Review of Literature on Asian Americans in Education." *Review of Research in Education* 31 (1): 95–130.

Nguyen, Toan Thanh, Yasuko Morinaga, Irene Hanson Frieze, Jessica Cheng, Manyu Li, Akiko Doi, Tatsuya Hirai, Eunsun Joo, and Cha Li. 2013. "College Students' Perceptions of Intimate Partner Violence: A Comparative Study of Japan, China, and the United States." *International Journal of Conflict and Violence* 7 (2): 261–73.

Nisbett, Richard E., and Dov Cohen. 1996. *Culture of Honor: The Psychology of Violence in the South*. Boulder: Westview Press.

Nishikawa, Saori, Elisabet Sundbom, and Bruno Hägglöf. 2010. "Influence of Perceived Parental Rearing on Adolescent Self-Concept and Internalizing and Externalizing Problems in Japan." *Journal of Child and Family Studies* 19 (1): 57–66.

Northeastern University. 2014. "The International Self-Report Delinquency Study" [online]. Available at https://web.northeastern.edu/isrd/. Accessed 10 December 2018.

Ogasawara, Kazumi. 2011. "Current Status of Sex Crimes and Measures for the Victims in Japan." *Journal of Medical Association Journal* 139 (3): 164–67.

Ohara, Takaharu, and Naomi Matsuura. 2016. "The Characteristics of Delinquent Behavior and Predictive Factors in Japanese Children's Homes." *Children and Youth Services Review* 61: 159–64.

Ohbuchi, Ken-ichi, and Hideo Kondo. 2015. "Psychological Analysis of Serious Juvenile Violence in Japan." *Asian Journal of Criminology* 10: 149–62.

Ohgi, Shohei, Tatsuya Takahashi, J. Kevin Nugent, and Kokichi Arisawa. 2003. "Neonatal Behavioral Characteristics and Later Behavioral Problems." *Clinical Pediatrics* 42 (8): 679–86.

Oka, Tatsushi. 2009. "Juvenile Crime and Punishment: Evidence from Japan." *Applied Economics* 41 (24): 3103–15.

Okabe, Takeshi. 2016. "The Quantitative Analysis of Juvenile Delinquency in Contemporary Japan (Part 1)." *Journal of the Literary Society of Yamaguchi University* 66: 121–60.

Okamura, Rie. 2016. "Filial Violence: An Unrevealed Problem for Decades." In *Family Violence in Japan: A Life Course Perspective*, edited by Fumie Kumagai and Masako Ishii-Kuntz, 103–22. New York: Springer.

Olweus, Dan. 1993. *Bullying at School: What We Know and What We Can Do.* Oxford: Basil Blackwell.

Ono, Yoshiro, and Andres J. Pumariega. 2008. "Violence in Youth." *International Review of Psychiatry* 20 (3): 305–16.

Ooki, Syuichi. 2013. "Characteristics of Fatal Child Maltreatment Associated with Multiple Births in Japan." *Twin Research and Human Genetics* 16 (3): 743–50.

Oshio, Takashi, Maki Umeda, and Norito Kawakami. 2013. "Childhood Adversity and Adulthood Subjective Well-Being: Evidence from Japan." *Journal of Happiness Studies* 14 (3): 843–60.

Osumi, Takahiro, and Hideki Ohira. 2010. "The Positive Side of Psychopathy: Emotional Detachment in Psychopathy and Rational Decision-Making in the Ultimatum Game." *Personality and Individual Differences* 49 (5): 451–56.

Osumi, Takahiro, Takashi Nakao, Yukinori Kasuya, and Jun Shinoda. 2012. "Amygdala Dysfunction Attenuates Frustration-Induced Aggression in Psychopathic Individuals in a Non-criminal Population." *Journal of Affective Disorders* 142 (1–3): 331–38.

Otani, Koichi, Akihito Suzuki, Yoshihiko Matsumoto, Naoshi Shibuya, Ryoichi Sadahiro, and Masanori Enokido. 2013. "Parental Overprotection Engenders Dysfunctional Attitudes About Achievement and Dependency in a Gender-Specific Manner." *BMC Psychiatry* 13 (1): 345.

Oyserman, Daphna, Heather M. Coon, and Markus Kemmelmeier. 2002. "Rethinking Individualism and Collectivism: Evaluation of Theoretical Assumptions and Meta-Analyses." *Psychological Bulletin* 128 (1): 3–72.

Ozawa-de Silva, Chikako. 2008. "Too Lonely to Die Alone: Internet Suicide Pacts and Existential Suffering in Japan." *Culture, Medicine, and Psychiatry* 32 (4): 516–51.

Pain, Rachel. 1995. "Fear of Crime and Local Contexts: Elderly People in North East England." *Northern Economic Review* 24: 96–111.

———. 2000. "Place, Social Relations and the Fear of Crime: A Review." *Progress in Human Geography* 24 (3): 365–87.

Pinker, Steven. 2015. "Behavior = Genes + Environment." In *This Idea Must Die*, edited by John Brockman, 188–91. New York: HarperCollins.

Piquero, Alex R. 2008. "Taking Stock of Developmental Trajectories of Criminal Activity Over the Life Course." In *The Long View of Crime: A Synthesis of Longitudinal Research*, edited by Akiva M. Liberman, 23–78. New York: Springer.

Piquero, Alex R., and Terrie E. Moffitt. 2014. "Moffitt's Developmental Taxonomy of Antisocial Behavior." In *Encyclopedia of Criminology and Criminal Justice*, edited by Gerben Bruinsma and David Weisburd, 3121–27. New York: Springer.

Piquero, Alex R., David P. Farrington, Alfred Blumstein. 2003. "The Criminal Career Paradigm." *Crime and Justice* 30: 359–506.

Piquero, Alex R., Wesley G. Jennings, and David P. Farrington. 2010. "On the Malleability of Self-Control: Theoretical and Policy Implications Regarding a General Theory of Crime." *Justice Quarterly* 27 (6): 803–34.

Pollard, John A., David J. Hawkins, and Michael W. Arthur. 1999. "Risk and Protection: Are Both Necessary to Understand Diverse Behavioral Outcomes in Adolescence?" *Social Work Research* 23 (3): 145–58.

Pontell, Henry N., and Gilbert Geis. 2007. "Black Mist and White Collars: Economic Crime in the United States and Japan." *Asian Journal of Criminology* 2 (2): 111–26.

Portnoy, Jill, Adrian Raine, Jianghong Liu, and Joseph R. Hibbeln. 2018. "Reductions of Intimate Partner Violence Resulting from Supplementing Children with Omega-3 Fatty Acids: A Randomised, Double-Blind, Placebo-Controlled, Stratified, Parallel-Group Trial." *Aggressive Behavior.* https://doi.org/10.1002/ab.21769.

Poudel-Tandukar, Kalpana, Akiko Nanri, Motoki Iwasaki, Tetsuya Mizoue, Yumi Matsushita, Yoshihiko Takahashi, Mitsuhiko Noda, Manami Inoue, and Shoichiro Tsugane. 2011a. "Long Chain N-3 Fatty Acids Intake, Fish Consumption and Suicide in a Cohort of Japanese Men and Women—The Japan Public Health Center-Based (JPHC) Prospective Study." *Journal of Affective Disorders* 129 (1–3): 282–88.

Poudel-Tandukar, Kalpana, Akiko Nanri, Tetsuya Mizoue, Yumi Matsushita, Yoshihiko Takahashi, Mitsuhiko Noda, Manami Inoue, and Shoichiro Tsugane. 2011b. "Social Support and Suicide in Japanese Men and Women E The Japan Public Health Center (JPHC)—Based Prospective Study." *Journal of Psychiatric Research* 45 (12): 1545–50.

Radzinowicz, Leon. 1962. *In Search of Criminology*. Cambridge: Harvard University Press.

———. 1999. *Adventures in Criminology*. London: Routledge.

Raine, Adrian. 2002a. "Biosocial Studies of Antisocial and Violent Behavior in Children and Adults: A Review." *Journal of Abnormal Child Psychology* 30 (4): 311–26.

———. 2002b. "The Basis Biological of Crime." In *Crime: Public Policies for Crime Control*, edited by James Q. Wilson and Joan Petersilia, 43–74. Oakland: ICS Press.

———. 2005. "The Interaction of Biological and Social Measures in the Explanation of Antisocial and Violent Behavior." In *Developmental Psychobiology of Aggression*, edited by David M. Stoff and Elizabeth J. Susman, 13–42. Cambridge: Cambridge University Press.

———. 2013. *The Anatomy of Violence: The Biological Roots of Crime*. New York: Vintage Books.

Raine, Adrian, Jill Portnoy, Jianghong Liu, Tashneem Mahoomed, and Joseph R. Hibbeln. 2015. "Reduction in Behavior Problems with Omega-3 Supplementation in Children Aged 8–16 Years: A Randomized, Double-Blind, Placebo-Controlled, Stratified, Parallel-Group Trial." *Journal of Child Psychology and Psychiatry and Allied Disciplines* 56 (5): 509–20.

Rake, Douglas D. E. 1987. "Crime Control and Police-Community Relations: A Cross-Cultural Comparison of Tokyo, Japan, and Santa Ana, California." *The Annals of the American Academy of Political and Social Science* 494: 148–54.

Ramirez, J. Martin, Jose Manuel Andreu, and Takehiro Fujihara. 2001. "Cultural and Sex Differences in Aggression: A Comparison Between Japanese and Spanish Students Using Two Different Inventories." *Aggressive Behavior* 27: 313–22.

Raynor, Peter. 2002. "Community Penalities: Probation, Punishment, and 'What Works.'" In *The Oxford Handbook of Criminology*, edited by Mike Maguire, Rod Morgan, and Robert Reiner, 1168–206. Oxford: Oxford University Press.

Reiss, Albert J., and David P. Farrington. 1991. "Advancing Knowledge About Co-offending: Results from a Prospective Longitudinal Survey of London Males." *Journal of Criminal Law and Criminology* 82 (2): 360–95.

Roberts, Aki, and Gary LaFree. 2004. "Explaining Japan's Postwar Violent Crime Trends." *Criminology* 42 (1): 179–210.

Rocque, Michael, Brandon C. Welsh, and Adrian Raine. 2012. "Biosocial Criminology and Modern Crime Prevention." *Journal of Criminal Justice* 40 (4): 306–12.

———. 2014. "Policy Implications of Biosocial Criminology: Crime Prevention and Offender Rehabilitation." In *The Nurture vs. Biosocial Debate in Criminology: On the Origins of Criminal Behavior and Criminality*, edited by Kevin M. Beaver, J. C. Barnes, Brian B. Boutwell, 431–45. New York: Sage.

Ronald, Richard, and Allison Alexy. 2011. "Continuity and Change in Japanese Homes and Families." In *Home and Family in Japan: Continuity and Transformation*, edited by Richard Ronald and Allison Alexy, 1–24. Oxon: Routledge.

Ryan, Trevor. 2005. "Creating 'Problem Kids': Juvenile Crime in Japan and Revisions to the Juvenile Act." *Journal of Japanese Law* 10 (19): 153–88.

Ryushima, Hidehiro, and Yuji Kaji. 2006. "Clinical Psychology-Based Community Support for Delinquency." *Japanese Journal of Clinical Psychology* 2 (2): 1–14.

Said, Edward. 1979. *Orientalism*. New York: Vintage Books.

Sakiyama, Mari, Hong Lu, and Bin Liang. 2011. "Reintegrative Shaming and Juvenile Delinquency in Japan." *Asian Journal of Criminology* 6 (2): 161–75.

Sampson, Robert J., and John H. Laub. 1993. *Crime in the Making: Pathways and Turning Points Through Life*. Cambridge: Harvard University Press.

Sampson, Robert J., and William Julius Wilson. 1995. "Toward a Theory of Race, Crime, and Urban Inequality." In *Crime and Inequality*, edited by John Hagan and Ruth D. Peterson, 37–56. Stanford: Stanford University Press.

Sasaki, Megumi, Yumiko Arai, Keigo Kumamoto, Koji Abe, Asuna Arai, and Yoko Mizuno. 2007. "Factors Related to Potentially Harmful Behaviors Towards Disabled Older People by Family Caregivers in Japan." *International Journal of Geriatric Psychiatry* 22: 250–57.

Sasaki, Takayo, and Masako Ishii-Kuntz. 2016. "Intimate Partner Violence: Domestic Violence from Japanese Perspective." In *Family Violence in Japan: A Life Course Perspective*, edited by Fumie Kamagai and Masako Ishii-Kuntz, 79–102. New York: Springer.

Schmitt, David P., Robert R. Mccrae, Kevin L. Bennett, and Karl Grammer. 2007. "The Geographic Distribution of Big Five Personality Traits: Patterns and Profiles of Human Self-Description Across 56 Nations." *Journal of Cross-Cultural Psychology* 38 (2): 173–212.

Schwarzenegger, Christian. 2003. "The Debate About the Reform of the Juvenile Law in Japan." In *Juvenile Delinquency in Japan: Reconsidering the "Crisis"*, edited by Gesine Foljanty-Jost, 173–98. Leiden: Brill.

Shahidullah, Shahid M. 2014. "Comparative Criminal Justice: Theoretical Perspectives." In *Comparative Criminal Justice Systems: Global and Local Perspectives*, 55–86. Burlington: Jones & Barnett Learning.

Sheptycki, James. 2008. "Transnationalisation, Orientalism and Crime." *Asian Journal of Criminology* 3 (1): 13–35.

Shiina, Akihiro, Aika Tomoto, Soichiro Omiya, Aiko Sato, Masaomi Iyo, and Yoshito Igarashi. 2017. "Differences Between British and Japanese Perspectives on Forensic Mental Health Systems: A Preliminary Study." *World Journal of Psychiatry* 7 (1): 8–11.

Shin, Young, Eric Fombonne, Yun-Joo Koh, Soo-Jeong Kim, Keun-Ah Cheon, and Bennett L. Leventhal. 2014. "A Comparison of DSM-IV Pervasive Developmental Disorder and DSM-5 Autism Spectrum Disorder Prevalence in an Epidemiologic Sample." *Journal of the American Academy of Child and Adolescent Psychiatry* 53 (5): 500–508.

Shiozaki, Arihiro, Yoshio Matsuda, Kunihiko Hayashi, Shoji Satoh, and Shigeru Saito. 2011. "Comparison of Risk Factors for Major Obstetric Complications Between Western Countries and Japan: A Case—Cohort Study." *Journal of Obstetrics and Gynaecology Research* 37 (10): 1447–54.

Shiraev, Eric B., and David A. Levy. 2010. *Cross-Cultural Psychology*. Boston: Pearson.

Siegel, Jane A., and Linda M. Williams. 2003. "The Relationship Between Child Sexual Abuse and Female Delinquency and Crime: A Prospective Study." *Journal of Research in Crime and Delinquency* 40 (1): 71–94.

Skeem, Jennifer L., Elizabeth Scott, and Edward P. Mulvey. 2014. "Justice Policy Reform for High-Risk Juveniles: Using Science to Achieve Large-Scale Crime Reduction." *Annual Review of Clinical Psychology* 10 (January): 709–39.

Smart, Carol. 1976. *Women, Crime, and Criminology: A Feminist Critique*. London: Routledge and Kegan Paul.

Smith, David, and Kiyoko Sueda. 2008. "The Killing of Children by Children as a Symptom of National Crisis: Reactions in Britain and Japan." *Criminology and Criminal Justice* 8 (1): 5–25.

Stamatel, Janet. 2009. "Contributions of Cross-National Research to Criminology at the Beginning of the 21st Century." In *Handbook on Crime and Deviance*, edited by Marvin D. Krohn, Alan J. Lizotte, and Gina Penly Hall, 3–22. Handbooks of Sociology and Social Research. New York: Springer.

Steinhoff, Patricia. 1993. "Pursuing the Japanese Police." *Law & Society Review* 27 (4): 827–50.

Stouthamer-Loeber, Magda, Rolf Loeber, David P. Farrington, Quanwu Zhang, Welmoet van Kammen, and Eugene Maguin. 1993. "The Double Edge of Protective and Risk Factors for Delinquency: Interrelations and Developmental Patterns." *Development and Psychopathology* 5: 683–701.

Stouthamer-Loeber, Magda, Rolf Loeber, Evelyn Wei, David P. Farrington, and Per-Olof H. Wikström. 2002. "Risk and Promotive Effects in the Explanation of Persistent Serious Delinquency in Boys." *Journal of Consulting and Clinical Psychology* 70 (1): 111–23.

Stuart, Heather. 2003. "Violence and Mental Illness: An Overview." *World Psychiatry* 2 (2): 121–24.

Sudo, Junya, Makoto Sato, Shugo Obata, and Akira Yamagami. 2006. "Exploring the Possibility of Risk Assessment of Japanese Sexual Offenders Using Static-99." *Criminal Behaviour and Mental Health* 16: 146–54.

Sugawara, Masumi, Toshinori Kitamura, Mari Aoki Toda, and Satoru Shima. 1999. "Longitudinal Relationship Between Maternal Depression and Infant Temperament in a Japanese Population." *Journal of Clinical Psychology* 55 (7): 869–80.

Sugie, Naomi F. 2017. "When the Elderly Turn to Petty Crime: Increasing Elderly Arrest Rates in an Aging Population." *International Criminal Justice Review* 27 (1): 19–39.

Sugimoto, Yoshio. 2014. *An Introduction to Japanese Society*. 4th ed. Cambridge, UK: Cambridge University Press.

Sugiura, Yoshinori, and Tomoko Sugiura. 2012. "Psychopathy and Looming Cognitive Style: Moderation by Attentional Control." *Personality and Individual Differences* 52 (3): 317–22.

Suwa, Mami, and Kunifumi Suzuki. 2013. "The Phenomenon of 'Hikikomori' (Social Withdrawal) and the Socio-Cultural Situation in Japan Today." *Journal of Psychopathology* 19 (3): 191–98.

Suzuki, Yumi E. 2016. "Sexual Violence in Japan: Implications of the Lay Judge System on Victims of Sexual Violence." *Journal of Law and Criminal Justice* 4 (1): 75–81.

Svensson, Thomas, Manami Inoue, Hadrien Charvat, Norie Sawada, Motoki Iwasaki, Shizuka Sasazuki, Taichi Shimazu, et al. 2014. "Coping Behaviors and Suicide in the Middle-Aged and Older Japanese General Population: The Japan Public Health Center-Based Prospective Study." *Annals of Epidemiology* 24: 199–205.

Tajan, Nicolas. 2015. "Social Withdrawal and Psychiatry: A Comprehensive Review of Hikikomori." *Neuropsychiatrie de L'enfance et de L'adolescence* 63: 324–31.

Takahashi, Hidehiko, Noriaki Yahata, Michihiko Koeda, Tetsuya Matsuda, Kunihiko Asai, and Yoshiro Okubo. 2004. "Brain Activation Associated with Evaluative Processes of Guilt and Embarrassment: An fMRI Study." *NeuroImage* 23 (3): 967–74.

Takahashi, Hidehiko, Takashi Ideno, Shigetaka Okubo, Hiroshi Matsui, Kazuhisa Takemura, Masato Matsuura, Motoichiro Kato, and Yoshiro Okubo. 2009. "Impact of Changing the Japanese Term for 'Schizophrenia' for Reasons of Stereotypical Beliefs of Schizophrenia in Japanese Youth." *Schizophrenia Research* 112 (1–3): 149–52.

Takahashi, Masura, Takemi Mori, and Daryl G. Kroner. 2013. "A Cross-Validation of the Youth Level of Service/Case Management Inventory (YLS/CMI) Among Japanese Juvenile Offenders." *Law and Human Behavior* 37 (6): 389–400.

Takahashi, Taiki, Haruto Takagishi, Hirofumi Nishinaka, Takaki Makino, and Hiroki Fukui. 2014. "Neuroeconomics of Psychopathy: Risk Taking in Probability Discounting of Gain and Loss Predicts Psychopathy." *Neuroendocrinology Letters* 35 (6): 510–17.

Takano, Yotaro, and Eiko Osaka. 1999. "An Unsupported Common View: Comparing Japan and the US on Individualism/Collectivism." *Asian Journal of Social Psychology* 2: 311–41.

Takeda, Yasuhisa, Ichiro Kawachi, Zentaro Yamagata, and Shuji Hashimoto. 2004. "Multigenerational Family Structure in Japanese Society: Impacts on Stress and Health Behaviors Among Women and Men." *Social Science and Medicine* 59: 69–81.

Takii, Yasutaka. 1992. "Sexual Abuse and Juvenile Delinquency." *Child Abuse Review* 1 (1): 43–48.

Tam, Frank Wai-ming, and Mitsuru Taki. 2007. "Bullying Among Girls in Japan and Hong Kong: An Examination of the Frustration-Aggression Model." *Educational Research and Evaluation* 13 (4): 373–99.

Tamura, Ayame, Yoshinori Sugiura, Tomoko Sugiura, and Jun Moriya. 2016. "Attention Moderates the Relationship Between Primary Psychopathy and Affective Empathy in Undergraduate Students." *Psychological Reports* 119 (3): 608–29.

Tamura, Ayame, Keiji Takata, Yoshinori Sugiura, Jun Moriya, Yoshitake Takebayashi, and Keisuke Tanaka. 2014. "Moderation of the Relationship Between Psychopathy and Empathy by Attention." *Personality and Individual Differences* 60 (April): S62.

Tanaka, Masako, Yumi E. Suzuki, Ikuko Aoyama, Kota Takaoka, and Harriet L. MacMillan. 2017. "Child Sexual Abuse in Japan: A Systematic Review and Future Directions." *Child Abuse & Neglect* 66 (April): 31–40.

Tanioka, Ichiro, and Daniel Glaser. 1991. "School Uniforms, Routine Activities, and the Social Control of Delinquency in Japan." *Youth & Society* 23 (1): 50–75.

Tanji, Fumiya, Masako Kakizaki, Yumi Sugawara, Ikue Watanabe, Naoki Nakaya, Yuko Minami, Akira Fukao, and Ichiro Tsuji. 2014. "Personality and Suicide Risk: The Impact of Economic Crisis in Japan." *Psychological Medicine* 45 (3): 559–73.

Tateno, Masaru, Norbert Skokauskas, Takahiro A. Kato, Alan R. Teo, and Anthony P. S. Guerrero. 2016. "New Game Software (Pokémon Go) May Help Youth with Severe Social Withdrawal, Hikikomori." *Psychiatry Research* 246: 848–49.

Thang, Leng Leng, and S. K. Gan. 2003. "Deconstructing 'Japanisation': Reflections from the 'Learn from Japan' Campaign in Singapore." *New Zealand Journal of Asian Studies* 5 (1): 91–106.

The Japan Times. 2017. "Waking Up to Child Abuse." Accessed 31 May. http://www.japantimes.co.jp/life/2014/09/13/lifestyle/waking-child-abuse/#.WS602BP1DPA.

Theobald, Delphine, David P. Farrington, and Alex R. Piquero. 2013. "Childhood Broken Homes and Adult Violence: An Analysis of Moderators and Mediators." *Journal of Criminal Justice* 41: 44–52.

Thornberry, Terence P., and Marvin D. Krohn. 2000. "The Self-Report Method for Measuring Delinquency and Crime." *Criminal Justice* 4 (1): 33–83.

Thornberry, Terence P., Adrienne Freeman-Gallant, and Peter Lovegrove. 2009. "Intergenerational Linkages in Antisocial Behaviour." *Criminal Behaviour and Mental Health* 93 (19): 80–93.

Thornton, Robert Y., and Katsuya Endo. 1992. *Preventing Crime in America and Japan: A Comparative Study*. Armonk: M.E. Sharpe Inc.

Toda, Yuichi. 2016. "Bullying (Ijime) and Related Problems in Japan: History and Research." In *School Bullying in Different Cultures: Eastern and Western Perspectives*, edited by Peter K. Smith, Keumjoo Kwak, and Yuichi Toda, 73–92. Cambridge: Cambridge University Press.

Towl, Graham J., and David A. Crighton. 2015. "Introduction." In *Forensic Psychology*, edited by David A. Crighton and Graham J. Towl, 2nd ed., 1–12. West Sussex: Wiley.

Toyama-Bialke, Chisaki. 2003. "The 'Japanese Triangle' for Preventing Adolescent Delinquency—Strengths and Weaknesses of the Family-School Adolescent Relationship from a Comparative Perspective." In *Juvenile Delinquency in Japan: Reconsidering the "Crisis"*, edited by Gesine Foljanty-Jost, 19–50. Leiden: Brill.

Treml, Jacqueline Noel. 2001. "Bullying as a Social Malady in Contemporary Japan." *International Social Work* 44 (1): 107–17.

Triandis, Harry C. 1989. "The Self and Social Behavior in Differing Cultural Contexts." *Psychological Review* 96 (3): 506–20.

Triandis, Harry C. 1994. *Individualism and Collectivism*. Boulder: Westview.

Triandis, Harry C. 2001. "Individualism-Collectivism and Personality." *Journal of Personality* 69 (6): 907–24.

Tsukada, Noriko, Yasuhiko Saito, and Toshio Tatara. 2001. "Japanese Older People's Perceptions of 'Elder Abuse.'" *Journal of Elder Abuse and Neglect* 13 (1): 71–89.

Tsushima, Masahiro. 1996. "Economic Structure and Crime: The Case of Japan." *Journal of Socio-Economics* 25 (4): 497–515.

Tsutomi, Hiroshi, Laura Bui, Mitsuaki Ueda, and David P. Farrington. 2013. "The Application of Criminological Theory to a Japanese Context: Power-Control Theory." *International Journal of Criminological and Sociological Theory* 6 (4): 128–44.

Ttofi, Maria M., and David P. Farrington. 2011. "Effectiveness of School-Based Programs to Reduce Bullying: A Systematic and Meta-Analytic Review." *Journal of Experimental Criminology* 7 (1): 27–56.

Ttofi, Maria M., David P. Farrington, and Friedrich Lösel. 2012. "School Bullying as a Predictor of Violence Later in Life: A Systematic Review and Meta-Analysis of Prospective Longitudinal Studies." *Aggression and Violent Behavior* 17: 405–18.

Umeda, Maki, Norito Kawakami, Ronald C. Kessler, and Elizabeth Miller. 2015. "Childhood Adversities and Adult Use of Potentially Injurious Physical Discipline in Japan." *Journal of Family Violence* 30 (4): 515–27.

United Nations, Department of Economic and Social Affairs, Population Division. 2017. "World Population Prospects: The 2017 Revision, Key Findings and Advance Tables." New York: Author.

United Nations Office on Drugs and Crime. 2016. "United Nations Office on Drugs and Crime Statistics on Crime." Vienna: Author.

Van Dorn, Richard, Jan Volavka, and Norman Johnson. 2012. "Mental Disorder and Violence: Is There a Relationship Beyond Substance Use?" *Social Psychiatry and Psychiatric Epidemiology* 47 (3): 487–503.

van Kesteren, John, Jan van Dijk, and Pat Mayhew. 2014. "The International Crime Victims Surveys: A Retrospective." *International Review of Victimization* 20 (1): 49–69.

Vazsonyi, Alexander T., and Lara M. Belliston. 2007. "The Family → Low Self-Control → Deviance: A Cross-Cultural and Cross-National Test of Self-Control Theory." *Criminal Justice and Behavior* 34 (4): 505–30.

Vazsonyi, Alexander T., Janice E. Clifford Wittekind, Lara M. Belliston, and Timothy D. Van Loh. 2004. "Extending the General Theory of Crime to 'The East:' Low Self-Control in Japanese Late Adolescents." *Journal of Quantitative Criminology* 20 (3): 189–216.

Virkkunen, Matti. E., David F. Horrobin, Douglas K. Jenkins, and Mehar S. Manku. 1987. "Plasma Phospholipids, Essential Fatty Acids and Prostaglandins in Alcoholic, Habitually Violent and Impulsive Offenders." *Biological Psychiatry* 22 (9): 1087–96.

Wacquant, Loïc. 2009. *Prisons of Poverty*. Minneapolis: University of Minnesota Press.

Wada, Ichiro, and Ataru Igarashi. 2014. "The Social Costs of Child Abuse in Japan." *Children and Youth Services Review* 46: 72–77.

Wagatsuma, Hiroshi, and George DeVos. 1984. *Heritage of Endurance: Family Patterns and Delinquency Formation in Japan*. Berkeley: University of California Press.

Walker, Nigel. 2003. *A Man Without Loyalties: A Penologist's Afterthoughts*. Chichester: Barry Rose Law Publishers.

Wallinius, Märta, Thomas Nilsson, Björn Hofvander, Henrik Anckarsäter, and Gunilla Stålenheim. 2012. "Facets of Psychopathy Among Mentally Disordered Offenders: Clinical Comorbidity Patterns and Prediction of Violent and Criminal Behavior." *Psychiatry Research* 198 (2): 279–84.

Walter, Glenn D. 1990. *The Crimina Lifestyle: Patterns of Serious Criminal Conduct*. Newbury Park: Sage.

Ward, Jeffrey T., John H. Boman, and Shayne Jones. 2012. "Hirschi's Redefined Self-Control: Assessing the Implications of the Merger Between Social- and Self-Control Theories." *Crime and Delinquency* 61 (9): 1206–33.

Watanabe, Norio. 2016. "Low Prevalence Rates of Common Mental Disorders in Japan: Does It Still Hold True?" *Epidemiology and Psychiatric Services* 25: 233–34.

Welsh, Brandon C., and David P. Farrington. 2010. *The Future of Crime Prevention: Developmental and Situational Strategies*. Bethesda: National Institute of Justice.

————. 2012a. "Crime Prevention and Public Policy." *Oxford Handbooks Online*, 1–19.

————. 2012b. "Science, Politics, and Crime Prevention: Toward a New Crime Policy." *Journal of Criminal Justice* 40 (2): 128–33.

West, Donald J., and David P. Farrington. 1973. *Who Becomes Delinquent?* London: Heinemann.

West, Donald J., and David P. Farrington. 1977. *The Delinquent Way of Life.* London: Heinemann.

Westermann, Ted D., and James W. Burfeind. 1991. *Crime and Justice in Two Societies.* Pacific Grove, CA: Brooks/Cole.

White, Merry I. 1994. *The Material Child: Coming of Age in Japan and America.* Berkeley: University of California Press.

————. 2002. *Perfectly Japanese: Making Families in an Era of Upheaval.* Berkeley: University of California Press.

Whitten, Tyson, Tara T. McGee, Ross Homel, David P. Farrington, Maria M. Ttofi. 2018. "Comparing the Criminal Careers and Childhood Risk Factors of Persistent, Chronic, and Persistent-Chronic Offenders." *Australian and New Zealand Journal of Criminology.* https://doi.org/10.1177/0004865818781203.

Wibbelink, Carlijn J. M., Machteld Hoeve, Geert Jan J. M. Stams, and Frans J. Oort. 2017. "A Meta-Analysis of the Association Between Mental Disorders and Juvenile Recidivism." *Aggression and Violent Behavior* 33: 78–90.

Widom, Cathy S. 1989a. "Child Abuse, Neglect, and Violent Criminal Behavior." *Criminology* 27 (2): 251–71.

Widom, Cathy S. 1989b. "The Cycle of Violence." *Science* 244 (4901): 160–66.

Wolfgang, Marvin E., Robert M. Figlio, and Thorsten Sellin. 1972. *Delinquency in a Birth Cohort.* Chicago: University of Chicago Press.

Wolfgang, Marvin E., Robert M. Figlio, Paul Tracy, and Simon I. Singer. 1985. *The National Survey of Crime Severity.* Washington, DC: U.S. Bureau of Justice Statistics.

World Health Organization. 1992. "The ICD-10 Classification of Mental and Behavioural Disorders Clinical Descriptions and Diagnostic Guidelines." Geneva: Author.

Wortley, Richard. 2011. *Psychological Criminology: An Integrative Approach.* Oxon: Routledge.

Wu, Ellen D. 2014. *The Color of Success: Asian Americans and the Origins of the Model Minority.* Princeton: Princeton University Press.

Xie, Liya. 2000. "Gender Difference in Mentally Ill Offenders: A Nationwide Japanese Study." *International Journal of Offender Therapy and Comparative Criminology* 44 (6): 714–24.

Yamagishi, Toshio. 1988. "The Provision of a Sanctioning System in the United States and Japan." *Social Psychology Quarterly* 51 (3): 265.

Yamagishi, Toshio, and Midori Yamagishi. 1994. "Trust and Commitment in the United States and Japan." *Motivation and Emotion* 18 (2): 129–66.

Yamagishi, Toshio, Karen S. Cook, and Motoki Watabe. 1998. "Uncertainty, Trust, and Commitment Formation in the United States and Japan." *American Journal of Sociology* 104 (1): 165–94.

Yamamiya, Yuko. 2003. "Juvenile Delinquency in Japan." *Journal of Prevention & Intervention in the Community* 25 (2): 27–46.

Yamamoto, Mana, and Takemi Mori. 2016. "Assessing the Effectiveness of the Correctional Sex Offender Treatment Program." *Online Journal of Japanese Clinical Psychology* 3: 1–13.

Yasumi, Katsuhiro, and Jinsuke Kageyama. 2009. "Filicide and Fatal Abuse in Japan, 1994–2005: Temporal Trends and Regional Distribution." *Journal of Forensic and Legal Medicine* 16 (2): 70–75.

Yoder, Robert S. 2004. *Youth Deviance in Japan: Class Reproduction of Nonconformity.* Victoria: Trans-Pacific Press.

———. 2011. *Deviance and Inequality in Japan: Japanese Youth and Foreign Migrants.* Bristol: The Policy Press.

Yokota, Kunihiro. 2012. "The Validity of a Three-Factor Model in PPI-R and Social Dominance Orientation in Japanese Sample." *Personality and Individual Differences* 53 (7): 907–11.

Yokoyama, Minoru. 2013. "Development of Criminology in Japan from a Sociological Perspective." In *Handbook of Asian Criminology*, edited by Jianhong Liu, Bill Hebenton, and Susyan Jou, 223–30. New York: Springer.

———. 2015. "Juvenile Justice and Juvenile Crime: An Overview of Japan." In *Juvenile Justice: International Perspectives, Models, and Trends*, edited by John A. Winterdyk, 179–208. London: CRC Press.

Yoneyama, Shoko. 2000. "Student Discourse on Tokokyohi (School Phobia/Refusal) in Japan: Burnout or Empowerment?" *British Journal of Sociology of Education* 21 (1): 77–94.

———. 2015. "Theorizing School Bullying: Insights from Japan." *Confero* 3 (2): 1–37.

Yoneyama, Shoko, and Asao Naito. 2003. "Problems with the Paradigm: The School as a Factor in Understanding Bullying (with Special Reference to Japan)." *British Journal of Sociology of Education* 24 (3): 315–30.

Yoo, Hyung Chol, Kimberly S. Burrola, and Michael F. Steger. 2010. "A Preliminary Report on a New Measure: Internalization of the Model Minority Myth Measure (IM-4) and Its Psychological Correlates among Asian American College Students." *Journal of Counseling Psychology* 57 (1): 114–27.

Yoshihama, Mieko, and Julie Horrocks. 2010. "Risk of Intimate Partner Violence: Role of Childhood Sexual Abuse and Sexual Initiation in Women in Japan." *Children and Youth Services Review* 32 (1): 28–37.

Yoshikawa, Kazuo, Pamela J. Taylor, Akira Yamagami, Takayuki Okada, Kumiko Ando, and Toshihiro Taruya. 2007. "Violent Recidivism Among Mentally Disordered Offenders in Japan." *Criminal Behaviour and Mental Health* 151: 137–51.

Yoshinaga, Chieko, Izumi Kadomoto, Toshiyuki Otani, Tsukasa Sasaki, and Nobumasa Kato. 2004. "Prevalence of Post-Traumatic Stress Disorder in Incarcerated Juvenile Delinquents in Japan." *Psychiatry and Clinical Neurosciences* 58 (4): 383–88.

Yoshino, Aihide, Taihei Fukuhara, and Motoichiro Kato. 2000. "Premorbid Risk Factors for Alcohol Dependence in Antisocial Personality Disorder." *Alcoholism: Clinical and Experimental Research* 24 (1): 34–38.

Yoshioka, Kumiko, Nicola J. Reavley, Andrew J. Mackinnon, and Anthony F. Jorm. 2014. "Stigmatising Attitudes Towards People with Mental Disorders: Results from a Survey of Japanese High School Students." *Psychiatry Research* 215 (1): 229–36.

Yu, Rongqin, John R. Geddes, and Seena Fazel. 2012. "Personality Disorders, Violence, and Antisocial Behavior: A Systematic Review and Meta-Regression Analysis." *Journal of Personality Disorders* 26 (5): 775–92.

Zedner, Lucia. 1995. "In Pursuit of the Vernacular: Comparing Law and Order Discourse in Britain and Germany." *Social & Legal Studies* 4: 517–34.

Index

Printed by Printforce, the Netherlands